CALVIN
AGAINST
HIMSELF

An Inquiry in Intellectual History

Suzanne Selinger

ARCHON BOOKS
1984

First published 1984 as an Archon Book,
an imprint of The Shoe String Press. Inc.,
Hamden, Connecticut 06514

Printed in the United States of America

Library of Congress Cataloging in Publication Data

Selinger, Suzanne.
    Calvin against himself.

    Bibliography: p.
    Includes index.
    1. Calvin, Jean, 1509–1564. I. Title.
BX9418.S4   230′.42′0924   83-21330
ISBN 0-208-01948-0

In memory of my cousin
1st Lt. Martin Bruce Keller, USAF
1939–1964

Who fetcheth God from without,
troubled is he by objects.

— Meister Eckhart

Contents

Illustrations
(Between pages 148–49)

14. Vasari: Screen from the Uffizi. Florence. Reproduced by permission of Alinari/Art Resource, Inc.

15. Michelangelo: The Laurentian Library Vestibule. Florence. Reproduced by permission of Alinari/Art Resource, Inc.

Acknowledgments

Marcia Colish and James Winn read early drafts of this study, offered helpful criticism, and provided decisive encouragement. William Bouwsma read a later version, and his commentary was stringent and startlingly generous. So, too, was the criticism of sections of the manuscript by Robert Ostroff, James Thorpe III, and Paolo Valesio; I benefited greatly from the perspectives of their fields.

The Rutgers Research Council gave me a summer grant for the reading with which this book began, and Sterling Memorial Library gave me two months of leave for further work: I thank them both for this support. To the Yale Divinity Library, I am grateful for a year of user's privileges and for the many kindnesses rendered by the staff. Every Calvin scholar is indebted to Peter De Klerk for his annual bibliography; my debt also includes long distance library service.

On the moral support side, I hardly know where to begin. I do know that John Harrison's support was crucial at the most difficult time in this enterprise. I hope also that Lois Banner, Janet and Robert Berls, Gretchen Mieszkowski, Deborah Shuler, and, in the very highest degree, my parents have some idea of how grateful I am for their various kinds of help.

Roland Bainton's contribution defies categorization. My earliest debt to him is recorded in note 23 of chapter 1, and I could add here — and am certain I am not the only one for whom it is true — that the seminar never ended.

Note on Quotations

Quotations are given in English in the text; those of literary relevance are included in the notes in the original Latin or French. In general, I have used standard translations for the Latin and translated the French myself; where no published source is cited, the translation is my own.

Introduction

Contexts

My primary interest in this study is in Calvin's immediate historical success such that Calvinism became the international form of Protestantism, though I will also concern myself with Calvin's weight and place in post-sixteenth-century history. Reformation historians have most often given one of two reasons, or variations thereof, to account for this success. The first is that it was actually not Calvin, but Luther, who succeeded. Calvin's historical role was to impart to Lutheranism the formal systematization of doctrine, the organization of church life, the discipline, and the dynamism that enabled Reform to spread, survive, take root, and flourish.[1] In the second view, Calvin was the creative synthesizer who molded ideas and impulses from his predecessors into a coherent whole, a totality greater than the sum of its parts and one that gave direction to both the inner and outer lives of adherents of Reform. The ingredients of this synthesis were gathered from late medieval movements for purification and renewal in religious life, from Erasmian humanism, from the spirituality of the French humanists, from Luther, Bucer, and certainly the church fathers—and eminently among the latter, Saint Augustine.[2]

This study began with a sense that Calvinism was neither virtually all Calvin nor virtually all Luther, but a third thing, Calvin's Luther. The agreement of Calvin's theology with Luther's, an agreement that includes not only ideas but also their systematic interrelations and weighting, renders Luther more than one of many important predecessors: it renders him decisive for Calvin. Yet Calvin's theology is not Luther's. The theology is that of a person very different from Luther; it is also the theology of a different time. As Reformation historians will point out, it is second-generation Reform.[3] It is also, as might usefully be stressed, thought and expression in Europe in the second third of the sixteenth century. And the most interesting aspect of a widened view of the context of Calvinist theology lies in the contingency of aspects of that context with aspects of Calvin the person which have always been seen as problematic — in the eyes of critics, his autocracy, repressive disciplinarianism, and fanaticism; to admirers, the single-minded absoluteness that could foreclose from judgments the perception of mitigating circumstances and could consider affective ties and personal damages to be secondary in the work of the Lord.[4]

The unifying theme running through Calvin's censoriousness at every level of communal life is an obsession with sin, with the pervasive corruption of human nature by its carnality, with the constant presence of a bodily life pitted against the spirit and threatening contamination and contagion. This extreme attitude in thought and action has often evoked the suspicion of dualism, an inherently troubling issue in studies of Calvin's theology because it is heretical to Christianity. However, the historical context of Calvinism makes dualism look historically orthodox, for the culture of the second third of the sixteenth century or late Renaissance period — and by culture I mean a totality of thought, values, and sensibilities — seems itself markedly dualistic in temper. Thus the possibility presents itself that Calvin succeeded, not despite, but somehow because of his extreme qualities.

Denials of dualism in Calvin do not resolve the question whether it may not be present and functioning in nondoctrinal ways, nor have such denials done so in other theologians. The Judaeo-Christian view of God as creator of the world contradicts the premise in religious dualism of two radically separate forms of reality that constitute good and evil, identified as God and the world or as spirit and matter — terms often interchanged with mind and body — and that share full ontological parity.[5] The Augustinian position on evil as the privation of good, following from the doctrine of creation, specifies the formal difference between Christian orthodoxy, whether Catholic or Protestant, and dualistic heresy. In the former, it is fallen human nature that results in evil; in the latter, the world of matter and the life of the flesh are inherently evil.[6] Within Christianity, however, evil can assume such palpable reality and be assigned to the life of the flesh so consistently that full commitment to the Christian economy of grace and redemption may be uncertain. On this ambiguous position, both Catholic and Protestant churches have found it difficult to render consistent judgment. The subject is a recurring thread in Calvin studies.

The conclusion of Calvinist historians has generally been that there is a spiritualizing tendency in Calvin, and nothing more than that.[7] Nicole Malet has cogently argued that the aversion expressed by Calvin toward bodiliness, and toward sexuality in particular, though unusually strong, was purposeful: it was a way to speak, through contrast, of God's transcendence and the glory of his being.[8] The same argument has been presented to explain the unmistakably Platonic imagery and phraseology that Calvin uses in his writings: his use was, more properly, an appropriation for his own purposes, to convey vividly and dramatically the overwhelming nature of God's goodness and sovereignty.[9]

Calvin's Protestantism was sufficiently orthodox to exist and continue to exist, in its totality, in mainstream church history. I think, however, that something is elided in the historiography of dualism in Calvin. The fact that historians have so often thought it necessary to rescue him from the charge may seem as striking as any of the individual analyses, and it reinforces my conclusion that a continuous and significant conflict between dualism and orthodoxy existed in Calvin.

Such a conflict is not unfamiliar in church history. Many aspects of the Reformers' view of the Middle Ages and later twentieth-century historiographical refinements prevent us from seeing the orthodox position on evil as normative in medieval thought and feeling. Studies of the late medieval church have indicated a cultural undercurrent that identified evil with sexuality and increasingly gained expression in confessional discourse.[10] The various forms of penance and the need to track sexual sins became a fairly widespread and dominant concern in the late Middle Ages. The disjunction between theology and religious life can perhaps be explained and understood pastorally. The whole value system of the medieval church, however, tended toward the suppression of the physical; Steven Ozment has suggested that the condemnation by the church of Eckhardt's teachings on transcendence was, ironically, the condemnation of ideas that were possibly "the logical conclusion of some of its most cherished beliefs."[11]

I find a parallel disjunction in Calvin between an orthodox position on dualism and an unorthodox one; however, it is one that exists within and runs through his theology, a psychologically engendered disjunction that colors and modulates that theology rather than producing contradictions. I think it is at the core of what I am calling Calvin's Luther. And the disjunction accounts for, and further attention to it might help to resolve, some of the internecine controversies in Calvin interpretation. One of our best Calvin historians remarks, in an article on Calvin's position on infant baptism, that the involvement of human intelligence in faith, for Calvin, is "not often recognized by Calvin scholars and still less by those determined to find fault with [him] on the basis of an exaggerated dialectic between God's sovereignty and our corrupt nature."[12] But suppose that Calvin's dialectic is, in historical perspective, only compensatorily exaggerated, and that, even discounting strategic exaggeration, it is still extreme. Could that extremism be realistic, healthy, and helpful? As Charles Partee has noted, "Calvin represents a religious response which a number of Christians have been able to identify with without always being able to identify."[13] The elusiveness in Calvin's appeal may involve just those areas that have been most resisted or regarded as preliminary obstacles to be dispatched on the way to the essential Calvin. This is the possibility that I want to explore, in psychological, intellectual, and historical contexts.

Several recent trends in Calvin scholarship are relevant to this study. One of these is reinterpretation in the form of image revision; in fact it is image reversal. I am referring to efforts, sometimes as parts of larger wholes, sometimes for this purpose alone, to revise by one hundred and eighty degrees the widespread negativism in Calvin's personal, political, and theological images in history. This work seeks to establish Calvin's humanity. He was not cold and callous, but warm and caring, and he was not puritanical. He was also not obsessed with the stark twin decrees of predestination and reprobation: his theology is, rather, christocentric. Richard Stauffer's work, in the forefront of the revisions, has focused upon Calvin's sermons. There the real but little-known Calvin concerned himself with God the creator and with his unceasing care of all that he created. On the whole, Calvin and his theology are being presented as gentler and more relaxed than commonly thought; Stauffer suggests that it is time for such a non-Calvinistic reading of Calvin — "une lecture non-calviniste de Calvin."[14]

The method of this work tends to be proof: the producing of evidence that disproves charges questioning Calvin's intellectual and emotional balance. Sometimes it is difficult not to see the proofs as self-directed arguments to quell nagging worries by counterforce. Yet that is certainly not the whole of these studies, for the revisionists consistently feel something wrong-headed in the accusations. I agree with that sense. On the other hand, the accusers consistently find something highly provocative in Calvin. But it is noteworthy that what they find gets easily tied up with what they consider to be wrong with the world or some part of it. Thus these debates are really conducted on two levels, that of substantive qualities and that of cultural and political attitudes toward those qualities, and the latter seem to cause pressure on both sides to see Calvin in particular ways. That is to say, the qualities exist, but they are rather abused by the context in which they are discussed.

A second historiographical trend, or an acceleration in an older trend, focuses upon aspects of Calvin other than his theology. This development involves both Calvin scholars and people outside the disciplines of history and religion, and there is in the former group a sense of unexplored richness, and in the latter, pleasure in the apprehension of a fertile field.

A smaller number of Calvin scholars have been using untried aspects of Calvin for new perspectives on his theology. Thus we are seeing a slowly increasing interest among historians in Calvin's writing (though it has long been appreciated by literary historians) and his interpretive methods are being looked at from the viewpoint of linguistics; philosophers and historians alike are showing interest in his logic.[15] Historians are also stressing once again the importance of his humanistic background, pointing to the effects of his philological and juridical training in his formalistic methods, his scriptural exegesis, and his full willingness to use classical materials in all his work.[16] These trends are compatible with the well-known and important view of Calvin as, in ways both deliberate and not, a major source and shaper of the secularism that increasingly characterizes the postmedieval European world. Sometimes with highly specific focuses, but more often generalized, it has been widely observed that Calvinists lived their religion and served their God in and through this world, not separated from it and not oriented beyond it. In Weber's view, an inner need to affirm election was a decisive behavioral factor; a secular orientation, at least, follows from Calvin's basic and thorough acceptance of the vast distance between human and divine nature. Humans can only be human.[17]

I think it true that Calvin is of high importance for the modern western world and specifically for the evolution of its secularism, but in a way that is different from these. I think it is precisely his religious thought that is important in this evolution, and the demonstrated substance of non-theological aspects of it—his thought processes, his mode of expression—may enable us to reach both deeper and wider dimensions of his theology.

I want further to investigate Calvin's theology at its innermost and outermost reaches: its psychological grounding and its formal expression. The latter being rhetorical, it brings us directly to the center of sixteenth-century culture. That turns out to be an intriguingly appropriate place to deal with the question of dualism in Calvin. A mode of expression that is adopted by the widest variety of individuals, as rhetoric was in the Renaissance period, may be peculiarly amenable and useful to particular individuals. I think it was such for Calvin. While rhetoric may hold ascendency in a very wide range of cultural situations, it may serve particularly important functions in particular situations, and I think it did so in the mid-sixteenth century. In both instances, it is the prominence of a dualistic vision which seems to render major techniques and figures of rhetoric eminently apt when they are used.

The culture of the late Renaissance in Italy—and the form of Renaissance culture transmitted directly to northern Europe—was characterized by a movement away from the humanist image of man, a movement toward intellectualism, order, and simplicity, a rejection of a civic ideal of culture that seems logical in a sharply deteriorated political environment.[18] Rhetoric, presented by earlier humanists as a device of public culture, was repudiated by many. A world view that William Bouwsma characterizes as Stoic became dominant, an endorsement of a life of reason in the face of what was felt to be both external and internal disorder.[19]

The late Renaissance is also the setting of Mannerist art, a highly intellectualized art, an art of deliberate artifice in contrast to an earlier sense of harmony and absorption in the world of nature. In different ways, both the Stoic and Mannerist tempers are dualistic. Bouwsma remarks that the late Renaissance seems to have been seeking to supply a defect in the culture of the earlier Renaissance.[20] I think Calvin supplied this defect; more than that, I think he synthesized high and late Renaissance impulses and realized very fully the potential in both. He combined a highly Stoic mentality, at a time when it was culturally dominant, *with* rhetoric, a rhetoric he applied to something other than public culture and applied in a singular and powerful way.

Let us recall the fundamental significance of rhetoric in Renaissance humanism. Structuralist critics as well as historians have turned our attention in the last two decades to the significance of the Renaissance discovery of the significance of language. The key phrase in the humanist sources is the union of wisdom and eloquence, and eloquence is emphasized because it was a new element in common consciousness about writing and discourse, first needing defense and ultimately gaining primary allegiance. Hannah Gray cited the implications of rhetoric for the Renaissance image of man, who came to be seen not merely as a creature of the intellect but as a creature of will and emotions, the objects of the persuasive powers of language; Jerrold Seigel described rhetoric as the core of civic humanism; Nancy Struever explored it intensively in its philosophical significance and found in it a shadow-side of skepticism. Bouwsma has used the concept and also cited Reformation figures as exemplars of Renaissance rhetoric.[21]

The image of the Renaissance that has emerged from this new perspective is one in which man became conscious of his power to shape his outer as well as his inner world, as language does and through language.[22] Renaissance historical consciousness, long well-known to historians, is now seen more precisely as the pluralism inherent in the belief that individuals can, and through language do, shape individual worlds. On the one hand, then, creativity and positive progress in this world; on the other hand, no universals or absolutes, and deep fears about the demagogic potential in language. This was a major development in consciousness.

Let us also recall that the words of men will be measured against and wondered about in relation to the Word of God in the Christian economy.[23] To a sixteenth-century theologian, literary expression could have been significant in multiple ways. I think that Calvin's rhetoric can be very fruitfully regarded from the standpoint of psychological purposefulness. The extremism that he so often demonstrated in life and thought can be comprised in the same perspective. Much of the extremism seems to be the circumscribed personal response of a particular psychological type, and it certainly veers to the neurotic; some of it may be compensation for adjustments made elsewhere. It is in the public sphere, as psychologists and historians have maintained, that an individual's psychic life can take the form of an intuitive and concentrated grasp of difficulties or problems such that their nature will be universally familiar and their solutions widely salutary.[24] Some of the intensity and energy with which such individuals do their work may be the result of what psychologists call overdetermination.[25] I think these considerations apply to Calvin. Ideas and expression, in his theology, seem to me to coexist in an internal dialogue. I think that Calvin's use of rhetoric constituted his fundamental personal response and adaptation to the conflict he seems to have felt between orthodox belief and dualistic experience — and he may have been listened to so attentively because his was a very ordinary conflict writ large and a widely relevant response.

Somewhere between feeling and expression lie ideas, and the final context for this study is intellectual; it is perhaps closest to what the Annalistes mean by *mentalité*. I want to know how Calvin's mind worked. I am interested in the interrelations among the different levels of his mental processes and among the different facets of his theology or the areas to which he devoted intellectual attention. It has increasingly appeared to me that nominalist philosophy is an important source for Calvin's thought and provides important clues to the nature of these interrelations and, indeed, to the genesis of the body of ideas that constitute Calvinist theology.

The consideration of Calvin in relation to nominalism also has bearing upon the historiographical question of the relation between the Renaissance and the Reformation. Historians of both have become increasingly interested in the impact of nominalism upon the understanding of language from the fourteenth century onward. Reformation historiography has long attributed doctrinal importance to Ockham's work. In the last decade, Renaissance historians have come predictably to associate Ockham's interest in language with the same interest in the Renaissance. The attention to language in nominalism is also now recognized as an integral part of nominalist opposition to the overreaching nature of scholastic metaphysics. Apparently in response to both these developments, Reformation historians have shifted their focus from doctrine to the nominalist stress upon verbal covenant and have pursued this concept in the scripturalism of the Reformers.[26]

The direct stimulus or reinforcement (historians have tended to see the relationship as one or the other) given by nominalist thought to the

concern with language in Italian humanism and to the centrality of
Scripture in Reformation theology suggests a quite precise and important
community in Renaissance and Reformation thinking despite those basic
differences between the movements which have seemed to historians to
limit the depth of common grounds.[27] I think this community could be
examined further through Calvin, and Calvin's theology better understood
in its light. Notably among Reformation figures, he believed in the significance of language, and the generally systematic nature of his thought
offers the possibility of considering fairly closely his conception of language
in its wider intellectual context. The significance that I am attributing to
his rhetoric is, I think, importantly shaped by this context.

My concern with the way in which Calvinism was able to take deep
root in sixteenth-century Europe will also involve consideration of the
effects of a material and changing historical environment upon its genesis
and early progress, though more often, social and political dimensions
will be implicit. Reformation historians have demonstrated fairly conclu-
sively that adherents of Reform knew more than summarily what they
were taking on.[28] It has been suggested that the printing press made the
sixteenth century "the most theologically informed and curious in Western
history, so that the laity, whether literate or not, saw more clearly than
ever before how seemingly abstract theological issues directly affected their
lives."[29] I am suggesting that it was Calvin's rhetoric—and by that I mean
his thought in its formal expression—that could so effectively communicate
the ideas of Reform to very large numbers of people in immediately varying
local situations. But this rhetoric did not merely persuade. I see it as a
functional part of Calvinism itself, the principal vehicle of that aspect of
Calvinism that seems to constitute a transformation of Lutheranism and
that seems to have been in particular need of expression in the late
Renaissance period. The reasons why Calvin has continued to find
audiences, and the reasons why there have been periods when his theology
has receded in its reach, seem also to include the resonance of this rhetoric
and changing receptivity to it.

I am focusing in the chapters that follow upon the *Institutes* of 1559,
though I will draw upon other editions and other writings. Calvin's
rhetoric, logic, and theology are quintessentially those of the *Institutes*.
The *Institutes* was published, read, and republished; lists of editions,
histories of printing, and booksellers' inventories record its history. The
names of students in the Academy of Geneva and exiles, refugees, visitors,
and recruits are part of its history. The history of theological faculties in
Europe is also part of its history. Multiple abridgments were published,
but biographical remarks place the original *Institutes* as influence in homes
as well as in the churches and schools of ministers whose education was
based upon it.[30]

The *Institutes* was alive, though definitely sequestered, in the adverse circumstances that seventeenth-century thought posed for it in Europe. The writings of New England Puritans do no merely reflect, but cite, Calvin's works.[31] It has been suggested that, even in the Calvinist theology that we call rationalist, Calvin's conception of the knowledge of God functioned as a buttress against the total incursion of Cartesianism into religious thought.[32]

The commentaries and, of course, the catechism were alive: they echo less emphatically the rhetoric of the *Institutes* and often present that text in the recognizable form of an author's abstract or separate elaboration. The constant in all these instances is Calvin's voice, or the voices of people who have heard it and who translate it into something comprised neither of words alone nor of doctrine alone, but of a relation between words and doctrine. It is this relation that is, I think, the most distinctive aspect of Calvinist theology and that points to Calvin's importance in modern western history.

The *Institutes* was intended by Calvin to teach his faith; his other works explicate aspects of this faith, as the successive editions of the *Institutes* are successive elaborations of an existing whole. For faith to change lives and for teachings to be learned, doctrine had to be received as a totality: in this sense the systematic nature of the *Institutes* is secondary to its rhetorical design and programmatic nature. Calvin's personality and his psychic life were such that leadership of the church in Geneva, the *vita activa* to which he was committed, was less than easy and spontaneous. The writing of the *Institutes*, I will be suggesting, was an unconscious and intuitively therapeutic *vita activa*. Calvin benefited profoundly from it. His readers certainly benefit from the intenseness of the talents which he concentrated in his theology; they have benefited also, I think, from the human relevance of its most subjective aspects. I think Calvin was indeed read calvinistically.

1

Calvin in Relation
to Luther

PHYSICAL LINKS

Calvin did not know German, and he never knew Luther personally. But he had close personal relationships with individuals who did know Luther—preeminently, Melanchthon—and, more important, we know that he read much of Luther in Latin. The influence to which this reading led is well borne out in the direct statements of Calvin on Luther. The statements are rare but significant, and there is reason for the rarity.

First, Calvin always associated the cause of the Genevan church with the Lutheran church, as he did not with the Zwinglian. In 1543 he spoke of the time "when God raised up Luther and others, who held forth a torch to light us into the way of salvation, and on whose ministry our churches are founded and built."[1] He overtly sided with the Saxon Lutherans in their struggles in the mid-1540s, asking Genevans from his pulpit, "May we set ourselves apart? May we say 'They are far away from us'? No, they belong to the church, and we are their members."[2] This is the sense of solidarity that led to Calvin's acceptance of the Augsburg Confession.[3] But it was not just identification: it was gratitude—gratitude for specific and crucial theological discoveries and gratitude for having the courage to make these discoveries the basis for a reform *ab radice*, a decisive break with Rome. It was Luther "through whose work and ministry, most of all, the purity of the gospel has been restored in our time."[4] The metaphor of clear light in utter darkness is frequent: "when all was totally dark, Luther let the Gospel shine forth and opened the way to salvation."[5]

Individual and central doctrines are identified: on predestination and the unfree will, "that which is most important in this question, and for the sake of which everything else is said, we defend today just as it was declared by Luther and others at the beginning."[6] Luther purged the church of godless superstition, that thick cloud of darkness that the doctrine of works constituted, and "in this course we still continue today."[7] And while Luther did not at first contemplate a total break, he came to see that the "fatal lethargy" in the church had gone so far that "what was needed to awaken it was not voices and words, but the trumpet-blast, thunder, and lightning."[8]

Certainly, Calvin thought, gratitude and admiration should not be carried too far. First, they are unhealthy and exacerbate a tendency in Luther toward intemperate, dogmatic, and hence uncharitable and inflexible self-assertion: "there is a bit of obstinacy mixed in with his firmness." Calvin said he revered Luther "from my heart, but am violently ashamed of him. . . . I admit we all owe him much. And I am not reluctant to let him be pre-eminent with the highest authority, provided he knows how to govern his own self."[9] Unfortunately, the followers of Luther are guilty of blind worship, making criticism, and hence progress, impossible. And progress is essential. Luther was indeed the beginning, but we have gone further since this beginning. Theological truth implies development: "our constant effort, day and night, is also to fashion, in the manner we think will be best, whatever is faithfully handed on by us."[10] It would have been "utterly ridiculous" for Calvin to undertake the work of exegesis if he had not been "permitted at any point to depart from the opinion of Luther."[11] Calvin most delightfully summarized his criticism when he asked, "Ah, Luther! How few imitators of your excellence have you left behind you — and how many apes of your holy belligerence!" and he most humanly summarized his eagerness to have his admiration reciprocated when he excitedly rejoiced at Luther's remark to Melanchthon that he had read Calvin's book (it is not certain which one) "with singular enjoyment."[12]

Theologically, there was a clear and simple reason for the rarity of Calvin's statements about Luther: human beings are instruments of God. "In the church we must always be on our guard, lest we pay too great a deference to men," Calvin wrote to Melanchthon.[13] Only close, personal friends could be individualized; only the ancients, such as Augustine, sanctified by time as authorities, could be revered. But Calvin's language in his relatively few direct utterances makes it abundantly clear that Luther was unique and special among men. He was not just "an illustrious servant of God"; he was, Calvin wrote, his "much respected father," his "ever-honored father," and, as distinctively and strongly, "a remarkable apostle of Christ."[14]

Luther was widely know in Paris, Orléans, and Bourges, where Calvin spent his student years. At Paris, Calvin heard John Major denounce

Luther—and specify his doctrines. His friend and teacher at Orléans, Melchior Wolmar, countered with an equally informative and, this time, encouraging endorsement of Luther, the first positive judgment to which Calvin was exposed, to be followed by many more in the humanist circles he frequented.[15] We know that Calvin read at least Luther's *Great Catechism*, the *Small Catechism* (the probable model for the first edition of the *Institutes* in 1536), *On the Freedom of a Christian*, *The Babylonian Captivity of the Church*, *On the Bondage of the Will*, and the major sermon on the Eucharist—all major works, and some minor works as well.[16]

Influence is an elusive matter. Historians who have maintained that Bucer exerted the decisive influence on Calvin have cited as evidence their close personal relationship, which is indeed evident in Calvin's letters to him, as well as the very concrete parallels between the organization of churches in Geneva and Strasbourg and the marked attachment to discipline that is reflected in this organization. The doctrine of predestination is also present in Bucer's writings. But against this interpretation it can be observed that the doctrinal parallels are either nonintegral matters (the external form of the visible church) or nonspecifiable: much of Bucer is in Augustine, Bradwardine, Gregory of Rimini—and Luther.[17] Again, the influence that is specifiable involves more than parallelisms of ideas and motifs: it involves their systematic interconnections and their relative weightings, and here the reading of texts alone will suffice.

SYSTEMATIC LINKS

Anthropological Foundation and Its Conclusion: Justification through Faith

Luther and Calvin each proceed from a conviction of radical disparity between man and God, between the human and the divine.[18] The disparity is first of all a matter of sin vis-à-vis perfection. This is more than a fact; it is a problem, because God and man are linked in a personal relationship and God is judgmental. He makes impossible demands for perfection; while he makes promises of salvation despite imperfection, he is at the same time inaccessible, and there is uncertainty for whom the promises are intended. Here religion as a relational matter turns into theology, with the impetus to theology being a need, indeed a craving, for certainty of salvation in light of sin and one's consequent impotence to effect this. So salvation must come from without. The solution is justification through faith—faith in God's promise of the substitutionary character of Christ's sacrifice. We can supply no righteousness of our own; rather, we must count entirely on the imputed righteousness of the Cross, in which Christ perfectly fulfilled the law (as we cannot) and God agreed to accept his righteousness as if it were ours.

However, as damnation would be just, because we are sinful, salvation through Christ is a matter of mercy, and this raises the question of God's discretion. To whom shall he grant it? Christ died for all men, but certainly the Old Testament makes it clear that God has always discriminated, as in the designation of the Jews as his people. This leads to predestination and thereby to God's power. There are, in human eyes, two kind of power—regulated and ordinate, on the one hand, and absolute and arbitrary, on the other. Both Luther and Calvin attribute both kinds to God and acquiesce in both: the salvation of some, not all, is just and reasonable because we all would merit only damnation without it; it is just but beyond human understanding, which perceives only that Christ died that all might live.

Human reason must bow before the justice that is opaque to it and seek enlightenment, and hence satisfaction, outside itself: next to *sola fide*, we come to *sola scriptura*. Scripture confirms all the above, and it historicizes it and thus renders it objective. Faith is the revelation of Christ as mediator, centered in the Cross, an event outside us, but for us. It is both absolutely objective, because it is circumscribed in time, place, and situation, and personal and relational: it has meaning only in relation to us, as external as it is.

So dependent are we on Scripture, and so determinative is the impact of the Cross on us to be, that the Word that is Christ, as presented in Scripture, is normative for our earthly life—the pilgrimage we are engaged in before our ultimate reconciliation with God. The Word is all of Scripture, and the Old and New Testaments define the church in which the Word lives and in which we live until the end of the world. A major part of scriptural exegesis in the Reformation, and one that permeates Calvin's commentaries especially, seeming to reflect a perception trained by and reinforcing his faith, is the harmonization of Old and New Testaments. What aspect of the new dispensation is foreshadowed her? What parts of the Old Testament give authority to, and thus verify and sanctify, this part of the New Testament? Asking these questions is a habit of faith, rendering Scripture a living whole for living beings. And the normative character of Scripture follows from the same anthropological consideration that leads to justification through faith—the total and radical disparity between the human and the divine. We do not know and are incapable of achieving the good; the evil in us has to be dealt with. Hence, the scripturally based church.

For Calvin as well as for Luther, justification through faith becomes the center of religion as the logical conclusion and culmination of an anthropology. Indeed, in the *Institutes*, it was first necessary to show man's true nature, and then to establish the implications that faith had for this nature, before discussing faith *per se*. Introducing the section on justification by faith, Calvin reviews the *Institutes* thus far. Until then, in Book III, "the theme of justification was... more lightly touched upon because it was more to the point to understand first how little devoid of good works is the faith through which alone we obtain free righteousness by the mercy of God.... Therefore we must now discuss these matters thoroughly. And we must so discuss them as to bear in mind that this is the main hinge on which religion turns."[19] For Calvin, as well as Luther, the "only" in *sola fide* was essential, and he was as characteristically stubborn about it:

> "Now the reader sees how fairly the Sophists today cavil against our doctrine when we say that man is justified by faith alone [Rom. 3:28]... Since the word 'alone' is nowhere expressed [in Scripture], they do not allow this additive to be made. Is it so?... If righteousness [i.e., Christ's imputed righteousness] is revealed in the Gospel, surely no mutilated or half-righteousness but a full and perfect righteousness is contained there.... Does not [Paul] who takes everything from works firmly enough ascribe everything to faith alone?"[20]

And for Luther as well as Calvin, predestination is the logical reflex of justification through faith: he expounded it thoroughly (as we shall see) in the treatise *On the Bondage of the Will*, his *Lectures on Romans*, and in many other writings, always in implicit but nevertheless systematic interconnection with his anthropology. The content, the order, and the weighting of this doctrinal sketch applies to both theologians.

Intellectual and Psychological Preconditions for Influence

The traditional picture of Luther and Calvin in historiography is that they are separate. Parallels between the two are often noted, yet without the establishment of a relationship. Exceptions to this pattern certainly exist. Brian Gerrish quotes with tentative approval a judgment that Calvin was Luther's greatest disciple.[21] The judgment was made by Peter Meinhold, who also maintains that Calvin was Luther's "only true" disciple.[22] Roland Bainton has said that no one understood Luther better than Calvin.[23] However, the precision of the relation remains unexplored and its possibilities neglected.[24]

The reason for the neglect may be largely a matter of biography, for the typical images of Luther and Calvin contain two radically different personal routes to Reform. Luther's route was experiential; his theology was the culmination of a long, agonizing, and determinative experience of sin and despair. Calvin's route was intellectual. His actual conversion occurred when he, the perpetual scholar, was quietly persuaded by the sudden apprehension of true doctrine, and his preparation for it was a long, careful exposure to late medieval thought. Indeed, Luther and Calvin themselves are probably responsible for these images. Luther talks continuously of his early and decisive religious experiences, and he maintained that "it is by living—no, rather, by dying and being damned—that a theologian is made, not by understanding, reading, or speculating."[25] Calvin always presented himself as a scholar by nature and, even when taken away from the scholarly life, as a student of Christ. He closed his introduction to the *Institutes* with Augustine's words, "I count myself one of the number of those who write as they learn and learn as they write."[26] However, Calvin had also been taught (probably by John Major) the Scotist doctrine that the intellect was incapable of attaining direct knowledge of God both because of its own infirmity and because of God's transcendent nature, and the more extreme doctrine of Ockham that knowledge of the transcendent divinity is necessarily available to us only through revealed truths and the church.[27] Major also transmitted the doctrine of predestination, drawing on Augustine, Bradwardine, and Gregory of Rimini.[28] Calvin was thus prepared for Lutheran ideas; additionally, the late medieval emphasis upon the limits of knowledge made him peculiarly open to the consideration of Luther's experience.

Calvin frequently depicted teachableness as accepting that which was contrary to natural inclinations: one learned through persuasion, through transforming impact. This notion is implicit in his presentation of his conversion, in his letters, and, indeed, in the *Institutes*. Both his conversion and Luther's impact were at the same time alien and prepared for: they were both experiential in the contrary sense and intellectually congenial. Moreover, it will be maintained that Luther's theology was in a very important sense experientially as well as intellectually plausible to Calvin, for Calvin had an experience of sin and despair comparable in intensity to Luther's. Different in nature, its sheer strength was, I think, decisive in making him accept the Lutheran influence.

Finally, Luther's experiential theology was intellectually compatible with Calvin's premises, not by coincidence, but because it was grounded in the same theological suppositions that Calvin had absorbed in Paris.[29] It is well known that Luther called Biel his master, and he cited Gregory of Rimini as the only one among the moderns who represented truly the unfree will.[30] The Lutheran and Calvinist anthropology was a radicalization of late medieval thought at the same time that it was a rejection of certain aspects of it—specifically, of the Pelagianism inherent in much of nominalism. The radicalization and revision were intellectual matters in an exact sense; they were also intellectual matters with an experiential base.

The certitude of salvation that Luther and Calvin sought had to answer an intellectual and experiential need in both. Which need was stronger? Or which was out of the ordinary? An answer emerges when one notes a qualification to the certitude at which they arrived and a logical dilemma in their stances, which we shall further explore. For neither Luther nor Calvin was the experience of certainty continuous: they accepted as inevitable the fact that experiences of despair accompanied them throughout life. Moreover, normal experience, as Luther and Calvin convincingly depict it, elides the issue of certainty. We do not naturally have a sense of sin; rather, we are proud (that is at the essence of sin) and deceive ourselves into oblivion to our sinful natures. If we have an inkling of a sense of sin, the same pride emerges as a defense mechanism. It seems highly likely that both Luther and Calvin had an experience of sin that was not usual in ordinary life — a sense of sin strong enough to make certainty an issue and affect the certainty they came to accept and proclaim.

Luther and Calvin are as closely linked in their doctrine of regeneration or sanctification. Sanctification is inseparable from and simultaneous with justification. As closely as Calvin is usually linked to discipline and exhortation, and as strong in traditional historiography as the image of his coldness and rigidity may be, sanctification is for him, as it is for Luther, spontaneous and activistic. Sanctification, like justification, springs from God-granted faith, and "faith cannot remain inoperative in the heart, but . . . must, of necessity, manifest itself."[31] Above all, for Luther and Calvin, sanctification is entirely separate from salvation and in dramatic contrast to the doctrine of salvation through works. Repeatedly, they tell us that a good man does good works, but he is not saved because of them: rather, he does them because he is saved.

Luther and Calvin are also very much alike on the related matter of love. But the differences with which we shall be concerning ourselves begin to emerge sharply here. For both of them, love is the paradigmatic Christian act. However, for Luther, love in man corresponds to the love that is constitutive of divinity, and he presents it as being as Christ to one's neighbor. Calvin, rather, derives it from the second table of the law. Sanctification is a rebirth away from sin, and the reborn man will love his neighbor. But that this is not a natural movement in the regenerate life is quite drastically reflected in the location, in the *Institutes*, of the realization of humanity in the sphere of civic authority. The church fosters love, but, to prevent men from being at each other's throats (the possibility of which would in no way have surprised Luther), civic authority governs the relations of men — their positive as well as negative interactions.

Calvinism is a systematization of Lutheranism, but some part of Calvin differed from Luther. The differences between the two actually emerge in areas where agreement seems to amount to congruence, and the similarities prevail even in those few areas in which they were in overt conflict: most notably, on the Eucharist. We must investigate the Calvinist experience of sin that made him open to Luther and the Calvinist personality that made him differ. But first we must further pursue the connections to establish the nature and extent of the influence more exactly, and only then will it make sense to talk, not of one versus the other, but of Calvin's Luther.

THE EXTENT OF THE INFLUENCE

STRICT IMPLICATIONS OF JUSTIFICATION THROUGH FAITH

So radically central was the concept of justification through faith to Luther that it was theologically prior to charity—even in this person who both apotheosized and felt naturally and spontaneously inclined to love. "This faith justifieth without and before charity," Luther wrote.

> We grant that we must teach also good works and charity, but it must be done in time and place, that is to say, when the question is concerning works, and toucheth not this article of justification. But here the question is, by what means we are justified and attain eternal life. To this we answer with Paul, that by faith only in Christ we are pronounced righteous, and not by the works of the law or charity. . . we will not suffer ourselves to be turned aside from the principal point of this matter as Satan most desireth.[32]

The way *must* be barred to the doctrine of salvation through works. That doctrine is, to Luther and to Calvin as well, the foremost work of the devil because it bases itself on self-assertion and, worse, self-reliance. We can do nothing. Faith is a gift of God, and it is efficacious, both theologians repeatedly tell us, only by virtue of the action of the Holy Spirit.

Calvin gave much attention to refuting the Catholic charge that faith in itself was tantamount to a work, representing an act of will in acquiescing, endorsing, and turning to God. Luther (having been exercised for the charge in his debate with Erasmus) had formulated his position in both formal and original theological terms. "This most excellent righteousness," he wrote, "which God through Christ, without works, imputeth unto us," is "neither political not ceremonial, not the righteousness of God's law, nor consisteth in our works, but is clean contrary; that is to say a mere passive righteousness, as the other above are active. For in this we work nothing, we render nothing unto God, but only we receive and suffer another to work in us, that is to say, God. Therefore it seemeth good unto me to call this righteousness of faith or Christian righteousness, the passive righteousness."[33]

The theme of nothingness in Calvin corresponds to the theme of

whatever else should be ascribed to one who is trusted. When this is done, the soul consents to his will. Then it hallows his name and allows itself to be treated according to God's good pleasure for, clinging to God's promises, it does not doubt that he who is true, just, and wise will do, dispose, and provide all things well."[56] We are left at this point with an extreme sense of sin in Calvin and Luther alike rendering damnation just and an extreme sense of God's possible injustice, his indisputable power, and his inscrutability. Predestination reinforces, even as it proceeds from, the anthropology in Luther's and Calvin's theology.

Characteristically, Calvin could, at the same time that he dreaded predestination, wonder at the fact of God's absolute transcendence and the fact of his sheer power. We should not search out God's secrets; rather we should accept them as "the sublimest wisdom, which he would have us revere but not understand, that through this also he should fill us with wonder."[57] This is a uniquely Calvinist, not Lutheran, note. But there is also in Calvin a note that is perhaps more Lutheran than Luther—or, rather, a carrying of Lutheranism to a logical extreme that Luther himself chose not to pursue. Some—undoubtedly Lutherans—have been guilty of making election depend on faith "as if it were doubtful and also ineffectual until confirmed by faith." Yet it is simply false "to say that election takes effect only after we have embraced the gospel, and takes its validity from this." But it is precisely the Lutheran conception of passive righteousness that is at the core of Calvin's argument, and he is only arguing against an Erasmian conception of faith as cooperation. "This rashness, therefore, must be restrained by the soberness of faith that in his outward Word, God may sufficiently witness his secret grace to us, provided only the pipe, from which water abundantly flows out for us to drink, does not hinder us from according its due honor to the fountain."[58] The connection between faith and predestination is clear, distinct, and Lutheran:

> Where we receive the promises in faith, we know that then and only then do they become effective in us. On the contrary, when faith is snuffed out, the promise is abolished at the same time.... God is said to have ordained from eternity those whom he wills to embrace in love, and those upon whom he wills to vent his wrath. Yet he announced salvation to all men indiscriminately. I maintain that these statements agree perfectly with each other. For by so promising he merely means that his mercy is extended to all, provided they seek after it and implore it. But only those whom he has illumined do this. And he illumines those whom he has predestined to salvation.[59]

Calvin systematized the Lutheran doctrine of predestination, including its basic anthropology and its integral relation to faith. It was a radically different answer to the question of salvation than that of the medieval Catholic church. But it is not yet clear how it leads to certainty, how it can be determined if salvation is *for me*. Was the substitution for me? Will faith, saving and *extra nos*, be granted to me? There is a need to know more about this God whose intentions are so unfathomable, and perhaps arbitrary and unjust. And exactly how was knowledge of God arrived at? Knowledge of the God we seem to be dealing with is clearly different from knowledge of earthly things. What was the nature of this knowledge?

KNOWLEDGE OF GOD

God's two wills and ultimate transcendence. I have referred to the importance of late medieval thought for Luther and Calvin. One of the clearest influencing motifs in this thought was its conception of God's omnipotence, of both an ordinate and an inordinate nature.[60] Both kinds of power were more extreme than in earlier conceptions. So omnipotent was the God of justice that knowledge of him necessitated obedience to him.[61] So omnipotent was the God beyond justice that one could speak of him only through the principle of noncontradiction:[62] God, as absolute being, could not annihilate himself. Scotus, unlike Aquinas, placed God's will before reason and distinguished two kinds of will: absolute and ordered. But God's essence was determined through love. Ockham discarded this qualification.[63] John Major retained the principle of moral indisputability in God, but taught all of Scotus and Ockham, too.[64]

Calvin deals with both kinds of power directly and frequently, and he does so more explicitly and systematically than Luther. He renounces inordinate power, "that absolute will of which the Sophists babble, by an impious and profane distinction separating his justice from his power."[65] But Calvin cannot maintain that God is just beyond controversy. He is definitionally just, and Calvin's is often a matter of literally blind faith. Speaking of the existence of evil, he writes, "When we do not grasp how God wills to take place what he forbids to be done, let us recall our mental incapacity, and at the same time consider that the light in which God dwells is not without reason called inapproachable [1 Tim. 6:16] because it is overspread with darkness."[66] He is virtually identical with the "Sophists" whom he rejects when he distinguishes between that will of God which we voluntarily obey and "his secret will, by which he controls all things and directs them to their end."[67] Luther was sometimes more succinct and epigrammatic than Calvin: of the God whose reasons were hidden or revealed only in paradoxes, he could only say "Unverstand ist der rechte Verstand."[68] The two wills are as clear in Luther as in Calvin: God "does not will the death of a sinner—in his Word, that is. But he does will it by that inscrutable will."[69]

Luther formulated a conception of the hiddenness of God, the unfathomable and unknowable God who was the essence of divinity in a naked and absolute sense, as distinct from the God of hidden revelation — the God hidden in the weakness and folly of the Cross. The God who hid himself outside Christ did not move him to trust — and yet this hidden God, like Christ, is "God himself."[70] The most intense experience of God's hiddenness for Luther was the *Anfechtungen*, the attacks of despair in which one lost the conviction of salvation that was at the same time relatedness to God: one was both damned and forsaken. Faith in the trial of the *Anfechtungen* was "a flight": one must dare against God to flee to God.[71] Somehow, God leads us, in order to make us content, "yet deeper into damnation, and hides his care within tempests."[72] Luther's experience of despair reinforced, as it sprang from, a conviction that divinity was not just different from, but contrary to, human nature. A craftsman doesn't work according to the form of the material: "No, the craftsman. . . destroys that substantial form so that he may introduce another form which is utterly contrary to the prior form of his material."[73] This is as close to the Calvinist conception of human versus divine nature as Calvin was to the related Lutheran experience of despair when he wrote, in the *Institutes*, that "surely no more terrifying abyss can be imagined than to feel yourself forsaken and estranged from God, and when you call upon him, not to be heard."[74]

The image of God as transcendent, of God as pure act, beyond the scrutiny of reason and perhaps contrary to the standards of justice inherent in reason, was reinforced in the writings of mystics, in the line running from Bernard of Clairvaux to Eckhardt, who stressed God's direct action, entirely apart from the church, entirely without agency. But the image was perhaps most intensively reinforced, and perhaps thereby made influential, by the epistemological foundation evolved by the late scholastics. Late medieval epistemology both proceeds from and results in an emphasis upon God's power as the expression of his transcendence. In the face of divine transcendence, human reason is severely limited, to say the least. Man also has no experience-grounded, intuitive knowledge of God; Ockham concluded that we cannot even approach God's essence.[75] Instead we can and must focus upon his effects. From Thomistic natural theology, in which we can learn of God's existence and basic attributes by a rational examination of the natural world, we move with Ockham to something akin to an existentialist concept of "presence." God is accessible to our minds through his experienced effects in the created world and his actions in Scripture.[76] Scotus drew the conclusion that the primary natural object of the intellect is not a thing's essence or quiddity; it is its evident existence.[77] He applied this logic to God and arrived at an entirely personalistic conception of him.[78] In it, knowledge of God became knowledge of a willed activity to which the human mind had no natural relation.[79]

The temper of knowledge. God's will is the basis of predestination. But in Luther and Calvin the link is otherwise important. Power, paradigmatically manifested as the sheer will of divine election, is the way God makes himself known to us: epistemology thus reinforces and is reinforced by anthropology, leading likewise to the dominant fact of predestination.

It is in late medieval thought that knowledge of a transcendent and omnipotent God and one's relationship to him become intertwined, inseparable, and equivalent. We know God through the effects of his will; man, in knowing God, is affected by him. It seems most probable that just this relational character of knowledge influenced Luther and Calvin, and could do so precisely because relating was tied to *scientia*, as it was not, necessarily, for the mystics, to whom the concept of the personal relation of man and God in Luther and Calvin is often attributed. Certainly, Jean Gerson evolved a "mystical theology" that was a synthesis of piety and *scientia*.[80] And religious knowledge for Luther and Calvin was always *scientia* and *devotio* or *pietas*. We must strive to attain the wisdom of God, Calvin writes, and that includes two things: "right affection and good understanding."[81] Luther directly learned of the need to combine knowledge and piety from the mystical tradition, notably in Tauler and Gerson; Calvin was also affected by the tradition, notably in Bernard of Clairvaux, the author of *The Imitation of Christ*, and the Brethren of the Common Life.[82] However, the thrust of mysticism was subjective, not objective. And Luther, and after him Calvin, centered religion on what Ozment calls "the objective context" of Scripture—the authoritative and unquestionable record, the Word objectified in the historical events constituting the Old and New Testaments.

Moreover, Luther and Calvin were very much in the humanist tradition of the Renaissance insofar as they believed that textual criticism could render historical records still more accurate and objective: the return to the painstakingly purified sources of truth was the basis of *pietas*. And yet if Scripture was objective knowledge of God through the Word, it was still more a matter of God speaking *to me*, personally. This implication is clear throughout Luther, and it is emphasized stylistically in his conversational paraphrases of Scripture: "Paul says to us . . ."; "Paul says for us here. . . ." Similarly for Calvin, John Major was probably the source who offered to him his auditive conception of Scripture, going beyond even Scotus in the presentation of Scripture as immediate, palpable, and personal.[83] The trinitarian corollary to this, and the corollary to the *sola fide* theology of Luther and Calvin, is that Scripture is God speaking to me; I have the capacity to hear and receive the Word by the grace and effectuating power of the Holy Spirit. Faith, as much *extra nos* as Scripture, renders Scripture truly mine. The subjectivity of mysticism is replaced by a personalized objectivism.

Finally, the intellectualism of late medieval theology would have been congenial to Luther as well as to Calvin. The importance of thorough, accurate, and specific knowledge for Calvin does not need to be stressed. As for Luther, despite his famous antiintellectual epithets and his strong polemics against "academicians," he was at the start and remained through his career "not a neurotic monk propounding riddles or a charismatic visionary privy to paradoxes, [but rather] a late medieval *doctor scripturae*."[84] Luther rejected Erasmus's skepticism, not his intellectualism, and against skepticism he raised a thoroughly intellectualist love of incontrovertible truths: "Not to delight in assertions is not the mark of a Christian heart. Indeed, one must delight in assertions to be a Christian at all!"[85] It is characteristic of Scripture and its strongest virtue that it is clear: "I hope you credit Luther with some acquaintance with and judgment in the sacred writings. . . . That there are in Scripture some things abstruse and not quite plain, was spread by the godless Sophists."[86]

Saving knowledge. For Luther and Calvin, God was known through his immediate presence. Knowing was living in this presence, and thus relational. The personalism in Calvin's concept of the knowledge of God is proclaimed, in the *Institutes*, in the motif that knowlege of God entails obedience to him.[87] That this personalism was suggested by the late medieval scholastics is reflected in Calvin's statements that specifically link a nonontological epistemology with a relational theology — as, for example, when he states that

> indeed faith ought not to fix upon the essence of Christ alone, so to speak, but should be intent upon his power and office. For there was little profit in knowing who Christ was unless this second thing happened, that Christ be known as he willed to be towards us and for what purpose he was sent by the Father. Hence it is that the Papists have no thing but a little shadow of Christ because while they were concerned to grasp the bare essence they neglected his kingdom.[88]

But Luther and Calvin rejected the Pelagianism in nominalist thought, and this rendered the core of relation to God — living in his presence — confrontational and judgmental. The radical contrast of perfection and sin meant that the inevitable judgment would include the possibility of damnation — a merited damnation — unless it were somehow obviated *extra nos*. God was judgmental and justly angry. And so knowing God was necessarily a soteriological question. Knowledge had to be saving knowledge.

The Case of Unio. The *extra nos* theme in both Luther and Calvin is grounded in an anthropology and a trinitarian theology. Faith is "the principal work of the Holy Spirit. . . . Paul shows the Spirit to be the inner teacher by whose effort the promise of salvation penetrates into our minds, a promise that would otherwise only strike the air or beat upon our ears."[89] This is as true of reading Scripture as of participating in the sacraments; it permeates the church and informs the whole Christian life. The penetration of faith is the core of our experience of union with God. Sometimes, in Luther and Calvin, *unio* sounds decidedly mystical. Luther can write, rhapsodically, that faith

> unites the soul with Christ as a bride is united with her bridegroom. . . . Christ is full of grace, life, and salvation. The soul is full of sins, death, and damnation. Now let faith come between them, and sins, death, and damnation will be Christ's, while grace, life, and salvation will be the soul's; for if Christ is a bridegroom, he must take upon himself the things which are his bride's and bestow upon her the things that are his. . . . By the wedding ring of faith he shares in the sins, death, and pains of hell which are his bride's. . . . The believing soul by means of the pledge of its faith is free in Christ, its bridegroom, free from all sins, secure against death and hell, and is endowed with the eternal righteousness, life, and salvation of Christ its bridegroom.[90]

Calvin can talk of the "secret union" with Christ—and that means the union that is beyond reason—in which "we leave our nature and go into Christ's." He writes lyrically of the "wonderful exchange" in the Eucharist, such that

> becoming Son of man with us, he has made us sons of God with him; that, by taking on our mortality, he has conferred his immortality upon us; that, accepting our weakness, he has strengthened us by his power; that, receiving our poverty unto himself, he has transferred his wealth to us; that, taking the weight of our iniquity upon himself (which oppressed us), he has clothed us with his righteousness.[91]

But *unio* is always based on a meeting of unlikenesses, as distinct from the paradigmatic mystical contact between divinity and the precreated spark of the soul.[92] Mysticism tended in the direction that Eckhardt carried to an extreme: toward a supraindividual conception of God. In Eckhardt's arresting assertion, in that return to precreated oneness with God, "I will be free in God and free from his will, that is, from God's works and from God himself."[93] The nothingness of which mystics often spoke referred to the obliteration of individual personality. "Our becoming like God is the cause of our union with him," Gerson wrote.[94] "Nothingness" also meant a leaving behind of all God's historical means of grace, notably, the sacraments and the Word in Scripture, Ozment's "objective context."

There are temporal and spatial dimensions to *unio* in Luther and Calvin: union is worked out in the course of sanctification and the regenerated life, and in the context of the church. It also has an eschatological dimension: it is not fulfillment in itself, but a foreshadowing of what will be the ultimate experience. Above all, *unio* consists of the reception of Christ's imputed righteousness. We are still sinners. To speak of leaving aside human nature means to construe this nature as irrelevant for justification: God will view us in the light of Christ's righteousness. Calvin clearly differentiates Adam's sin, which is actually in us such that we, individually, are guilty, from the gift of Christ's grace, which is "not a quality with which God endows us, as some [he has been speaking of the Schoolmen] absurdly explain it, but a gratuitous imputation of righteousness."[95] *Unio* is effected by the Holy Spirit through faith and does not substantially transform us, while it does most profoundly affect us.

Like *unio*, knowledge of God comes through faith for Luther and Calvin. Its effects are radical: knowledge itself is soteriological. In Calvin's words, "where [God] has shone, we possess Him by Faith and also enter into the possession of life, and this is why the knowledge of Him is truly and justly called saving."[96] But that is the theology of the two. There is also to be examined a biographical aspect, a historical dimension inherent in any theory of knowledge that is affective and personal as well as intellectual and objective. Examination of this historical dimension is further necessitated by the theological premise, ultimately derived from Augustine, with which the *Institutes* begins and which is implicit in the writings of the very Augustinian Luther: that knowledge of God depends upon, proceeds from, and is interwoven with self-knowledge. Here we must return to the concept of saving knowledge, for it is ultimately one with self-knowledge in its full theological dimension, a theological dimension necessarily and naturally grounded in personal history.

SELF-KNOWLEDGE

Saving knowledge, self-knowledge, and knowledge of sin. Saving knowledge is, precisely, effective knowledge of sin. It contains two mysteries. First, it consists of real knowledge of sin—comprehensive, accurate, and specific—despite the psychic tendencies and mechanisms that make such knowledge totally unnatural, contrary to nature, and impossible. Second, it necessarily leads, because it is simultaneously linked, to knowledge of Christ as Redeemer, which is the solution to the problem of living with sin—of living with sin in the face of God's potential and entirely just damnation.

Sin is the totality of human nature, not just the flesh and the fleshly. To exist is to be sinful. Luther herein broke with the dualistically tempered medieval conception of sin. Tentler has pointed out that "the capitulation to dualism" in medieval theology, however extreme it appears, was never complete.[97] Yet the dualistic suspicion of the evils of the natural physical function of sex persisted throughout medieval moral theology, and indeed "sexuality holds a special place in medieval religion": the medieval church, in both its literature and the records of its confessional practices, was "inordinately concerned with the sexual."[98] The disparagement of the bodily and of all temporal existence is reflected in the pervasive medieval conviction that likeness to God was the way to salvation—hence the precept of *imitatio* as well as the mystical transcendence by withdrawal into the soul.[99] The Lutheran conception of sin dissolved that conviction: it was the human and the divine that were different, and morality as well as salvation had to be understood accordingly.

In his changed conception of sin, Luther also anticipated insights in existential thought. One makes a choice, and the choice is determinative of the whole of one's existence. It does not affect an abstract essence; it does not affect specific behavior; it affects being-in-life. Faith, for Luther, is a turning—a turning from existence as sin to life under the guidance and in the power of the Spirit. For what truly defines man is not what he is in essence or the acts he performs, but what he looks for and expects. Ozment suggests that this does not transform, but rather substantiates, man.[100] The same totalistic conception of sin and existentialist motif of determinative turning are clear in Calvin. It is significant to him, and would have been impressive to read, that sin that is bodily and sin that is of the spirit can be described through the same metaphors: "For as the body is weighed down with dissipation and drunkenness and becomes fit for nothing, so the cares and passions of the world, sloth or indifference, are like a spiritual drunkenness, which overpowers the mind."[101] That pervasive sameness is the basis for his conclusion that "the whole man is naturally flesh, until by the grace of regeneration he begins to be spiritual."[102] The source of the turning is *extra nos*—it is God-granted faith. But it constitutes a commitment—to believe in Christ as Redeemer— that redefines existence totally.

The existentialist parallel includes the nature of the new life. It is not determined once and for all by the turning, but has to be renewed at every moment: commitment is not at once, not intermittent, but continuous. That is because it is commitment in the face of a continuous threat: the continuous possibility, and sometimes the actuality, of despair.

Obstacles to self-knowledge. If the whole concept of justification in Luther "excelleth all reason,"[103] there are indications that the most problematic part of it was arriving at the knowledge of sin that would lead one to turn to Christ. Sin is continuously conceived as the pride that is the denial of sin, "this monster and this mad beast (I mean the presumption of righteousness and religion) which naturally maketh men proud."[104] It is inordinately and decisively strong:

> For as long as the opinion of righteousness abideth in man, so
> long there abideth also in him incomprehensible pride, presump-
> tion, security, hatred of God, contempt of his grace and mercy,
> ignorance of the promises and of Christ. The preaching of free
> remission of sins for Christ's sake, cannot enter into the heart
> of such a one, neither can he feel any taste or savour thereof.
> For that mighty rock and adamant wall, to wit, the opinion of
> righteousness, wherewith the heart is environed, doth resist it.[105]

Calvin takes the same starting point, conceptualizes the theology of self-
knowledge, and systematizes it in its theological context: the theology of
sola fide and ultimately of predestination.

The *Institutes* of 1559 opens with the statement that knowledge of
God and knowledge of ourselves, which constitute "true and sound
wisdom," are intertwined, and while it is "not easy to discern" which is
prior, Calvin's first statement is that knowledge of self leads to God. The
gifts with which we are endowed lead us to knowledge of the donor—of
God the Creator—and then "the miserable ruin, into which the rebellion
of the first man cast us, especially compels us to look upward."[106]
However, pride and self-condemnation are in contradiction; moreover,
they are presented nonexperientially. Even before the opening of the text,
the preface to King Francis, retained in the final edition, asks

> what is more consonant with faith than to recognize that we are
> naked of all virtue, in order to be clothed by God? That we are
> empty of all good, to be filled by him? That we are slaves of
> sin, to be freed by him? Blind to be illumined by him? Lame,
> to be made straight by him? Weak to be sustained by him? To
> take away from us all occasion for glorying, that he alone may
> stand forth gloriously and we glory in him?[107]

We condemn ourselves in order to render glory and attribute power unto
God.

This is nonexperiential: what experience demonstrates is the opposite.
Man is innately proud; so surrounded is he by misery that even the smallest
talent will be the cause for pride.[108] Ungratefully, perversely, he misinter-
prets the great gifts of God—of reason, of creativity, of worldly capabilities—as his own: "we flatter ourselves most sweetly, and fancy ourselves
all but demigods."[109] Indeed, the theme of man's impulse to self-
deification—to which self-reliance, reliance on one's works for salvation,
is tantamount—runs through the *Institutes*. But some of us have an inkling
of sin: the law, after all, spells it out and condemns us. Yet so devastating
would it be to admit it, and so prone are we to pride, that the mechanism

of self-defense against the accusation goes into effect: despair leads back again to pride. "What man does not remain as he is. . .either ignorant or unmindful of his own misery?"[110]

Calvin changed the order of the *Institutes* considerably after the first edition of 1536; finally in 1559 he expressed satisfaction with its arrangement.[111] He refers to "the order of right teaching" in Book I which requires that he place knowledge of God the Creator before knowledge of man. But this is a formality that doesn't work. God the Creator's gifts are abundant, in both the universe and man, but man's pride rejects the message that these gifts are divine creations and proceeds to take the universe for granted and his gifts for his own powers. The actual changes Calvin made in the 1559 *Institutes* speak to this problem and go beyond it.

Theological solution to the problem of self-knowledge. The major change is in Book II, Knowledge of God the Redeemer. It opens with a discussion of original sin—chapters i through v. But, radically breaking the original order, two chapters on redemption through Christ are introduced before proceeding to the discussion of the law and the way in which it reveals sin.[112] *Then* comes the section on the law, with its extended definition of sin. And then the section on the law is itself interrupted with a new chapter, chapter ix, on Christ the Redeemer as revealed in the New Testament. The discussion of the Old Testament is then resumed, and then comes the final and extended discussion of Christ as Redeemer. This deliberate and uncharacteristically disorderly interweaving of sin-redemption-sin-redemption is a statement about saving knowledge: that its two parts are equally necessary and, in fact, simultaneous. Knowledge of sin cannot exist without knowledge of salvation; knowledge of salvation depends upon knowledge of sin. Calvin's general presupposition that knowledge must be "useful" and "fruitful" and "profitable" is eminently realized here.

Calvin maintains, and quotes Augustine as his authority, that the function of the law is to kill and the function of faith is to save: "'If the Spirit of grace is absent, the law is present only to accuse and kill us.'"[113] More exactly, the law brings death to those not chosen, and despair, and then faith—the two constituents of saving knowledge—to the elect. It condemns the sins of the nonelect and elect alike, but the result in the nonelect is not despair, faith, and regeneration, but the opposite: deeper and deeper transgression and more and more certain death. For it is not just a matter of our pride and resultant oblivion to sin; we have psychic defense mechanisms against any accusation of weakness:

> There is no doubt that the more clearly the conscience is struck with awareness of its sin, the more the iniquity grows. For stubborn disobedience against the Lawgiver is then added to

transgression. . . . Since our carnal and corrupted nature contends violently against God's spiritual law and is in no way corrected by its discipline, it follows that the law which had been given for salvation, provided it meet with suitable hearers, turns into an occasion for sin and death.[114]

So devastating is the knowledge of sin that we cannot accept it.

The grace granted in justification is that we do not resist the accusations of the law, that we allow ourselves to be overwhelmed with despair. And despair is precisely the psychic mechanism that now makes us turn for salvation outside ourselves, *extra nos* — since we now see there is nothing within. At the same time we know that salvation exists, through Christ's righteousness. It is as if we see that God has made us see. Faith both effectuates the law and reveals the grace of Christ the Redeemer. Faith makes despair over sin natural, for it abolishes our pride and pride-provoking defenses. And it provides the answer to despair. We would reject the answer as unnecessary without our despair. Faith effectuates our turning to God the Redeemer. Justification is the imputed righteousness that we fully know that we need. The link between self-knowledge and knowledge of Christ as Redeemer is now a natural movement; it is a necessary movement; and, insofar as it is grounded in the objectivity of Scripture, it is a realistic movement. What is "there" becomes "there for us."

Luther proceeds unsystematically in his theology, but elaborates and makes clear his feelings about the ingredients, indicating their relative weightings — which Calvin could absorb, acquiesce in, and systematize.

Sometimes self-knowledge does not sound like a problem in Luther. Human nature "knows no shame," but "the preacher's message must [i.e., can] show men their own selves and their lamentable state, so as to make them humble and yearn for help."[115] But we know from other contexts that the Word is made effective by faith, and so it remains a matter of divine intervention: "To preach Christ means to feed the soul, make it righteous, set it free, and save it, provided it believes the preaching."[116] The most obvious impediment to self-knowledge is pride, and it is the most widespread. It is natural to all men, and, moreover, it is reinforced by historical circumstances:

> Since human nature and natural reason, as it is called, are by nature superstitious and ready to imagine, when laws and works are prescribed, that righteousness must be obtained through laws and works; and further, since they are trained and confirmed in this opinion by the practice of all earthly lawgivers, it is impossible that they should of themselves escape from the slavery of works and come to a knowledge of the freedom of faith

. . . . Nature can only condemn [God's wisdom] and judge it to be heretical because nature is offended by it and regards it as foolishness.[117]

More subtly, the law increases transgression when it actually does arouse subconscious, but nonefficacious, acknowledgment: the natural inclination in man, when it is not counteracted by faith, is to retaliate against accusation, to resist painful truths. Recognition of impotence, of incapacity to merit salvation, incites self-deceiving denial and rebellion. "A man only hates the law the more, the more it demands what he cannot perform."[118] Hatred of the law is rejection of God: it is unbelief, and unbelief is "the very source of all sin."[119] It is the source of sin because its counterpart is self-assertion — either as overt evil or in the conviction that external works can merit salvation. The exact theological equivalency of doing evil and doing good for the wrong reason is as basic to Luther as to Calvin.

Righteousness of works, as distinct from passive righteousness, was a perilously strong temptation to Luther. His experience of sin must have included just this pride, and he never felt an easy triumph: "for in the hour of death, or in other agonies of the conscience, these two sorts of righteousness do encounter more near together than thou wouldest wish or desire.[120] Self-knowledge was indeed radically unnatural. Yet it was saving knowledge.

Saving knowledge was an ordeal. The law "is that hammer, that fire, that mighty strong wind, and that terrible earthquake rending the mountains and breaking the rocks, that is to say, the proud and obstinate hypocrites." But it behoves "that the tempest of fire, of wind, and the earthquake should pass, before the Lord should reveal himself in that gracious wind."[121] Ozment has stressed the motif of crying out in Luther: "one cries out of a God-awakened recognition of his utter soteriological impotence"; one cries out of faith that God will hear him.[122]

Calvin, like Luther, responded to the strong emotional expressions of despair in the Old Testament. His *Commentary on Psalms* dwells on David's agonized sense of impurity and weakness, and at the same time he marvels at David's faith that he will be saved despite his sins, that the Lord will be true to his promises. He systematized that experience in a formal theology. But he was following most strictly the logical interconnections in Luther. "Faith alone," Luther wrote,

is the saving and efficacious use of the Word of God. . . . The moment you begin to have faith you learn that all things in you are altogether blameworthy, sinful, and damnable. . . . When you have learned this you will know that you need Christ, who suffered and rose again for you so that, if you believe in him,

you may through this faith become a new man insofar as your
sins are forgiven and you are justified by the merits of another,
namely, of Christ alone.[123]

A sense of sin as the substance of self-knowledge was central in
Luther's and Calvin's theology. And it is the psychological solution, as
distinct from the theological, to the circularity in the relation between
knowledge of self and knowledge of God. Self-knowledge leads to
knowledge of God; knowledge of God leads to self-knowledge. If the circle
is ever to get started, if the theology is ever to get written, it depends upon
an initiating theologian's felt sense of sin.

The intricate concept of self-knowledge that we have seen thus far
has been neglected, yet it is essential to an understanding of Luther and
Calvin and of their relationship: it is the key to understanding both Luther's
great influence and Calvin's transformation of Luther. It seems fair to say
that each one's sense of sin must have been a personally central experience, and there is much evidence for this conclusion.

Excursus in the history of philosophy. The centrality of the self-
knowledge problem in Luther and Calvin corresponds very closely to that
of the general problem of knowledge in nominalism and may be its implicit
core—one that came to the surface in the sixteenth century.

Both awareness and definition of the limits of knowledge were fundamental to nominalist thought. Gabriel Biel perceived "the tragedy of
man," Oberman stresses, "as centered in a lack of knowledge which is
not primarily explained as a result of his fall and loss of original justice,
but as a natural consequence of his status as creature."[124] Nominalism
derived the limits of human knowledge first from divine liberty and
omnipotence. The latter was one of the bases for Ockham's attack on the
theory of essences.[125] On the one hand, there was in Ockham a certain
Pelagian strain, and his rejection of universals supported it even when
talking about God's power: "One man," he wrote, "can be annihilated
by God without any other man being annihilated or destroyed. Therefore
there is not anything common to both, because (if there were) it would
be annihilated, and consequently no other man would retain his essential
nature."[126] But more centrally, the human intellect, attempting to deduce
a priori the order of the world, is sensed as an infringement on divine power
and choice.[127] And God must know creatures and be free to create without
the intervention and constraints of independently existing ideas and
essences alike. There is a sense here, in regard to God, of the primacy
of will *per se* over intellect. However, God's omnipotence, for Ockham,
seems most often to consist specifically in his omniscience, and the limits
to our power, correspondingly, to consist in our limited intellectual
capacity: "it is to be held indubitably that God knows all future contingents

certainly and evidently. But to explain this clearly and to describe the way in which He knows all future contingents is impossible for any intellect in this [present] condition.[128]

Clearly articulated in this statement and recurring throughout Ockham's writings is the sense of what Oberman has called "the incommeasurability between Creator and creation."[129] This sense is neither in contradiction to nor overridden by the Pelagian thread in his thought. Rather, the latter seems to heighten the incommeasurability in a somewhat ironic way. God's power consists in his knowledge; our will is not unfree to choose but is insignificant in the light of that divine knowledge—for our freedom to decide and to act is limited by the state of our knowledge. A major instance of our limited capacity is the real uncertainty in which Ockham can find himself when he confronts two equally valid sets of data or experience that lead to contradictory conclusions—the double truth that is one way of knowing versus another. A recurring pattern in his treatment of irreconcilable positions is to extend an argument, hypothetically, a step beyond the actual reach of evidence, then to prove that, even if we knew that much more, it would still be insufficient for certainty.[130] The limits of knowledge are thus demonstrated by the unlimited space for questions between the human mind and its target.

There is also a continuous interweaving of the different kinds of evidence in Ockham's writings, and they may sometimes be part of the same argument. The principle of economy precludes redundant proof.[131] However, "an aggregate formed of all those *habitūs* [i.e., the natural *habitus* and the theological, existing in the same intellect] which have a definite order as regards one conclusion" is valid.[132] In all instances, Ockham moves with ease from one realm of truth to the other and deploys his arguments with sureness and adeptness: they are resources which he knows how to use. And their use depends upon the distinct identity of their referents. For explicitly or implicitly, these writings assert both the disparity and the disconnectedness between the divine and human natures. The disconnectedness is as real as that within the natural sphere of individual, atomistic existence. The concomitant of such disconnectedness is that we cannot know God or anything else "through our natural powers in a simple concept proper to itself, unless the thing is known in itself. For otherwise we could say that colour can be known in a concept proper to colours by a man born blind."[133] Thus, although we have various ways of knowing things about God—through analogies of different kinds to things that are within our experience—we are, because of what we still do not and cannot know, as if blind.

There is as much uncertainty at the innermost reach of knowledge as at its outer reach. It is often maintained that God, in nominalist thought, can be trusted not to act *de potentia absoluta* but will adhere to the covenantal order spelled out in Scripture. Yet how far can we trust that our trust is not based upon self-deception? While Ockham retained the basic medieval tenet that God is ultimately limited by the law of contradiction, he extended his concept of *potentia absoluta* to include the power to cause things that *seemingly* contradicted the divine benevolence and justice.[134]

Interior knowledge is only more certain and clearer by degree than sensory evidence. Ockham held that we have evident and direct knowledge of the soul's acts; however, the knowledge is merely of those acts and not of the soul's states.[135] The formal position that God can produce in us intuitive knowledge of a nonexistent object, that "God can produce an assent which belongs to the same species as that evident assent to the contingent proposition 'this whiteness exists', when it does not exist,"[136] affirms the possibility of total and unavoidable deception—"assent" is the key word.

The context of this limited capacity is a position on causality neither original with Ockham nor incompatible with Thomism or, indeed, with the basic medieval attention to another and invisible reality that may be a decisive dimension in every consideration and decision. In its elaboration and philosophical centering, however, the position became a characteristic nominalist motif: "Whatever God can produce by means of secondary causes he can directly produce and preserve without them."[137] The nominalist trust that God will not act *de potentia absoluta* thus coexists with an acceptance of that constant possibility. Disruptions and breaches of the natural order were numerous and extensive enough in the late Middle Ages—breaches of the order of nature and society, questioning (in which Ockham was involved) of the validity of the order of the hierarchical church—to constitute counterevidence to Scripture, and it seems not a radical deviation from the logical emphasis upon contingency in nominalism for Gregory of Rimini and others to have held, and with the tenet to render less firm and steady the rock of Scripture, that God could make a past thing to have not been.[138] This dimension of nominalism is surely echoed in Calvin's sense of total dependency upon God's choice and power. Calvin notes in his commentary on Genesis that, as prone as we are to tie down the power of God to those instruments whose agency he employs, "the Lord, by the very order of creation, bears witness that he holds in his hand the light which he is able to impart to us without the sun and the moon."[139]

Ockham's criticism of scholasticism and his method of economy purposefully cleared the mental atmosphere of a great deal of obstructive clutter—knowledge that was not knowledge—and may also have heightened and made habitual an awareness not only of the precariousness of existence but of something other than the immediately evident in that atmosphere: the phenomenon of the mediation of the self in acts of knowing. Ockham stated that "neither the divine essence . . . nor anything intrinsic to God nor anything which is really God can be known by us without something other than God being involved as object."[140] Later thinkers were to draw this conclusion explicitly of our knowledge of all objects; it is implicit in Ockham, sounding a sense of distance and separation of subject from object.

F. Edward Cranz has traced an awareness already evident in Abelard of a subjectivity sufficient to challenge the established classical assumption of rapport between being and thinking, the presupposition of "a substantial relationship resulting in the union or conjunction of the knower with the known."[141] Nominalist thought intensified the sense that Cranz sees evolving ineluctably and finally necessitating a break with Aristotelian metaphysics and epistemology, the sense of a "duality or disjunction between [that which] senses or intellects and what is sensed or intellected."[142] The response, as it clearly seems to be, of Ockham and his followers to the reality of this disjunction was to focus attention upon thinking and discourse, upon the mental and verbal signs that mediate our experience. Ockham's logic proceeds from classification and comparing of kinds of referencing—or degrees of distance from the things to which words are ordinarily taken to refer. It is as if this attention is both an experiencing of indirection and a *modus vivendi* in its light.

Nominalism has been linked to Reformation theology by the question that arises from the gap it describes between God and man: the question of whether we can count upon a divine benevolence.[143] Also very closely paralleled in Luther and Calvin is the nominalist determination to arrive at clear knowledge, not despite, but because of, our intellectual limits. Ockham raised the criteria for certainty at the same time that the areas in which it could be attained were restricted, not only for stronger theological analysis, not only to avoid the absurdities of the sort that Calvin liked to point out in the questions of the Schoolmen, and Ockham, to state in the most extreme forms, but to avoid being certain of that which we could not be certain of through any means of verification. The leitmotiv in Calvin's writings of caution against being overcurious may be evidence of a particularly strong sympathy with the temper of nominalist thought. Luther and Calvin both traced the doctrine of righteousness through works to an erroneous conception of human nature. They were, thereby, responding to the same urgency that underlies nominalist philosophy: to clear the air of delusion.

Medieval thought before and outside of nominalism included awareness of the many conflicting and limiting aspects of human nature, already adumbrated in Saint Paul's observations. However, what was not immediately fathomable was more awesome than disconcerting, and existed within the context of a trusted mediating church. Others in the sixteenth century besides the Protestant reformers could extensively describe the phenomenon of self-deception and trace its recurrence — one thinks especially of Erasmus and *The Praise of Folly*. But Luther's and Calvin's descriptions of the same phenomenon concentrate upon its vast and potentially murderous implications, approximating more closely than hitherto the conception of the unconscious in modern psychology. The Reformation could arguably be attributed to these descriptions; they were tantamount to discovering the self's alienation from the self. It also seems arguable that nominalism more than any preceding movement of thought made separation and distance between knower and object of knowledge unavoidable and of central significance. That sense of distance is made vivid in Dürer's observation that "there is falsehood in our knowledge, and darkness is so firmly planted in us that even our groping fails."[144] Montaigne went a step further when he said, "And there is as much difference between us and ourselves as between us and others."[145] The persistent difficulty of self-knowledge is at the core of the general problem of the limits of knowledge in modern thought. First you have to know that you don't know. The particular unease that this problem has presented corresponds to much in the purpose and substance of nominalist writings.

In their views of the problem of self-knowledge, Luther and Calvin stand together and in contrast to the theologian closely associated with both and especially with Calvin: Saint Augustine. Calvin once wrote that "Augustine is so fully on our side that if I had to write a confession of faith it would suffice for me to put down a collection of passages from his writings."[146] Such a collection could be assembled readily, for Calvin, like Luther, quoted him extensively on major doctrinal matters, and historians have assembled lists of close parallels as well as quotations[147]. However, the implicit links between the passages would be quite different for Calvin (and Luther) from those that existed in Augustine's mind. The difference is epistemological; it is in the incompatibility between the post-Ockhamist epistemology of Luther and Calvin and the Augustinian theory of divine illumination through which we are able to see the necessity of eternal truths.[148] And the context of Augustine's theory was the medieval presupposition of the unity of thought, language, and reality. The knowledge of God and the soul which the three theologians valued above everything was, for Luther and Calvin, not only narrower in substantive scope, but tempered by an anxiety which the limits to knowledge presented.

The problem posed by these limits may have been still more extreme for Calvin than for Luther. Gerd Babelotsky has drawn some convincing parallels in Calvin's writings to Plato's myth of the cave: Calvin's frequent use of sharp dark/light contrasts and the image of the sun as the source of both light and life may be a direct reflection of the shattering and dazzling contrast Plato posited between life in the cave and life after release into the light of knowledge. As in Calvin, Plato's prisoners realize the misery of their previous existence only after they leave the cave and learn to see. The contrast of the two lives in Plato is certainly an ascent from a kind of unreality to reality, and this may be reflected in Calvin's contrasts of life before and after true self-knowledge in faith.

Most directly, sin is tantamount to lack of knowledge in Calvin, as it was in Plato. We also sin out of bodiliness, and Calvin dissociates himself from Plato's conception of the human problem as lack of knowledge.[149] But Plato would agree that mind is mind only insofar as it is not body, and the two are actually most akin in their specific opposition of bodiliness and knowledge — an affinity that will be explored below. But more exactly, sin, for Calvin, is ignorance of ignorance; it is the pride that keeps us from questioning and seeing through our illusions about ourselves. So the solution is more difficult than in Plato, where knowledge, and it is specifically reason, transmitted through the philosophers, is a sufficient motor for the ascent to the light, and our eyes gradually, but naturally, adjust to the light to which our reason can impel us. Hence the continuous emphasis in Calvin on the blindness and errors, the absurdities and the inevitable sinfulness of the human mind unaided, unenlightened by revelation and faith: only from without can we attain the likeness of God that Babelotsky finds identified, in both Plato and Calvin, with knowledge. We have the potential to receive the light, and that is all.

SENSE OF SIN: LUTHER, CALVIN, AND THEIR ENVIRONMENT

SENSE OF SIN IN LUTHER AND CALVIN

Luther's sense of sin proceeded from a personally conditioned dilemma. Scripture demanded righteousness in absolute terms: one must obey the totality of the law in order to merit salvation. At the same time, Luther was convinced that all sins, each and every one, must be expiated to merit salvation. The formal position of the medieval church that knowledge and consent were necessary for an act to constitute sin had ceased to be an operative principle in pastoral practice in the late Middle Ages and had, in fact, always been elusive and ambiguous. That Abelard was censured for his insistence upon testing the subjective intention in an act rather than its nature and effects is evidence of this ambiguity.[150] To Luther, the occurrence of a single sin was an impediment to salvation and a negation of all previous work toward this end: time itself seemed to be an enemy. "When I was a monk," he records,

I thought by and by that I was utterly cast away, if at any time
I felt the concupiscence of the flesh: that is to say, if I felt any
evil motion, fleshly lust, wrath, hatred, or envy against any
brother. I assayed many ways. I went to confession daily, etc.,
but it profited me not; for the concupiscence of my flesh did
always return, so that I could not rest, but was continuously
vexed with these thoughts: This or that sin thou hast committed;
thou art infected with envy, with impatiency, and such other sins;
therefore thou art entered into this holy order in vain, and all
thy good works are unprofitable.[151]

But Luther's spiritual crisis was ultimately more than a logical
difficulty. It was an intense conviction that, though there was a solution
to the problem of sin, it somehow did not apply to *me* because I am
uniquely unworthy. Salvation was not a logical problem; it was *my*
problem.

Though I lived as a monk without reproach, I felt that I was a
sinner before God with an extremely disturbed conscience. I could
not believe that he was placated by my satisfaction. I did not
love, yes, I hated the righteous God who punishes sinners, and
secretly, if not blasphemously, certainly murmuring greatly, I was
angry with God, and said, "As if, indeed, it is not enough, that
miserable sinners, eternally lost through original sin, are crushed
by every kind of calamity by the law of the decalogue, without
having God add pain to pain by the gospel and also by the gospel
threatening us with his righteousness and wrath!" Thus I raged
with a fierce and troubled conscience.[152]

It is this acute sense of personal guilt, of guilt beyond redemption, that
Erikson has explored and traced to Luther's earliest childhood experience:
if one is not a thoroughgoing Freudian, one is at least convinced that there
were unusual ingredients in Luther's biography, forming the consciousness
that he ultimately placed vis-à-vis God's judgment—if not driving him to
pit himself against his own father, extrapolated into God, and to posit
the compensatory experience of Christ.

Calvin's sense of sin seems to me to have a very different origin and
nature than Luther's, and I think that the difference accounts in great part
for the distinctive nature of Calvin's version of Lutheranism. But in the
development and structure of their theology, this sense of sin has the same
function. As for Luther, for Calvin, too, sin was a logical problem and
a personal problem. Every sin had to be atoned for, but even atonement
would somehow not suffice for *me*: "I believed, as I had been taught, that
I was redeemed by the death of thy Son from liability to eternal death,

but the redemption I thought of was one whose virtue could never reach me. I expected a future day of resurrection, but hated to think of it, as a most dreadful event."[153]

So extreme was the sense of sin in Luther and Calvin that it led each to a concept of human nature itself as sin. Sin was not additive; it was not the sum of individual, separately occurring, and performed sins; it was existence itself, for life was led by one whose total being was sin. Works and actions did not define a man; rather, his being defined his works and actions. "Good works do not make a good man, but a good man does good works; evil works do not make a wicked man, but a wicked man does evil works."[154] Coping with the problem of the totality of sin, Luther made definitional statements, and they abound in Calvin: over and over, we are told that, being human, we sin. The totality of sin was similarly expressed by the concept of infinity: "When," Calvin writes, "the sinner has poured out himself entirely before God, let him earnestly and sincerely consider that still more sins remain, and that the recesses of these evils are deep beyond fathoming."[155]

Luther's totalistic conception of sin was inherently antidualistic. Mind and heart were as much sin as body — just as mind, heart, and body alike were involved in the "turning" of faith. Here, Luther was nonmedieval. Yet he spoke the same language as the medieval church, words that had been increasingly invested with sexual connotations in late medieval theory and practice of confessing. If mind and heart were sinful, it was as the "carnal mind," the "carnal heart." Sin for Luther remained somehow rooted in sexuality.

The very generality of sin suggests also a determinative role for sexuality in human feeling. Luther uses the term "flesh" to include "the entire self, body and soul, including our reason and all our senses," because "everything in us leans to the flesh."[156] As in Freud, sexuality is decisive. Additionally, as in Freud, action and thought are radically complex; motivations are multileveled; the laws of contradiction do not apply to the totality of impulses in individual human lives.

Calvin rejected dualism and anticipated discoveries of Freud in the same ways. He speaks repeatedly of the evil mind and evil heart; they are interchangeable with the carnal mind and the carnal heart. The disobedience of Adam was "wicked lust," though it consisted of pride.[157] Succinctly, Calvin maintained that "the whole man is overwhelmed — as by a deluge — from head to foot, so that no part is immune from sin and all that proceeds from him is to be imputed to sin. As Paul says, all turnings of the thoughts to the flesh are enmities against God [Rom. 8:7] and are therefore death [Rom. 8:6]."[158] We will later ask again, as we already have, whether Calvin's rejection of dualism may not have been highly ambivalent. But his conception of human nature, if it may turn out to be more extremely and directly sexually determined than Luther's, was still totalistic. Man *as* man sinned.

Just this totalistic conception of sin raised more acutely and also solved the problem of certainty of salvation. Salvation was now an existential concern, for merely to live was to merit damnation. But this is to admit that we can do nothing toward the attainment of salvation, and so it must come from without. It must also be different in focus from specific atonement for individual sins: given the totality of sinful nature we must deal not with the sins but with the sinner. What alone is possible, since we cannot change, is a change in God's decision to damn us. He can change our status before him. Rather than appearing as justly and inevitably condemned sinners, we can be considered righteous: the righteousness of Christ can be imputed to us. Thus we do not solve the problem of sins but of the implications of sinning. Thus the totalization of sin alleviates guilt and anxiety alike.

Luther makes it clear that the logical problem he felt, the problem of the need for total satisfaction in light of the power of one occurring sin to wipe out all previous satisfaction, was historically engendered. The "sophisters" of his day

> constrained men to work well so long until they should feel in themselves no sin at all. Whereby they gave occasion to many (which, striving with all their endeavors to be perfectly righteous, could not attain thereunto) to become stark mad; yea an infinite number also of those which were the authors of this devilish opinion, at the hour of death were driven into desperation. Which thing had happened unto me also, if Christ had not mercifully looked upon me, and delivered me out of this error.[159]

In light of the human propensity to sin, the sophisters could only produce guilt and anxiety, not satisfaction and salvation—or an absolute reliance on the church, and yet a reliance to which the church could not convincingly respond.

Sense of Sin in the Pre-Reform and Reformation Environment

Ozment has demonstrated at length that the late medieval church first aroused and intensified anxiety about sin, and thereby aroused a craving for certainty of salvation; second, it burdened its members overwhelmingly with the atoning and satisfying remedies and apparatuses it offered as a solution to this anxiety and craving for certainty.[160] The eve of the Reformation thus saw an anxiety-ridden and heavily burdened populace, one which doubtless also resented the burden.

By the time of the high Middle Ages, the issue of salvation had been raised and joined to the church. Clerical standards were prescribed and accepted for determining states of the soul; the use of church apparatus (for example, the sacraments and indulgences) was prescribed and accepted to affect the state of the soul. But the churchly solution was asserted more strongly and more exclusively in the late Middle Ages because the claims of the church were seriously challenged. Immorality and inefficiency in the clergy — perhaps increasing because of success itself; certainly, increasingly apparent — stimulated religious protest movements. The jurisdictional claims of the church increasingly aroused challenges from political powers, partly to correct abuses and partly because the powers themselves had new claims. The church, eminently threatened, could react only by asserting its claims all the more strongly. And the principal means was to impose absolute dependency on its members by making the church apparatus the logical solution to their problems. To attain salvation, sins had to be atoned for — every sin, trivial or great, hidden or overt. The church could ferret out the sins in the confessional and exact satisfaction — at its discretion and dependent upon its ratification. The means of satisfaction ranged from fastings, to acts of charity, to pilgrimages; absolutely basic was complete, comprehensive, specific confession. Lists of sins raised possibilities ranging from the trivial and usual to the absurd. Thoughts, inclinations, and half-impulses, on the one hand, and careless words, on the other, had to be atoned for as thoroughly as sins against the Holy Ghost and murder of one's parents or of the Holy Roman Emperor. The worst sins were imperfect participation in the sacraments: incomplete confession was a sin, and the guilt from it was added to the guilt of the unconfessed sin. Satisfying the church — through complete confession and the prescribed atonement — became identified with satisfying God. This was a confusion doubtless intended and carefully established in the catechisms used from earliest childhood, where games, sentiments, and literal violations of the Ten Commandments were all potential causes of eternal damnation, and all alike had to be remembered, confessed, and atoned for. And all the atonements were wiped out by a new lapse, which then called for a new prescription.

The late medieval church created a problem and offered a solution at the same time. Anxiety and a feeling of being overwhelmed, of being hopelessly and perhaps uselessly burdened, rather than the desired dependency, were the results.

Ozment presents this situation as the background of the Reformation in general, and particularly of Luther. That it was the background for Calvin as well is clear. In an important defense of the Reformers' break with Rome, Calvin wrote of a personal despair of salvation, which he related to the despair "derived from the doctrine which was then uniformly delivered to the people by their Christian teachers." They preached God's mercy:

> They informed us we were miserable sinners dependent on this mercy; reconciliation was to come through the righteousness of works. . . [but above all] the method of obtaining [God's mercy] which they pointed out was by making satisfactions to thee for offences. Then satisfaction was enjoined upon us: first, that after confessing all our sins to a priest, we suppliantly ask pardon and absolution; and second, that by good deeds we efface from thy remembrance our bad; lastly, that in order to supply what was still wanting, we add sacrifices and solemn expiations. Then, because thou wert a stern judge and strict avenger of iniquity, they showed how dreadful thy presence must be. Hence they bade us flee first to the saints, that by this intercession thou mightest be easily entreated and propitious toward us.[161]

Calvin clearly differentiated his conception of sin from that of the Catholic church. He maintained that there was "an abyss of sins in us" while "the Papists think they can bundle up their sins once a year"; all those who truly fear God "must necessarily be overwhelmed with despair, so long as they think themselves bound to enumerate all their sins" in order to be pardoned.[162] In light of a conception of sin as a totality, as the nature of man, the solution of the church was irrelevant. It was also immoral: it was a claim for absolute power, a tyranny bad in itself, robbing God of his claims, and worse even than the temporal claims of the church. Above all, the solution was psychically destructive, just as it was self-defeating: guilt, and the torment of despair, were only increased. And so the Lutheran and Calvinist solution was a direct response to a felt, objective need for certainty and disburdenment. It was at the same time a great simplification: anxieties about many different kinds of sins and their many different solutions were channeled into anxiety about sin *per se*; and there was a sure as well as single solution to that.

DESACRALIZATION

The Lutheran and Calvinist solution was also tantamount to a desacralization of society and thereby reinforced a major historical trend. The desacralization was experienced as a release from the tyranny of the church, a very real tyranny of induced dependence. The Lutheran anthropology broke down the distinction between clergy and laity by raising the determinative distinction between human nature and the divine: we are all human; moreover, we are all priests. More exactly, all believers are priests, constituting an invisible church of the elect. Calvin only carried to a logical conclusion Luther's incipient doctrines of the priesthood of all believers and the calling. And, just as we are all priests, the clergy are all, necessarily, good citizens: here Luther's logical conclusion answered a felt resentment of his time, resentment not just against clerical indolence but against the clergy's privileged exemption from taxation. Finally, the secularization inherent in the Reformation reinforced a practical trend in the secular sphere, extraneous to criticism of the church. Increasingly, city magistrates were taking over as their responsibility and a concomitant of their power the welfare functions traditionally assumed by the church. In many cities, charity and education were already in the hands of lay authorities. The Reformation provided further justification for this trend.[163]

The trend toward desacralization, moreover, may have among its determining causes precisely that intellectual tradition to which I have related the core problem in Lutheran and Calvinist theology, nominalism, and may thus point to another facet of the link between the Reformation and late medieval thought. There was a pronounced antihierarchical thrust in the substitution in nominalism of physical explanation of the world and logical explanation of knowledge for the traditional metaphysical explanations of both.[164] Among the effects of this change were closer scrutiny of the physical world (and within it, of individual physical existents) and of thinking itself. Together, these formed a basis for the acceptance of the possibility of positive change in this world—a fundamental ingredient in any doctrine of secularism and the constructive side of desacralization.

Two Men and Their Times: The Problem of Anxiety

Self-knowledge, or knowledge of sin, was a central problem for Luther and Calvin. A natural impossibility, it was engendered in their theology by faith. Historically, both Luther and Calvin attained self-knowledge through an intense, extreme, and unusual sense of sin. Their personal evolutions were paralleled by a situation in which an objective force, the late medieval church, took the place of the individual unconscious and instilled a most extreme and unusual sense of sin in great numbers of people. A related matter, the craving for certainty in Luther, who heatedly told Erasmus that the Holy Spirit was no skeptic, and in Calvin, whose dogmatism is famous, found an echo in their times—again, the work of the existing church. Anxieties were alleviated, in two individual theologians and their eager mass audience.

It should not be forgotten that Luther and Calvin would have been psychologists for any time. They anticipated the Freudian discovery of psychosexual determinism, and they anticipated many of the specific mechanisms of Freudian psychology. Calvin seems to have sensed the full complexity of psychic life in the phenomenon of ambivalent motivation and the psychic equivalency of the potential and the actual. "For as the body, so long as it nourishes in itself the cause and matter of disease (even though pain does not yet rage), will not be called healthy, so also will the soul not be considered healthy while it abounds with so many fevers of vice."[165] His discussion of the nature of conscience is a good indicator of the import to him of every latent velleity in the soul: his discussion is etymological. Knowledge (*scientia*) is the grasp of the conception (*notitia*) of things by the mind and understanding (*mens, intelligentia*). Conscience is such an awareness by virtue of "the divine judgment adjoined to [men] as a witness. . . . It is a certain mean between God and man."[166] Conscience, then, is a conveyor of knowledge.

Calvin was acutely aware of the phenomenon of repression and of a conscience that convicted repressed guilt.[167] Associating himself with "traditional wisdom" and specifically Saint Paul, his special measure of the strength of the unconscious was its continuous action: we cannot rest for a moment, he so often tells us.

Luther, too, knew the unconscious; thus he could speak to Calvin's concerns, and both of them to their audience. The absence of conscious feelings of guilt in individuals was the strongest indication of depravity — or of the uncontrolled power and activity of the unconscious.[168] Both Luther and Calvin saw that the despair-provoking demand for perfection was at the core of the doctrine of works righteousness, and thereupon they incorporated into their doctrine of justification the psychological conception that acceptance of inadequacy could be transforming — and more productive of good works in the end than the ethic of performance.[169] Works could be superlative just because they did not have to be superlative.

Indeed the grounding of theology in psychological insight had positive historical effects. The noneudaemonistic ethic was both admirable and responsive. Men and women in the sixteenth century were acting on the basis of their convictions, and could do so because the ethic represented both an immediate alleviation of the anxiety engendered by the church and a long-range alleviation of the pressure engendered by the psychology underlying the doctrine of works righteousness. It is both plausible and admirable that immediate satisfaction and concrete results were rejected for something more idealistic and ultimately more deeply satisfying. And it is clear that people know what they were doing when they chose reformed theology. The popular literature of the day demonstrates that Luther and Calvin were understood, accepted, and internalized. Admirably and realistically, people were living up to their convictions, and one of the convictions was the disinterested performance of good works. There was to be sure an utterly regressive counterpart to the ethic that Luther and Calvin endorsed, and that was doubtless responsible for much

Protestant fanaticism: if a good man does good works, an evil man, one not of the elect, does evil works. This, despite their apparent perfection. This is a motif in the *Institutes*, and it recalls Luther's stubborn dogmatism: "It follows that what is done in the absence of faith on the one hand, or in consequence of unbelief on the other, is naught but falsity, self-deception, and sin, Romans 14:23, no matter how well it is gilded over."[170] With less theology and more overt irrationalism, Luther states that unless faith illumines a man, he is "not able to will, have, or do anything good. All he does is evil, even when he does what is good."[171] Intolerance was the price immediately paid for sanctification.

The alleviation of anxiety that Luther and Calvin presented was far more subtle that a simple cancellation. It was perhaps a cancellation of anxiety about anxiety. Regeneration is never fully accomplished in this life. Justification is necessary,

> first, because we are not yet perfectly righteous, but while we remain in this life, sin dwelleth still in our flesh; and this remnant of sin God purgeth in us. Moreover, we are sometimes left of the Holy Ghost, and fall into sins, as did Peter, David, and other holy men. Notwithstanding we have always recourse to this article: that our sins are covered, and that God will not lay them to our charge, Rom. 4. Not that sin is not in us (as the sophisters have taught, saying that we must be always working well until we feel that there is not sin remaining in us): yea, sin is indeed always in us, and the godly do feel it, but it is covered, and is not imputed unto us of God for Christ's sake; whom because we do apprehend by faith, all our sins are now no sins.[172]

The newness of Luther's concept of sin is only underlined in his ingrained references to isolated lapses. But they are the symptoms of sin, not sin itself. The consistent Lutheran anthropology at its base is manifest.

SIMULTANEOUS SIN AND SANCTIFICATION

Sin and guilt remain, and remain as a felt problem, at the same time that faith is effecting good works in us. The Holy Spirit "makes us spiritual, constrains the flesh, and assures us that, no matter how violently sin rages within us, we are the children of God as long as we obey the spirit and strive to put sin to death."[173] Sanctification is the spontaneous doing of good works; it is also the strict disciplining of our human nature. In this life, a man

> must control his own body and have dealings with men. Here the works begin; here a man cannot enjoy leisure; here he must indeed take care to discipline his body by fastings, watchings, labors, and other reasonable disciplines and to subject it to the

Spirit so that it will obey and conform to the inner man and faith and not revolt against faith and hinder the inner man, as it is the nature of the body to do if it is not held in check.[174]

The flesh cannot be transformed into spirit. However, the regenerated man can "watch and wrestle in Spirit against [the flesh], that if he cannot altogether bridle it, yet at the least he does not fulfil the lust thereof."[175] But if the struggle is constant and extreme, there is no doubt about its theological meaning — and Luther can anticipate Calvin's reading of the Psalms, just as his remarks on discipline foreshadow an extreme strain in Calvin:

> The flesh is accused, exercised with temptations, oppressed with heaviness and sorrow, bruised by the active righteousness of the law; but the spirit reigneth, rejoiceth and is saved by this passive and Christian righteousness, because it knoweth that it hath a Lord in heaven at the right hand of the Father, who hath abolished the law, sin, death, and hath trodden under his feet all evil, led them captive and triumphed over them in himself, Col. 2:15.[176]

Luther is both at his most medieval and his most modern in his conception of the persistence of sin in regenerate man. Commitment to the new life must be continuous, and it is the very commitment, rather than the concrete actions in which it results, that is transforming; what it determines is a mode of existence. Conversely, in rigorously Augustinian terms, sin is a concomitant of earthly existence. The earthly city is, was, and always will be corrupt, and it is abstracted into the equivalent of sin. We of the city of God, engaged in a pilgrimage through the earthly city, in our earthly bodies, reflect, as we participate in, this universal corruption. Our end is secure; it is also remote and does not yet substantively affect our nature. The Augustinian philosophy of history is implicit in Luther and emerges in his references to our earthly bodies; the pilgrimage motif is explicit and recurrent in Calvin.

The struggle of the elect against the flesh is continuous and intense. It is clear that sin is not an abstraction but a power, and the Reformers' treatment of it is parallel to their nonessentialist approach to God. Here, again, is a coming together of epistemology and experience. Ozment has emphasized the *simul iustus et peccator* theme in Luther. Because the human and divine evoke, indeed require, the full opposition of each other to manifest themselves, we must be in continuous movement. "We who are righteous are always in movement, always to be made righteous." We are always going from a point of departure, sin, and always going to a point of destination, righteousness.[177]

Calvin even physicalizes the movement in his exhortations to castigate the flesh. The very exhortations to do good works—which a regenerate man will in fact do spontaneously—emphasize the urgency of the struggle against the flesh and its inescapability: sin arises as spontaneously in regenerate man as his good works. As is frequently the case, Calvin, in systematizing the Lutheran theology, provided his own emphasis: here, upon persistence. Sanctification contains two aspects, and they are simultaneous, not consecutive. "First [the Spirit] has been given to us for sanctification in order that he may bring us, purged of uncleanness and defilement, into obedience to god's righteousness. . . . Second, we are purged by his sanctification in such a way that we are besieged by many vices and much weakness so long as we are encumbered with our body."[178] The first aspect is a traditional and metaphorical expression of the imputed righteousness that results in the right (that is, faithful) orientation toward God and in good works. The second aspect is the basis for persistence:

> Thus it comes about that, far removed from perfection, we must move steadily forward, and though entangled in vices, daily fighting against them. From this it also follows that we must shake off sloth and carelessness, and watch with intent minds lest, unaware, we be overwhelmed by the stratagems of our flesh. Unless, perchance, we are confident that we have made greater progress than the apostle, who was still harassed by an angel of Satan [2 Cor. 12:7] "whereby his power was made perfect in weakness" [2 Cor. 12:9] and who in his own flesh unfeignedly represented that division between flesh and spirit [cf. Rom. 7:6ff].[179]

SIMULTANEOUS FAITH AND DESPAIR

There was another *simul* theme in Luther and Calvin, exactly parallel to that of *simul iustus et peccator*, and also grounded in the Lutheran anthropology: the simultaneity of faith and despair. Luther experienced the deepest despair, which he likened to death, in his *Anfechtungen*, throughout life. Generally, he charcterized the despair as occasional and recurrent, intermittent with periods of faith. Sometimes, as we saw when he spoke of the flight, he described the actual experiencing of simultaneity. Calvin records the same experience, both analytically and dramatically. In the *Institutes* he can write that,

> while we teach that faith ought to be certain and assured, we cannot imagine any certainty that is not tinged with doubt, or any assurance that is not assailed by some anxiety. On the other hand, we say that believers are in perpetual conflict with their

own belief. Far, indeed, are we from putting their consciences in any peaceful repose, undisturbed by any tumult at all. Yet, once again, we deny that, in whatever way they are afflicted, they fall away and depart from the certain assurance received from God's mercy.[180]

The anthropological base is then made clear, and so too is a quiet intensity indicating deep inner acceptance of this situation:

Therefore the godly heart feels in itself a division because it is partly imbued with sweetness from its recognition of the divine goodness, partly grieves in bitterness from an awareness of its calamity; partly rests upon the promise of the gospel, partly trembles at the evidence of its own iniquity; partly rejoices at the expectation of life, partly shudders at death. This variation arises from imperfection of faith, since in the course of the present life, it never goes so well with us that we are wholly cured of the disease of unbelief and entirely filled and possessed by faith. Hence arise those conflicts; when unbelief, which reposes in the remains of the flesh, rises up to attack the faith that has been inwardly conceived.[181]

Calvin sometimes expressed the simultaneity with the metaphor of weak faith progressing toward greater strength. "The more we advance as we ought continually to advance, with steady progress, as it were, the nearer and thus surer sight of him we obtain; and by the very contrivance he is made even more familiar to us."[182] But the end of the passage in which this statement occurs drops the motif of progress and offers weak faith in itself as the metaphor: "bound with the fetters of an earthly body, however much we are shadowed on every side with great darkness, we are nevertheless illumined as much as need be for firm assurance when, to show forth his mercy, the light of God sheds even a little of its radiance."[183]

Perseverance in unheard prayer, in which God, "even though he does not answer, . . . is always present to us," indicates graphically this simultaneity.

By deferring our hope with a well-tempered evenness of mind, let us follow hard upon that perseverance which Scripture strongly commends to us. For in the Psalms we can often see that David and other believers, when they are almost worn out with praying and seem to have beaten the air with their prayers as if pouring forth words to a deaf God, still do not cease to pray.[184]

Light and darkness become life and death in Calvin's commentaries. In faith, we go forth "partly exulting in the apprehension of life, partly terrified by death"; again, "even our life is a sort of continual death."[185]

Related motifs juxtapose contradictory statements. The life of the faithful is joy, is sorrow, is sometimes grasped directly as joy in sorrow; the "cheerfulness [of the believer] shines if, wounded by sorrow and grief, he rests in the spiritual consolation of God."[186]

Life amid death became for Luther and Calvin the believer's *modus vivendi*. It was death now made conscious in its facticity and totality, and life made meaningful in its relation to death, as at the same time to God. Thus the Reformation revealed the full difficulty of life in order to offer a more meaningful and appropriate solution; this solution replaced the late medieval panacaea for difficulties *in* life.

TOWARD CALVIN'S TRANSFORMATION
OF LUTHER

A Significant Motif

The systematic ordering of Calvin's *Institutes*, a systematization of Lutheranism, was frequently broken by some very real obsessive concerns, and these concerns are part of the Calvin who was different from Luther. In the earliest part of the *Institutes*, Calvin introduces the first of a recurring series of polemics with the decidedly minor theological figure, Osiander. Calvin is obsessed with Osiander, and keeps interrupting the majestic course of the *Institutes* to argue with him. At the core of the disagreement is an altogether Lutheran objection to Osiander's doctrine of "essential righteousness." Osiander has "clearly expressed himself as not content with that righteousness which has been acquired for us by Christ's obedience and sacrificial death, but pretends that we are substantially righteous in God by the infusion both of his essence and of his quality."[187] Here are the Lutheran anthropology and the objective context of the Cross. But Calvin has an abbreviated phrase to refer to Osiander's position, throughout the *Institutes*: he "mingles heaven and earth." Moreover, this phrase is indiscriminately, and frequently inappropriately, applied to other theologians: it is evidently an obsessive concern. Referring to the relationship between the human and the divine and certainly corresponding to Luther's anthropology, it may also indicate a variation in conception of the human and divine natures on which the relationship is based. There is a hint of dualism in this horror of mingling.

Calvin's Positive
Conception of the Law

It is instructive to compare Calvin's and Luther's commentaries on a circumscribed text. In the *Commentary on Galatians*, Luther draws a distinct and strong contrast between the law and the Gospel. First, the flesh is indeed subject to the law despite our Christain freedom from it: *simul iustus et peccator*, man will always need discipline. But the language in which the indisputable disciplinary service of the law is expressed is most significant. It is negative, and the law is, additionally, alien to us. Defensively, Luther writes,

> the law in a Christian ought not to pass his bounds, but ought to have dominion only over the flesh, which is in subjection unto it, and remaineth under the same. Where it is thus, the law is kept within his bounds. But if it shall presume to creep into thy conscience, and there seek to reign, see thou play the cunning logician, and make the true division. Give no more to the law then belongeth unto it.[188]

Succinctly stated, "the flesh may not be at liberty, but must remain in the grave, the prison, the couch: it must be in subjection to the law, and exercised by the Egyptians."[189] More exactly, we must become "ignorant of the law"; Christ is presented in the commentary as the conqueror of the law.

Calvin's conception of the law in Galatians is far different: it is a positive part of the Christian life. The law, "so far as it is a rule of life, a bridle to keep us in the fear of the Lord, a spur to correct the sluggishness of our flesh . . . is as much in force as ever, and remains untouched."[190] Although we are not subject to the law as of old, in our Christian freedom "the law is the everlasting rule of a good and holy life."[191] Moreover, in the *Commentary on Galatians*, the other commentaries, and throughout the *Institutes*, the term "law" itself has a different meaning to Calvin: not just the Decalogue, it includes the Old and New Testament covenants as well. Clearly, Calvin has a positive and decidedly un-Lutheran attitude toward law *pe se*. Of course, this reflects his juristic background. But it is also indicative of a psychological inclination. Constraint and control are not necessary evils; they are positive parts of Christianity. Self-control, moderation, temperance are virtues. Moreover, the contradictorily extreme modes of control—asceticism, "bridling"—have positive connotations.

CALVIN'S FORMALISTIC EXEGESIS

There is a certain parallel to Calvin's and Luther's different attitudes toward discipline and law in itself in the ways in which they treat the scriptural text. Luther's exegesis is both free and personal. Calvin's, in comparison, is distanced. The personal voice in the commentaries is restrained, for Calvin is, above all, a teacher, though one who will make personal observations that the lessons may be better learned, in the same way that he will (and more often does) introduce philological commentary when it is useful. Luther could bring in broader, sometimes even apparently extraneous concerns, when he made an association or saw a connotation. He could also introduce his own concepts. Passive righteousness is Luther's translation of Paul's "righteousness of faith"; Calvin adhered to the more traditional imputed righteousness. Not only is this less free; but it can be observed that, while passive and imputed righteousness are theologically the same, Luther's concept is experiential and subjective, while Calvin's is formally relational and legal.

THE ISSUES OF PERSONALISM, EMOTION, AND INTEGRATION IN THEOLOGY

Luther made liberal use of autobiographical reflections in his commentary. The theme "when I was monk" echoes throughout; personal observations are inserted unselfconsciously, as when he states, in a discussion of righteousness, "I also do wish myself to have a more valiant and constant heart."[192] Paul was speaking directly to Luther; Luther understood him in the light of his own experience and then offered this corroborating experience to his readers.

Luther could also perceive a personal, feeling individual behind the Pauline Epistles. He knew and could record that Paul was concerned with anguish of conscience, with the way in which the law increased terror. He could also empathize even with those whom Paul the moralist condemned. Like Paul, he rejected the evil of righteousness of works, but knew that, while the distinction between the two kinds of righteousness was "easy to attest in words,... in use and experience it is very hard, although it be never so diligently exercised and practiced"[193]; he knew "these things are easily said: but blessed is he which knoweth how to lay sure hold on them in distress of conscience."[194] For Calvin, ever judgmental, works righteousness was, in the kindest light, an arrogant mistake.

To Luther, emotions were natural and acceptable and had positive connotations: human beings were not "stocks and stones."[195] He could speak with wonder of the great joy in faith; he could speak of "our longing to be free from the flesh and from sin."[196] Calvin also speaks of joy in faith, but the style in which the remarks appear is an impersonal, controlled formality.

Luther's style is natural and conversational, even colloquial. It is often blunt. Sometimes the down-to-earthness and bluntness are staged: he is also a natural performer. Luther paraphrases continuously. It is "as if Paul were saying..." or "as if one were to say...." He has dialogues with Satan; he records dialogues, in decidedly unscriptural language, between God the Father and Christ. He is always direct. Instead of exhorting, he records for encouragement and inspiration realistic and empathetic inner monologues that will strike a note of recognition in his reader. "When a man feeleth this battle of the flesh, let him not be discouraged therewith, but let him resist in the Spirit, and say: I am a sinner, and I feel sin in me, for I have not yet put off the flesh, in which sin dwelleth so long as it liveth; but I will obey the spirit and not the flesh."[197] Luther wants to personalize the Bible and doctrine: his concern is that Christ is to be preached "that he may not only be Christ, but be Christ for you and me."[198]

Luther does not write as an intellectual or a judge. This is partly the result of his consciousness of the involvement of reason in sin, and even, insofar as it gives rise to pride, of its centrality in sin.[199] It is also the result of his propensity for the concrete and palpable, as distinct from the abstract. His image of God as a mighty fortress is typical in integrating the material and spiritual and rendering the spiritual real.

Just as Luther made evident his personal involvement in his theology, he stresses the full humanity of Christ:

> And this, no doubt, all the prophets did foresee in spirit, that
> Christ should become the greatest transgressor, murderer,
> adulterer, thief, rebel, blasphemer, etc., that ever was or could
> be in all the world. For he being made a sacrifice for the sins
> of the whole world, is not now an innocent person and without
> sins, is not now the Son of God born of the Virgin Mary; but
> a sinner, which hath and carrieth the sin of Paul, who was a
> blasphemer, an oppressor and a persecutor; of Peter, which
> denied Christ; of David, which was an adulterer, a murderer,
> and caused the Gentiles to blaspheme the name of the Lord: and
> briefly, which hath and beareth all the sins of all men in his body,
> that he might make satisfaction for them with his own blood...
> we must as well wrap Christ, and know him to be wrapped, in
> our sins, our maledictions, our death, and all our evils, as he
> is wrapped in our flesh and blood.[200]

Calvin did not speak this way; rather, he chose to speak of Christ's offices, of Christ as king, prophet, and priest.

Christ's felt humanity was the basis, for Luther, not, of course, of substantial union, but of effective identification and imitation. "The example of Christ" was rendered further real by being fully and substantively the model for the positive content, not just the stance, of the Christian life.[201] To Calvin, the imitation of Christ meant obedience to God; to Luther, the imitation of Christ meant loving one's neighbor as Christ loved mankind. Love was not merely a commandment; it was constitutive of divinity. It made divinity accessible because it was unformidable, at the same time that it affected the believer's life. Luther's writings reflect a person both less estranged from divinity and more intimate and comfortable with humanity than Calvin's.

The part of Calvin that made his Lutheranism hard won is often marked within the most crucial of shared Reformation concepts when he elaborates them with reasons that differ from Luther's, and their explications are mutually supportive because of this difference. The acceptance of grace implied wonder at God's goodness and power to save one otherwise justly damned. But that wonder could be expressed in different ways. Luther is moved and enraptured by the gift; Calvin most typically focuses not upon the gift but upon its unmeritedness. For him, really strong emotion seems only, or best, expressible in close connection with a sense of unworthiness.

I am proposing that the distinctiveness of Calvin's theology and religion is psychologically rooted, and that the cultural preference (that is Jung's term) of his time favored this theology and religion. But I have dwelt on the likeness and agreement of Calvin and Luther because Calvin's Luther seems an instance of preservation through transformation. If this echoes the logic of Hegel, it is not always, but sometimes, the matter of history.

2

Calvin's
Religion

GLORY UNTO GOD

The motif of rendering glory unto God is absolutely dominant in Calvin's theology and in his personal writings as well. Two aspects of the motif are striking: the explicit conception of God's absolute transcendence, and the formality and impersonality of the response. But emotion is sometimes involved: we must love God. However, the nature of our love of God is not spontaneous, warm, and positive; rather, it is a matter of reverence, a mixture of honor and fear. "Fear is the beginning of love."[1] Glory to God, moreover, is the core of religion—indeed, the content of religion. Love is enjoined, but it is always secondary. "Why do we live except to serve God's glory?"[2] Or again, "one must put aside all humanity when it is a matter of fighting for his glory."[3]

The conception of God's absolute transcendence is, as we have seen, a strong presence in late medieval thought. It could in particular be said of Calvin, as it has been said of Ockham, that he emphasized so strongly God's immediate creative relationship to everything he made that the ideas of creation and of the preservation of creation are inseparable.[4] We cannot cease to worship for a moment. It is also likely that Calvin's legal background was influential here. Sixteenth-century jurisprudence incorporated and emphasized the newly discovered concept of sovereignty, a fact the New Monarchs appreciated, if they did not inspire it. The ruler was answerable to no one outside himself; he set his own standards of behavior, asserted his power through activity, and elicited a response of unquestioning obedience. But Calvin's acceptance of, and even delight in, God's sovereignty goes beyond these influences.

What Then of Man?

The corollaries to God's transcendence are man's total abjectness and total dependence on God. It is a matter of self-abnegation: we are as nothing before God. The mysticism that Eckhardt exemplified was also self-abnegating, but without the abjectness; it was union between the divine spark in man and an equally depersonalized divinity. There is no divine spark for Calvin; there is, moreover, always positive corruption and evil present in the "nothingness" he brought to God. It was, rather than nothingness, worthlessness, with a strong substantive character of damn-worthiness and loathsomeness.

Calvin repeatedly says that man must be reduced to nothing in his own estimate in order not to deprive God of his glory. Man has no free will: that would be to attribute something to man that is God's exclusive possession. Man has no goodness: that would be to attribute something to man that is God's exclusive characteristic. "For, so long as man has anything to say in his own defense, he detracts. . . from God's glory."[5] That it is a deep-rooted conviction of the highest emotional intensity is clear when Calvin asks of the scholastics, "what place have these most pestilent Sophists left to Christ to exert his power?" They maintain "that he deserved for us the first grace, that is, the occasion of deserving, but that it is now our part not to fail the occasion offered. O overweening and shameless impiety! Who would have thought that those who professed the name of Christ would dare so strip him of his power and virtually trample him underfoot?"[6] Three qualities stand out in these remarks (and are paralleled through the course of the *Institutes*, the commentaries, and even Calvin's personal letters): man's lowly abjectness, God's perfection and power, and the logic in which they are formulated, which is *a priori*. Man's abjectness is not presented as a felt and observable experience; it is a logical necessity, given God's claims to his attributes.

There is, accompanying the theme of abjectness, an emphasis upon the need for self-punishment and punishment by God that has a distinctively masochistic strain. Evils will always prevail in this world. We should, of course, pray for deliverance. But suffering serves positive purposes. Luther stressed the identification of personal sufferings with the suffering of Christ. Calvin stresses its disciplinary nature. We also bear the Cross "for righteousness' sake."[7] And more: with a neat theological twist, we suffer, and God can thereby demonstrate his power when light comes into the darkness. It is "the peculiar work of God to bring light out of darkness."[8] "If [God] did not keep his people in suspense and waiting long for deliverance from affliction, it could not be said that it is his prerogative to save the afflicted."[9]

The language Calvin uses to express self-discipline is significant. It describes an attack upon the self. It is, moreover, violent. Mortification of the flesh consists of beating and pummeling. "When the spirit has been broken . . . through a felt sense of the anger of the Lord, a man is brought to genuine fear and self-loathing, with a deep conviction that of himself he can do or deserve nothing, and must be indebted unconditionally for salvation to Divine mercy."[10] In a parallel way, the positive manifestations of the Christian life that seem to attract him most, away from their institutional context in the medieval church, are asceticism, poverty, and fasting. In his letters, Calvin pointed to his own poverty as evidence of the life of faith, and he held up as an example to the extravagance and wealth of the Roman church the frugality and poverty of the early church, "which both the nature of sacred things prescribes and the apostles and other holy fathers have prescribed both by teaching and by example."[11] The early church also understood the virtue of combining prayer and fasting: "their sole purpose in this kind of fasting is to render themselves more eager and unencumbered for prayer."[12]

THE NATURE OF REALITY

The Lord knows that one of the forms of self-discipline is to resist temptation. He sends us temptations daily; they are needed to test our steadfastness. They are also needed to strengthen, indeed to insure the existence of, our faith. For reality is antagonistic. Life is a struggle in which forces are defined by asserting themselves against resistance. Luther also knew of a struggle between God and Satan; occasionally he sounds like Calvin, but more usually the struggle is, rather, an inevitability, the necessary tragedy *in* life rather than the mode *of* life. The latter perception underlies and appears as a leitmotiv throughout Calvin's writings; it is also communicated in the catechism of the Genevan church, in which deliverance from evil, by the Lord and through our own constant vigilance, resistance, and pressing ahead, are required lest we be overcome by the devil "or by the desires of the flesh which wage constant war with us."[13] Calvin's reference for this is Galatians 5:17; it is, as often, a tightening of a less acutely or less specifically polarized view.[14] The related motif of the "exercise" of faith runs through the *Institutes*, and it permeates Calvin's interpretation of the trials of the Lord's people in his *Commentary on Psalms*. Parallel to this is a conception of suffering as medicine: "as we do not recover from our vices to spiritual health in one day, God prolongs his chastisements: without which we would be in danger of a speedy relapse."[15]

The *Imago* and Obedience

Calvin believed scripturally that man was created in God's image and that the *imago dei* shone in Adam. But the *imago* was affected decisively in the fall. A remnant remains, but so removed is it from its former glory that man is but a ruin. The image is, however, restored in regenerated man through the new creation of faith. Sometimes Calvin sounds as if the image consisted in the substantive gifts of God—the talents for whose abundance man must render gratitude to his creator. Calvin was affected by Renaissance humanism, and this is reflected in the *Commentary on Genesis*, where he compares the unfallen Adam to "a world in miniature," and the *Institutes*, where he states that "although the primary seat of the divine image was in the mind and heart, or in the soul and its powers, yet there was no part of man, not even the body itself, in which some sparks did not glow."[16] But the emphasis even here is on spiritual gifts; in fact, the image consists not in man's being graced with reason and will, but in the fact that, in unfallen Adam and regenerate man, reason and will are directed wholly to the knowledge of God and obedience to God.[17] The term Calvin characteristically applies to prefall Adam is "rectitude." The image consists in "the light of the mind," "the uprightness of the heart," and "soundness of all the parts"; when Adam became "alienated from God," the image "was so corrupted that whatever remains is frightful deformity."[18] Rectitude is gratitude to God for his creation, worship of God's power, and acquiescence in a constant dependence upon God:[19] above all, it is obedience.

The theme of obedience, a self-limiting and deferential quality, is stressed far more than the theme of freedom in the conception of Christian liberty that Calvin adopted from Luther. And it has an exact christological parallel—and foundation. For the decisive character of the Cross was Christ's obedience to God the Father: hence the content of the *imago* and the nature of the imitation of Christ.

Willis has reminded us that Luther opposed a *theologia crucis* to a *theologia gloriae*.[20] While Calvin's was, certainly, a theology of glory unto God, he would reject such a characterization of his theology if it implied one which did not take as its starting point the nature of God's revelation in Christ. Nevertheless Christ himself is differently perceived than in Luther. To Luther, the wisdom and strength of God were hidden in the folly and weakness, the sheer humility, of the Cross. The humility was for us: it was an act of love to become fully man so that man could be fully redeemed. To Calvin, the orientation of the Cross is to God, and Christ announces and perfectly demonstrates, in his perfect obedience, the correct relationship of man to God. The Cross is seen as an act of worship.

Love is constitutive of divinity and is dominant, natural, and spontaneous in regenerated man, for Luther. Calvin could exclaim, "As if we could think of anything more difficult than to love God with all our heart, all our soul, and all our strength."[21] Luther said that he once hated God: his crisis was an overcoming of that. Calvin here shows some shrewd human insight, but he also manifests the extremely problematic character that love *per se* represented for him throughout life—in the positive times of faith as well as in despair.

BEING OVERWHELMED

The decisive event in Calvin's life was his conversion. And, like his call and recall to Geneva, this "sudden conversion" was experienced as imposed from without, an intervention demanding total submission and acquiescence (again, everything versus nothing) and a response, based upon evaluation of the human vis-à-vis the divine, of obedience of a life-constituting nature—this in contrast to Luther's gradual uncovering of truth, in which the entry to Paradise came only after he "beat importunately upon Paul at that place [Roman 1:7] most ardently desiring to know what Saint Paul wanted."[22] The theme of being overpowered, and evidence that this is appropriate and even perversely satisfying, is clear in Calvin's treatment of natural theology—the ways in which the universe serves to reveal God the Creator. On the one hand, the very great beauty and harmony in the regularity, constancy, and dependence of the heavens is stressed. Adam perceived it and thanked the Lord; while postfall man is too blinded by sin to see it, its evidence is so strong and absolute that it renders him inexcusable. But there is a countertheme. If God the Creator reveals his love of and adherence to rules, to pattern, to law in the universe, he can also use the universe as a stage to reveal and proclaim power definitely *inordinata*. Storms, lightning, the shaking of the heavens, "sudden and unforeseen changes," are most salutary disasters: "if natural things always followed in an even and uniform course, the power of God would not be so perceptible."[23] The counterpart to this theme is the idea that disasters such as floods would result "were the restraint imposed upon the sea by the hand of God removed."[24] The universe depends upon God's arbitrary decisions; God's arbitrary power (and his ability to annihilate us) is evidence of his majesty and is incitement to thanksgiving and worship. These effects are also evidence of a power than can counteract, as we are unable to, the inner turmoil that is the natural effect of sin. In both ways, one senses that a great deal of Calvin's attraction to being overwhelmed lies in self-aversion.

ORTHODOXY AND FEELING IN DOCTRINE

There is in all these themes a strong hint of theological dualism, of good and evil as two equal powers whose struggle, in the form of spirit versus flesh, dominates life, and an unusual personal sense of sin. The psychological reflex of dualism in its western historical context has tended strongly to be guilt about creatureliness itself.

Calvin as well as Luther knew what the orthodox position on dualism was and endorsed it. However, there is a very notable presence of tension in Calvin. The tension can, I think, be traced to the presence of unconscious dualism versus conscious Lutheran orthodoxy. From this viewpoint, Calvin's obsessive and sometimes inappropriate attribution of Manichae-anism to opponents and his singling out for polemic such figures as the neoplatonic Origen indicate both a hard-won orthodoxy — an orthodoxy won against itself and perhaps reinforcing itself — and unconscious guilt, projected and being dealt with. Jung said of Tertullian: "the intellectuality of the Gnosis, its specifically rational coinage of the dynamic phenomenon of the soul, must necessarily have been odious to him, for that was just the way he had to forsake, in order to recognize the principle of feeling."[25]

Calvin is disgusted with the foulness of human nature; Luther despairs at its weakness. Calvin, like Luther, uses the term "flesh" to characterize mind and spirit as well as body. But he seems to have had a horror of the flesh in itself and as sheer matter, in a Platonic sense, as Luther did not. This seems to me to make more impressive the strength of the Lutheran influence: it was persuasive enough to overcome psychic resistance.

Calvin manifests both strict Chalcedonian and Lutheran orthodoxy when he writes directly of the two natures of Christ: "we affirm his divinity so joined and united with his humanity that each retains its distinctive nature unimpaired, and yet these two natures constitute one Christ." But it remains "a very great mystery."[26] He is similarly orthodox about the origin and nature of evil: "let us remember that this malice, which we attribute to [the devil's] nature, came not from his creation but from his perversion."[27] But we are not to investigate the matter more deeply: "although these things are briefly and not very clearly stated [in Scripture], they are more than enough to clear God's majesty of all slander. And what concern is it to us to know anything more about devils or to know it for another purpose?"[28]

The orthodox doctrine of the dual nature of Christ is beyond human understanding, questioning, and feeling, Calvin repeatedly tells us. But there could be impulses to the contrary. These could only be controlled — and they eminently were — but they could not be obliterated.

THE EXTRA-CALVINISTICUM

The doctrine in Calvin that has most often brought into question his orthodoxy, and that suggests, I think, the presence of dualism, is the so-called extra-Calvinisticum. This is the idea that the Son's reign in heaven at the right hand of the Father did not cease and was not suspended during the Incarnation:

For even if the Word in his immeasurable essence united with the nature of man into one person, we do not imagine that he was confined therein. Here is something marvelous: the Son of God descended from heaven in such a way that, without leaving heaven, he willed to be born in the virgin's womb, to go about the earth, and to hang upon the cross; yet he continuously filled the world even as he had done from the beginning.[29]

Moreover, Calvin speaks of "the divine glory, which at that time [during the earthly life of Christ] shone in the Father only, for in Christ it was concealed."[30]

Willis has demonstrated the unquestionable and strict orthodoxy of this doctrine: it can be traced from the church fathers onward. There is indeed a balancing parallel for its emphasis in Calvin: he maintains that Christ was Mediator even before the world was created.[31] Taken together with the extra-Calvinisticum, this is an orthodox statement about the equivalency of incarnate and nonincarnate God. It is also a reflection of Calvin's tendency to formalize: he perceives life in roles, offices, and callings; truth is perceived in categories. Rather than speculate on the dual nature of Christ, Calvin prefers to speak of his offices of priest, prophet, and king. But there is more to the extra-Calvinisticum. It is orthodox, but it represents a choice and an emphasis abstracted from the richness of the orthodox position. The extra-Calvinisticum could indeed represent an orthodox and Lutheran statement on the full humanity of Christ Incarnate, and thereby of his satisfaction of the law, as son of man, for *us*. Rather, it represents in Calvin a reserve in christology and Christian philosophy of history.

The union of human and divine in Christ was a fact. Each nature, not totally constitutive, was still fully present. The fullness of divinity was necessary soteriologically: Christ's divinity was necessary to enable him to satisfy the law, just as his special relation to the Father, his being truly of his essence, is necessary in the continuing intercession of Christ's prayers for us. But was Christ Incarnate fully divine? Did God's will that divinity become incarnate manifest itself by full participation in the Incarnation? The formulations of the extra-Calvinisticum suggest a negative answer.

There is a related reserve in Calvin about the significance of the Cross. Christian philosophy of history is linear, marked by the unique, decisive events of Creation, the Cross, and the Last Judgment. The Cross imparted meaning into time. The meaning was not extraneous; to use a term of Ozment's, it was substantiating, changing man's relation to God for all time. In this sense, the life of the world was contained in the Cross. Is the extra-Calvinisticum compatible with this historicity? One may wonder whether Calvin does not tend to define divinity exclusively as absolute transcendence and perceive humanity as both incompatible with and a threat to transcendence. That this is the case is suggested by a parallel to the doctrine of the reign of Christ during the Incarnation *etiam extra carnem*: the reign of Christ not just in the church, his body, but *etiam extra ecclesiam*. God reigns through the kingdom of Christ; Christ has lordship particularly over the church and generally over mankind.[32] The lordship of Christ in the church is hidden: the true church is invisible. But corresponding and appropriate to his manifest glory, God reigns through the world. And so does Christ.

There is an emphasis here on sheer power: Oberman has linked the "beyond" motif, the *extra-*, to God's power *inordinata*.[33] He has also pointed out that, while the late scholastics spoke of the possibility of absolute power, Calvin, with this motif, shows such power realized. The counterparts to Calvin's relatively rare statements about absolute power (he more usually speaks of lawfulness beyond human comprehension) are his statements about "great mysteries," such as the manifestation of God's power in the sacraments, and his prohibitions against probing into divine verities with questions.

THE INCARNATION

Calvin retained doubts about whether the Incarnation was a worthy and thus truly essential part of divinity. One can always find orthodox statements — and it is this very orthodoxy that must have rendered the doubts a cause of conflict and heightens their presence by contrast. Salvation depends upon the Incarnation: "this life resides in His flesh so that it may be drawn from it. It is a wonderful purpose of God that He has set life before us in that flesh, where before there had only been the material of death."[34] Although righteousness flows from God alone, "we shall not have the full manifestation of it anywhere else than in Christ's flesh."[35] However, there is another note. "In discussing Christ's merit, we do not consider the beginning of merit to be in him, but we go back to God's ordinance, the first cause. For God solely of his own good pleasure appointed him Mediator to obtain salvation for us."[36] There is a clear echo here of Scotus, who maintained that "apart from God's good pleasure [in accepting the sacrifice of the Cross] Christ could not merit anything."[37]

There seems to be in Calvin a certain negative attitude toward Christ Incarnate and a qualification of the nature of the union of the human and divine in Christ. Just as the divine does not commit itself to and participate fully in the Incarnation, the human here does not participate in divinity (as is implied in union) but rather depends upon, or petitions, the divine. A complement to the hierarchical relation between Christ and God is the relation between Christ and the Holy Spirit. It is one thing to say that the Spirit renders God's grace efficacious; it is another to assert that "without the illumination of the Holy Spirit, the Word can do nothing."[38]

There is still another reflection of the divine reserve, of Calvin's reluctance to conceive that God would become fully human, in the fact that the human nature in which God does participate in the Incarnation is a qualified humanity. Christ suffered, but he did not suffer in an altogether human way. Christ certainly experienced, "together with external evils, the feelings of the soul, such as fear, sorrow, the dread of death and similar things."[39] But, as certainly, there is a quantitative difference in the feelings. Stated negatively, "one greatly lessens the benefit of our redemption, in imagining that Christ was altogether exempted from the terrors which the judgment of God strikes into sinners."[40] In fact, there is more than a quantitative difference in Christ's suffering and ours: there is a difference in nature. Christ's feelings differed from ours in that they were "without sin while ours are sinful because they rush on unrestrainedly and immoderately";[41] Christ experienced "human affections but without disorder."[42]

Christ's full humanity is further qualified by a special sanctification by the Holy Spirit: "For we make Christ free of all stain not just because he was begotten of his mother without copulation with man, but because he was sanctified by the Spirit that the generation might be pure and undefiled as would have been true before Adam's fall."[43] It is no wonder that Calvin can refer to the incarnate body "which Christ inhabits like a temple."[44]

Calvin can be very specific about the qualified participation of divinity in the Incarnation. Divinity was communicated to the human nature "in such measure as was needed for our salvation,"[45] and he can be very specific about the separation, as well as the distinction, between the two natures: "the divine nature rested and did not exert itself at all whenever it was necessary in discharging the office of Mediator that the human nature should act separately according to its peculiar character."[46] The strength and also the reason for the reserve are clear in contrast with Luther. Luther's paradox of the hidden God—the God who hid his power beneath the weakness and in the humility of the Cross—and the consequent possibility of identification with Christ are, in Calvin, curiously short-circuited and, by emphasis, turned into the contradictory rejection of humanity as unworthy of God. "To prevent the offence of the Cross, God not only promises that the death of Christ will be glorious . . . but also commends the many honors with which He had already adorned it."[47] Although, in the crucifixion,

> the weakness of the flesh concealed the glory of His divinity for
> a short time, and though the Son of God was disfigured by shame
> and contempt, and, as Paul says, was emptied, yet the Heavenly
> Father did not cease to distinguish Him by some marks, and

during His lowest humiliation prepared some indications of His future glory, in order to support the minds of the godly against the offence of the Cross.[48]

THE ASCENDED CHRIST

The final measure of Calvin's reserve is in his formulations of the doctrine that the ascended Christ is more beneficial to us than was Christ Incarnate in his time. Christ laid aside "the mean and lowly state of mortal life and the shame of the Cross," and "by rising again began to show forth his glory and power more fully. Yet he truly inaugurated his Kingdom only at his ascension into heaven. . . . For Christ left us in such a way that his presence might be more useful to us—a presence that had been confined in a humble abode of flesh so long as he sojourned on earth."[49] One piece of evidence for Christ's greater usefulness in heaven than on earth is that his ascension "was soon followed by the wonderful conversion of the world, in which His divinity was displayed more powerfully than when He lived among men."[50] Additionally, and of greater personal relevance, it can be said that Christ serves as intermediary between us and the Father in a way that is more efficacious than the Cross: "Why, then, does Christ assign a new hour wherein his disciples shall begin to pray in his name unless it is that this grace, as it is more resplendent today, so deserves more approval among us? . . . Christ by his very ascension into heaven would be a surer advocate of the church than he had been before."[51] Quite parallel is the way in which Calvin recasts 2 Corinthians 5:16 ("from now on . . . we regard no one from a human point of view; even though we once regarded Christ from a human point of view, we regard him thus no longer"). Calvin's assertion differs in more than tone: the distastefulness of carnal thinking seems to make some part of him want not to remember Christ Incarnate when he writes of "the ascension of Christ, by which he withdrew the presence of his body from our sight and company, to shake from us all carnal thinking of him."[52]

ACCOMMODATION AS LOWERING

The theme of accommodation runs strongly throughout the *Institutes*. God knows that we can conceive of the spiritual only physically, and so he translates his manifestations and commandments into physical terms. At one level, it is because divinity, so transcendent and glorious, would overwhelm us: it would simply be too much. The Incarnation was necessary "not only to draw us near to God but to prevent us from being overwhelmed and utterly destroyed by his majesty."[53] More fundamentally, it is a necessary translation into our language. The created universe is a book of revelation in itself, in accommodated form: "we know the most perfect way of seeking God, and the most suitable order, is not for us to attempt with bold curiousity to penetrate to the investigation of his essence, which we ought more to adore than meticulously to search out, but for us to contemplate him in his works whereby he renders himself near and familiar to us and in some manner communicates himself."[54]

There are, however, pejorative connotations in this accommodation. It is lowering, for God is responding to our intellectual weakness which requires that things be palpable: "The Lord, well knowing that, if he spoke to us as would be appropriate to his majesty, our intelligence would not be capable of attaining to such heights, accommodates himself to our small-ness, and he uses a gross means of speaking to us, in order to be under-stood."[55] In his *Commentary on Psalms*, Calvin repeatedly notes that David adapted himself to his people's need for the concrete and physical. The law and ceremonies were the language they could understand and were the necessary dispensation before the new covenant, which they grossly foreshadowed, could take effect. Moreover, despite the contrast of Old and New Testaments, of the physical and the spiritual, there is accom-modation in the New Testament as well. For the Incarnation and the Cross are the maximum accommodation and the epitome of lowering. It is the flesh itself, it is matter, not intellectual weakness, that stands between us and the spiritual. Matter is abhorrent; the Incarnation was necessary. But what was needed in order that it could be effective made it also, in Calvin's eyes, to his sensibilities and despite his convictions, a regrettable and degrading condescension.

Vocabulary is significant. The physical concept of heaven was nec-essary because "our minds, so crass are they, could not have conceived his unspeakable glory otherwise."[56] God had no other choice, in dealing with men, but the Cross. Justification proceeds,

> not according to his divine nature but in accordance with the dispensation enjoined upon him. For even though God alone is the source of righteousness, and we are righteous only by parti-cipation in him, yet, because we have been estranged from his righteousness by unhappy disagreement, we must have recourse to the lower remedy that Christ may justify us by the power of his death and resurrection.[57]

And the nature of the lowering is the assumption of flesh, of matter, of "that abject and contemptible condition, by which he became clothed in our flesh."[58] Exactly parallel to this thinking is Calvin's conception of the sacraments. Not just a dramatic concretization, a rendering vivid of the divine power, they are a condescension to and a compromise with our lowliness. In the joining of Word and sign,

> our merciful Lord, according to his infinite kindness, so tempers himself to our capacity that, since we are creatures who always

creep on the ground, cleave to the flesh, and do not think about
or even conceive of anything spiritual, he condescends to lead
us to himself even by these earthly elements, and to set before
us in the flesh a mirror of spiritual blessings.[59]

Matter in itself, as much as the fall, seems to be the trouble.

Parallel to the theme of accommodation is the emphasis in Calvin
upon the idea that, in the Cross, God acted out of pity for us rather than
out of love for us, and it was pity for our lowliness, our creatureliness
in itself, rather than for our weaknesses. The more "wretched and
despicable our condition is, the more inclined is God to show mercy, for
the remembrance that we are clay and dust is enough to incite him to do
us good."[60]

HISTORICITY VERSUS ESSENTIALISM

There is also reserve about historicity *per se*. A dispute arose in the
sixteenth century between Calvinists and Lutherans, and within later
Calvinism, about whether perseverance was reliable and definite or whether
one could lapse from faith.[61] Luther and Calvin were both consistent to
their theology: the answer to the latter question was no. Faith did not
mean absence of despair, but it assuredly meant triumph over despair.
Eternal election could not be changed; the faith of justification was truly
efficacious and decisive. But Lutherans came to say that faith could be
lost, and Calvinists to say that, not only could it not be lost, it could also
not be shaken. Both these deviations from orthodoxy can be traced to
tendencies and impulses in Luther and Calvin. Luther emphasized the
historicity of the Cross and the parallel need for the believer to win his
faith and conquer his despair, ever anew in time. Calvin, rather, focused
upon God's eternal decision, made before all time. Persistence depended
for its certainty on God's fidelity to his promise. It is as if God's action —
his decision in election — was, insofar as it was eternal, a manifestation
of God's essence. And we have seen that Calvin had a very marked
propensity for an *a priori*, nonexperiential essentialism that belied both
the logic and the theology he was taught and formally accepted. The congeniality to him of the assimilation of Old and New Testaments — both
in regard to perseverance, where the two Testaments manifest God's fidelity
to his covenant, and especially in regard to the law — indicates also an
abstracting, essentialist mind, a tendency to deindividualize and dehistori-
cize. *A priori* abstractions, preeminently the abstractions of good and evil,
were as real to Calvin as historical and even soteriological events.

CREATURELINESS IN BODY AND IN EMOTIONS

There is further evidence of reserve about creatureliness in Calvin where one would most expect it and where one would least expect it. Although the body partakes of the divine image, "yet there is no doubt that the proper seat of his image is in the soul."[62] Osiander, an obsession of Calvin's, comes into the picture at this point. For, in "indiscriminately extending God's image both to the body and to the soul, [he] mingles heaven and earth."[63] Moses rightly reminds us in Scripture that man's body was taken out of the earth. Thereby, we learn that "this advantage [being created in God's image] was adventitious; for Moses relates that man had been, in the beginning, dust of the earth. Let foolish men now go and boast of the excellency of their nature!"[64]

Emotions, despite their location in the soul, are also, to Calvin, an important sign of creatureliness. Servetus made the "devilish" mistake of declaring the soul to be a derivative of God's substance. But,

if man's soul be from the essence of God through derivation, it will follow that God's nature is subject not only to change and passions, but also to ignorance, wicked desires, infirmity, and all manner of vices. Nothing is more inconstant than man. Contrary motions stir up and variously distract his soul. Repeatedly he is led astray by ignorance. He yields, overcome by the slightest temptation. We know his mind to be a sink and lurking place for every sort of filth. All these things one must attribute to God's nature, if we understand the soul to be from God's essence, or to be a secret inflowing of divinity. Who would not shudder at this monstrous thing.[65]

We are told, parallel to this, that God allows himself to be depicted, in Scripture, with emotions. To speak of God's anger is simply another example of accommodation: God is beyond emotion; man understands only the language of emotion, and that is a sign of his lowliness. When God seems to change from avenging to merciful, we must be reminded that God does not change. Scripture, here, "speaks only after the manner of man."[66]

UNFALLEN ADAM AND REGENERATE MAN

Following Augustine, regenerate man possesses the greater grace of the *donum perseverantiae*.[67] "The grace of persisting in good would have been given to Adam if [God] had so willed. . . . To us it is given both to will and to be able. The original freedom was to be able not to sin; but ours is much greater, not to be able to sin."[68] Additionally, there is evidence in Calvin that regenerate man is simply worthier than unfallen Adam despite the definition of regeneration as restoration of the *imago dei* obliterated in the fall. It is "a peculiar benefit conferred by Christ, that we may be renewed to a life which is celestial whereas before the fall of Adam, man's life was only earthly, seeing it had no firm and settled constancy."[69]

Adam, for his very creatureliness, had needed the Word to be able to recognize God as Creator: even before the fall, God had provided him with the symbols of the tree of life and the tree of knowledge.[70] More broadly, Adam needed the Son as Mediator:

> [The Son] was always the Head of the Church and held primacy even over the angels and was the first born of all creatures. Whence we conclude that he began to perform the office of Mediator not only after the fall of Adam but insofar as he is the Eternal Son of God, angels as well as men were joined to God in order that they might remain upright.[71]

To be sure, as Willis points out, Calvin construes "Mediator" in the sense of preserving and ordering Creation, and he is concerned in a most orthodox way with maintaining the full equality of Eternal Son with God the Father.[72] But the words "upright" and "ordering" have moral connotations to Calvin, and he can make clear his conviction of the need of unfallen Adam and of Creation itself for redemption when he states that, "even if man had remained free from all stains, his condition would have been too lowly for him to reach God without a Mediator."[73]

Luther, Calvin, Integration, and Reserve

In the context of the many hints of dualism in Calvin, his idea that regenerate man is superior to unfallen man evokes also the idea that Creation itself was a fall—as in the pure, dualistic mysticism of Tauler. Luther sometimes sounds dualistic: as long as we are in the flesh, he will say, sin remains. But it is always the fallen flesh. Luther's style, we have seen, is naturally and easily integrated; it includes graphic physical metaphors and is frequently conversational or colloquial. He considers emotions to be a positive part of even the regenerate life. He reminds us that the saints sinned and had feelings; we must take care not to be like those who labored to attain such perfection "that they might be without all feeling of temptations or sin: that is to say, very stocks and stones. The like imagination the monks and schoolmen had of their saints, as though they had been very senseless blocks and without all affections."[74] Luther loved the Psalms above all other books because they were a mirror of the human soul. For Calvin, this mirror of the soul draws "to the life all the griefs, sorrows, fears, doubts, hopes, cares, perplexities, in short all the distracting emotions with which the minds of men are wont to be agitated."[75] We lapse from patience in the face of adversity; "in condescension to our infirmity, [God] permits us to supplicate him to make haste."[76]

Luther's doctrine is integrated. The evil heart symbolizes a totalistic conception of sin which he has internalized. Its counterpart is the possibility of the spiritual direction of the physical. Luther's integration can sometimes seem to render havoc to all traditional bounds, and it seems intended to have that effect in order to emphasize further its rejection of the traditional lines of thought about body and soul and especially those lines running toward dualism:

> If Christ was able to suffer and die on earth while at the same time he was a part of the godhead, one with God, well then, what is to prevent his suffering on earth today, even though he is in heaven?...Now, what if I should not only say that Christ was in heaven while walking upon earth, but that the apostles were too—and all of us, even while we are mortal on earth, just as long as we have faith in Christ? Wouldn't that stir up a tempest in Zwingli's bag of tricks?[77]

In contrast to the praises of man frequently sounded in Italian humanist writing, Luther's evaluation of human nature vis-à-vis God was emphatically negative. But his totalistic conception of sin was as much a break with the past as were its implications for the possibility of the new life. Erikson has associated the integrated conception of man in Luther's restatement of the boundaries between the human and the divine with the integration that characterized Renaissance art—with Dürer's depiction of his own features in Christ's face, or Leonardo's theory of interplay between the intellectual and the sensory.[78] Although Luther often distinguishes between the inner and outer man and never believed that the temporal political order could be fully regenerated, his political thought was quite separate from his moral thought. The equivalent of total regeneration is indeed possible: regenerate man is capable of the spontaneous expression of love, and the flesh which he inhabits is not an impediment. It will be part of this love.

On the resurrection of the body, Luther and Calvin were orthodox. But in Calvin there is again a reserve, and it indicates a different attitude toward the body. In the *Institutes* he presents this resurrection as dogma but also as mystery; in the *Commentary on Corinthians*, he dwells upon it in language that suggests that the idea of the salvation of the body is as distasteful as the incomprehensibility of the means toward that end. The dead are raised, but

> nothing is more repugnant to human reason than this tenet of faith. For nobody else, except God, can convince us that, after our bodies, which are already subject to corruption, have rotted away, or been consumed by fire, or been torn to pieces by wild animals, they will be restored in their wholeness, but in a far

better nature. Does not our whole cast of mind reject it as in-
credible, even as absurd in the extreme?[79]

Lutheranism found root in a mind characterized by the extreme presence
of something that was only one of the facets of Lutheranism.

I think that recognition of the presence of dualism renders Calvin's
version of Reform less puzzling and actually more coherent than historiography has taken it to be. W. Fred Graham has argued in a parallel way
that the Nestorian tendencies in Calvin's christology constitute a unifying
thread running through the contradictions that have been most frequently
cited in him—the apparently harsh and self-righteous autocrat, on the one
hand, and the profoundly humble believer who also considered every action
he took in the perspective of the social implications of faith, on the other.
And Graham looks right on target about cause and effect when he states
that "there is in Calvin's Christology a lack of divine involvement in the
sin and despair of humanity which is curiously like the lack of rapport
with sinful man seen in Calvin's Geneva."[80] Perhaps a small difference
between Calvin and Saint Paul is a microcosm of this problem and points
in the direction in which I want to proceed. Calvin will assert his "paternal
affection" to and for the church of Geneva; Paul will say, even in
admonition, "my children." I want to carry my analysis to the root of the
doctrinal cause that Graham stresses, to another kind of cause that is
probably the reason why this life-long student and introspective and keen
analyst could not resolve these contradictions—contradictions that would
otherwise have posed for him a challenge and exercise in faith.

TOWARD CALVIN THE PERSON

AN ANALYTIC FRAMEWORK

The motifs of the prisonhouse of the body and the corruptibility of
the flesh run through all of Calvin's writings. I do not believe the prison
to be his particular, relatively frail constitution, as it has sometimes been
taken to be. Calvin's ideas were formed before his health became a critical
concern; the ideas were always more reflected in his treatment of bodily
complaints than reflections of them.[81] It is, rather, a psychic life with other
determinants that seems to explain considerably the presence of dualism
in his theology. Those aspects of Calvin the religious leader that have
seemed unpleasantly, harmfully, or neurotically extremist and have
alienated many can also be associated with dualism and can also be looked
at psychologically: these are his censorious attitude toward sexuality and
anything that can be associated with it, and the absolutism of his censoriousness.[82] And the most salient characteristics of Calvin's personality, in
his own accounts and the accounts of many others, his introversion and

his intellectualism, can be closely correlated with a dualistic sense of life. Both also contain qualities or kinds of experience that are very common, but in Calvin they are dominant.

The censoriousness and moralism seem to me part of his adaptation to reality as he experienced it. But they are only part, though very prominent, and the course of history may have disfavored attention to less prominent parts. Calvin in some remarkable ways dealt with troubling and troublesome aspects of his temperament, just as, in ways as exasperating as distressing, he often did not. Yet I do not think it is a matter of a trade-off. Rather, if we take all the perceptible parts, we may get better access to something else that contains them.

My guiding sense in dealing with Calvin the person has been of something I can only call an almost all rightness, psychologically. One can always find in him something that sounds thoroughly unbalanced, but if one stays with the text in which it appears, it will be absorbed into a balanced totality. Then when one proceeds confidently to another text, one will, before that balanced totality takes on a new dimension or further substance, trip over something—something that may seem a psychological malapropism, or a note one would like to ignore. Reading Calvin for an admirer is a sure course, but never an even course; that pattern of surprise is probably true also for his strongest critics.

The impression of almost all rightness is the result, I think, of the coexistence of two very different psychological processes. They are part of what psychoanalytic theory calls character—the aspect of personality that reflects an individual's habitual modes of bringing into harmony his inner needs and the demands of his external world.[83] One of the processes indeed partakes of the quality called character disorder or neurosis, while the other, in significant contrast, seems to me the equivalent of a quite successful kind of self-help. The first comprises the censoriousness and moralism; the second, the personal use to which Calvin put his writing. Certainly a major inference of psychology since Freud is that the deviousness that characterizes neurotic psychic life and manifests itself as character neurosis, the elaborately and painfully wrought economies and calculuses, are only variants upon a basic quality of instinctive purposefulness in human life. The character neuroses, however, are self-perpetuating, through economies so carefully and fearfully worked out that they appear to be the only way their deviser can safely live.

The two psychic processes I find in Calvin, one neurotic and the other not, interact considerably. The first one gives the second its color and temper, and it is this effect that has, I think, led to much misreading of Calvin. One may assume that the second process eased, but did not totally transform the experience indicated in the first. Rather, I think that a fairly distinctive character trait in Calvin, his formalism, served for him as a kind of bridge (and frequent compromise) between the two. The second process, a therapeutic one, was, more broadly, a successful and successfully communicated response to the general human problem that he clearly seems to have inferred from all of his experience, just as he found evidences of that problem in the writings of others.

There are qualities in Calvin that resemble the classic obsessive-compulsive and paranoid neuroses, but the match is not exact; it is also contradicted by other qualities. While he seems, in many of his reactions, to have all the cognitive rigidity of the obsessive-compulsive type, he also has, eminently, the decision-making capacity that is wanting in that type.[84] While his conspicuous guardedness and defensiveness often suggest the totally mobilized defensiveness of the paranoid type,[85] it is as conspicuous to students of Calvin that this was not his only mode of behavior in interpersonal relations—and to students of sixteenth-century church history that his immediate environment, and his role in it, were cause for some guardedness. The very unwary and responsive Calvin known to his friends and the Calvin who maintained an onerous correspondence with Protestants in exile and persecution, sustaining them not just with spiritual counsel and political advice but with graciousness and cordiality, suggest a closer look at the other Calvin. There is indeed some kind of arbitrary division of the human world into good and bad at the base of his behavior. However, "bad" is lacking in the specificity that characterizes the paranoid perception of enmity. For Calvin, it very often seems merely otherness that is the problem when he reacts with defensiveness: something has intruded or is constituting an obstacle.

I suggest that the Jungian conception of introversion as a psychological type,[86] with cognitive, affective, and behavioral dimensions, provides the most accurate and comprehensive psychological description of Calvin. Jung's elaboration of variants within the model of introversion—specifically, of the thinking or intellectual type—is of the greatest usefulness in offering a unifying framework for the different and seemingly disparate things that variously point toward the same dualistic sense. The framework also provides a single perspective for the theologically, behaviorally, and personally problematic sides of Calvin. Through it, they can be seen as his perception and evaluation of otherness, which may be the core of his dualistic sense, and his way (we shall see that it is, rather, ways) of relating to otherness. In the terminology of general psychological theory, we will be dealing primarily with the area of object relations—an individual's attitude and behavior toward the persons and things of the external environment that are significant to his psychic life.[87]

It is the implication of Jung's typology that introversion, as a psychological type, is innate, and much of the work in psychoanalytic theory on the origins of character structure reinforces that conclusion. Agreement does not exist on exactly how much of an individual's characteristic psychic life is innate; agreement does exist that the formation of character occurs "through the interaction of an [individual's] biologically transmitted predispositions with the environment."[88] David Shapiro's particularly useful formulation posits an initial structure consisting in a distinct disposition or tendency toward the organizing of experience.[89] The innate psychological equipment of the structure will include such things as tension and sensory thresholds and cognitive apparatus; it may include other things—for example, a disproportion between sexual and aggressive drives.[90] And the initial organizing configuration will develop interactively with environment in a very general, yet recognizable, way.[91] It can be expected that early childhood will provide determining stimuli and objects for the particular refinements and crystallization of an individual's psychic life—for its shaping—as it may also provide the stimuli and objects for the neurotic economies that can be part of that life. It is important to note, of the interaction of environment and character structure, that the latter serves to screen the input of the former: "certain developmental influences 'take,'. . . whereas others, no matter how forceful or compelling they may seem from an objective standpoint, do not 'take,' that is, are inconsistent with or lack foundation in the existing forms of functioning."[92]

Like Calvin's intellectual temper, his early personal life has a quality of psychological almost all rightness. That, and its specific composition, suggest a highly interesting contingency of psychological type and an environment that sharpened and concentrated some of its elements. I have chosen first to delineate the basic constituents in this psychic life and their interrelations. We can then take advantage of the light his early environment sheds upon them, and from there we can move to the weighting of these qualities in his later life and writings. This seems a logical way to get at the Calvin who was read by vast numbers of people and certainly read within a definable but variable range and intensity of impression.

INTELLECTUALISM

Calvin's intellectualism is as clear in the general pattern of his polemics, in both letters and theological writings, in which he attacks first the ideas and only later the upholders of the ideas, as it is in his obvious attraction to the extraneous, but highly intellectualist, formulation of Aristotelian causality to express the relations of the Trinity.[93] It is also clearly present in his autobiographical statements. In contrast to Luther's, Calvin's statements are rare, but those that we have are convincing in their consistency with each other and with all the qualities of his theology. The most extended of these is the preface to his *Commentary on Psalms*, where he records the story of his "sudden conversion" and relates it to his earlier and later life. First, there was intellectual resistance to the conversion: "I was too obstinately devoted to the superstitions of popery to be easily extricated from so profound an abyss of mire." But it was not merely Calvin's habituating exposure to orthodox theology in Paris that created the intellectual resistance: there is a hint of an unusually strong intellectualism in itself — of attention and response to the power of ideas *as* ideas. Calvin's conversion necessarily had two stages. First he had to be made open to new ideas; then he had to acquiesce in them: "God by a sudden conversion subdued and brought my mind to a teachable frame, which was more hardened in such matters than might have been expected from one at my early period of life."[94] The picture of a strong and unusual personality emerges as we read on, and is reinforced by other evidence.

INTROVERSION

Calvin was an intellectual: he resisted the call to Geneva because he wanted to pursue a life of study and scholarship, the *vita contemplativa*. Over and over again, in his letters as well as the preface to the *Commentary on Psalms*, he depicts himself as a scholar by nature who found the active life of the Genevan church simply alien. Yet there is more here than intellectualism versus involvement and activity. For the role in Geneva, which (Farel convinced him) was God's calling, and which he resisted both stubbornly and sadly, from which he rejoiced at being released when he went into exile in Strasbourg, and which he found doubly hard and even repugnant to return to, was — and this is its overwhelming characteristic for Calvin — a public role. Calvin did not only crave time for study; he craved quiet — removal from the distractions of people. And it can be said that it was not just distraction that people represented: Calvin was uncomfortable with them in all relations. People were preeminently involved in his role in Geneva, and Calvin resisted this aspect of the role as unpleasant, discomforting, and threatening. He was an introvert to an extreme.

> Being of a disposition somewhat unpolished and bashful, which led me always to love the shade and retirement, I then began to seek some secluded course where I might be withdrawn from the public view; but so far from being able to accomplish the object of my desire, all my retreats were like public schools. In short, whilst my one great object was to live in seclusion without being known, God so led me about through different turnings and changes that He never permitted me to rest in any place, until, in spite of my natural disposition, He brought me forth to public notice.[95]

Not just being left alone, but not being known: that is radical isolation.

The deep-rootedness of his introversion is clear in the emotional language that breaks through in a letter to du Tillet in 1538, in which he declares that "there is nothing I dread more than returning to the charge from which I have been set free. For while, when first I entered upon it I could discern the calling of God which held me fast bound, with which I consoled myself, now, on the contrary, I am in fear lest I tempt him if I resume so great a burden, which has already been felt to be insupportable."[96]

INTROVERTED INTELLECTUALISM AND DUALISM

Dualism and introversion have been linked historically. Though universal and varied, the mystic personality, in the intensity of the inner experience to which it responds, as if leaving its world, is characteristically introverted.[97] Further, studies of the psychological base of dualism (in Manichaeanism, in particular) have stressed a sense of sin that equates matter and sexuality.[98] Some very intriguing evidence for the presence of dualism in the introvert exists in the highly introverted Jung himself, despite himself. In his general psychological theory, he describes, in strikingly dualistic language, a basic sense of alienation from others, the world, and within the self:

> The shadow [part of the psyche] is a moral problem that challenges the whole ego personality, for no one can become conscious of the shadow without considerable moral effort. To become conscious of it involves recognizing the dark aspect of the personality as present and real. This act is the essential condition for any kind of self-knowledge, and it therefore, as a rule, meets with considerable resistance. . . .
>
> Closer examination of the dark characteristics—that is, the inferiorities constituting the shadow—reveals that they have an *emotional* nature, a kind of *autonomy*, and accordingly an *obsessive* or, better, *possessive* quality. Emotion, incidentally, is not an activity of the individual but something that happens to him. Affects occur usually where adaptation is weakest, and at the same time they reveal the reason for its weakness, namely a certain degree of inferiority and the existence of a lower level of personality. On this lower level with its uncontrolled or scarcely controlled emotions one behaves more or less like a primitive, who is not only the passive victim of his affects but also singularly incapable of moral judgments. . . . [While it can generally be assimilated, the shadow will sometimes assert itself with] the most obstinate resistance to moral control and prove almost impossible to influence. These resistances are usually bound up with *projections*, which are not recognized as such, and their recognition is a moral achievement beyond the ordinary. . . .
>
> As we know, it is not the conscious subject but the unconscious which does the projecting. *Hence one encounters projec-*

tions, one does not make them. The effect of projection is to *isolate the subject* from his environment, since instead of a real relation to it there is now only an illusory one. Projections change the world into the replica of one's own unknown face.[99]

There seems ample reason for the frequent concurrence of dualistic experience and the introverted thinking type. The intellectual will tend toward identification of self and mind: mind certainly represents strength for him. It is also his highest value, and, in relation to it, emotional and sensory experience are devalued. That he may experience mind as a better self and body and feeling as an inferior self (from which to take refuge in mind) seems highly plausible for an intellectual who is also an introvert. Recent studies of introversion have emphasized that the introvert feels radically disjunct from otherness insofar as subjective, rather than objective, factors are primary in his experience. The introvert also strongly feels as such the mediating nature of his experience of the world (and feels that others are equally preoccupied with their experience of it). He will feel a sharp distance from others when his experiencing of the other interrupts the encounter.[100] So important is the mediation that the introvert does not distinguish, as experience, between people and things.[101] It is consistent that, under stress, the introvert will typically retreat within[102] — and it seems likely that a sudden shift to impersonality, as often in Calvin, is a version of this by force of circumstances.

It is also characteristic of the introvert to abstract, and this approach to reality is intensified in the introverted intellectual. To the introvert, "the object has secondary importance; occasionally it even represents merely an outward objective token of a subjective content, the embodiment of an idea. . . . or it is the object of a feeling, where, however, the feeling experience is the chief thing, and not the object in its own individuality."[103] Thus the first distinction that the introvert draws is between external and internal reality rather than among individual objects; the distinction will be structurally akin to, and, in the introverted intellectual, very likely associated with, the traditional dualistic dichotomies of mind and body, mind and matter, or spirit and matter.

It is the premise of dualistic thought that the relation between the two kinds of reality is inherently one of conflict. In light of the sheer impact made by confrontation with otherness, the same is likely for the dichotomies experienced by the introverted intellectual — the confrontation will be felt as an intrusion into his inner life. Jung formulated the introvert's problem as "the problem of how libido can be withdrawn from the object, as though an attempted ascendency on the part of the object had to be continually frustrated."[104] The abstraction of the object by the introverted thinking type "abolishes both the burdensome relation and the compulsion it evokes."[105] Jung also observed the tendency of the introverted thinking type toward projection: introverted thinking "can also create the idea which, though not present in the external facts, is yet the most suitable abstract expression of them."[106] Indeed, introverted thinking has "a dangerous tendency to coerce facts into the shape of its image."[107]

The paradigm for abstracting the threat of otherness into enmity would seem to be, exactly, the quality of the emotional life of the introverted intellectual. The introverted intellectual abstracts "in order to escape affectedness."[108] But this is just what he cannot do—and thereby tries to do all the more—because his emotional life is unusually intense. He presents "a stout defense against a chaotic and passionate emotional life" precisely because it is there.[109] We can recall that Calvin identified emotion with creatureliness and that he specifically distrusted his own emotions. He often consciously overrode them in personal decisions; it can be assumed that he often tried to suppress them. When his wife died, he reminded Viret of what he knew well enough: "how tender, or rather soft, my mind is." And, "had not a powerful self-control, therefore, been vouchsafed to me, I could not have borne up so long."[110]

The character of emotional life in Jungian psychology is one of polarity. Emotions exist as opposites; they coexist and, more frequently, clash. The polarity is at an extreme in the introverted intellectual; moreover, "the emotional life of the introvert is generally his weak side; it is not absolutely trustworthy."[111] The qualities of the introvert's intense, unconscious feelings "are primarily infantile and archaic."[112] Extremes rather than subtleties are its character, and the extreme emotions, in the presence of their radical opposites, clash. The primitive, archaic nature of Calvin's emotional life may be reflected in his attraction to the Old Testament—to the elemental crying and raging—and it is reflected in the welling up of his own violent temper, which he regretted but could not control: he speaks of his "*affections trop véhémentes*."[113]

Emotional life was both intense and painful for Calvin and was a major source of his desire for isolation: aloneness meant peace insofar as interaction with people meant inner conflict. In Geneva, emotional interchange with others would be made manageable through formalization. However, isolation itself would have been only a partial solution despite the very strong desire and need for it that Calvin's wishes indicate. The *Institutes* is in many ways a vivid and consistent depiction of the inner life of Calvin's psychological type finding expression in the vocabulary and experience—the objects and their valuation—of radical dualism.

Calvin felt himself pitted against God from the viewpoint of his creatureliness, and against his body from the viewpoint of his spiritual life. These were his abstractions as realities. God, in his very transcendence, was alien, threatening, and overwhelming. The motif of rendering glory to God reflects both the actuality of his transcendence and a means of confronting it: it is a formalization of the charged relationship. Communal worship was further formal. One was a member of a congregation rather than an individual; expression of one's intense love of God was full and subtle, but not spontaneous: emotions were controlled and responses reliable.

The body was alien to Calvin; the flesh, alien to the regenerated man of faith. Abstraction in Calvin the introverted intellectual was above all a dephysicalizing. The physical was, first, symbolic of an individualism that had to be depotentiated and, secondly, a determining constituent of it. Calvin's mind opposed itself to matter. He expressed his detachment in a loathing of the body, but he could never escape "this prison-house"; he expressed his total distrust of the body in detachment. The alienness of the body, and because of it the alienness of God, in this introverted intellectual, seems the basis of the tension that runs through his writings. Jung has linked "the tense attitude that is characteristic for the introvert" with his distrust of the outer world.[114] He fears otherness; in face of it, his inner life is mortally threatened. But such a threat comes not only from the outer world. Annihilation is a possibility through guilt—through the meriting of annihilation. Let us remember that the *Institutes* is fraught with the background of predestination. Typically, it is hinted at obliquely; sometimes it erupts in all its dreadfulness—God's response to creatureliness. Pitted against his God and his creatureliness, Calvin capitulated to one and fought to subdue the other.

This intellectual's maximum capitulation—for it is tantamount to self-annihilation—was to follow God's commands, accept his judgments, and acquiesce in his proclamations even when they clashed with reason—in fact exactly because they clashed with reason. "God, for the better trial of our obedience, has lifted his deep and mysterious judgments far above our conceptions."[115] Obedience was somewhat perversely measured by the difficulty it caused: Calvin the intellectual scourged his mind. This was total acceptance of God; it was acceptance of him precisely in his nature as sheer power, asserting itself against the believer, asserting itself in total control of him.

With words, Calvin also scourged his body. It was an attempt to control it; indeed, as it were, to annihilate it. The thinking type's exclusively intellectualist values cause him to evaluate the body negatively; to the introvert, it can also be hateful, threatening to his self—his real, inner self—and murderous. Bodiliness is the form in which otherness announces itself in the world; matter, constitutive of otherness, is determinative.

And matter, for Calvin, is active and assertive; life is a struggle between the spirit and the flesh, between mind and matter; it is tantamount to a raging war, and the war is between good and evil. Calvin felt the strongest distrust of the flesh and of the emotions stemming from the flesh.

He felt a need to control the flesh as it was actively trying to control him. Pauline rhetoric was entirely congenial to him. "As soon as we cast off the burden of the body this strife of spirit and flesh ceases. Therefore the slaying of the flesh releases the spirit into life."[116] For life was violence; the form of process was dialectical. Order was control of the extremes, of the clashing polarities. As Luther did often, Calvin sometimes personified evil in the figure of Satan. But Luther directly wrestled with Satan, while Calvin led battle. "We have been forewarned that an enemy relentlessly threatens us. . . [we must] stand our ground in combat."[117] Chaos threatened continuously: we have seen that only God's hand arbitrarily prevented the waters of the world from overflowing into disastrous floods.[118] The nature of God, bringing light out of darkness to manifest his power, reinforced this world view. He operated in extreme actions, and he was continuously assertive: there was no resting of power. And that the flesh never rested only reflected its own very real power; the experience of evil rendered evil more than just the fallen good. Reality being what it is, we have to annihilate the self to save the self. That is the self-contradictory logic of Calvin's sense of sin.

Emotion and Sexuality. As much as Calvin will talk about the corruptibility of the flesh, he will also talk of the "radical corruption of the mind," and he will say that "sin is properly of the mind."[119] In a very particular sense, sin is emotion. It is inclination in the direction of evil; it consists of the emotions that surprise us, the emotions that we do not will, the "violent and lawless movements which war with the order of God."[120] We cannot prepare against them. Thus, "I do not what I want, but I do the very thing I hate" (Rom. 7:15).

Emotions are contrary to faith; they are also alien and threatening to an intellectual because they impinge upon, interfere with, try to take control of his mind. So contrary are they that Calvin automatically distrusts them: a theme running through his letters is that he will follow God on a particular matter since, his own feelings drawing him in a contrary direction, he suspects himself.[121] God must be right and personal inclination must be wrong.

Emotions are also excessive in nature: they are always inordinate. Perseverance, the gift of faith, is defined negatively as not being swayed by extremes. Calvin's writings are permeated by antitheses such as moderate versus inordinate, prudent versus rash, steady versus inconstant. He revered moderation; it is the quality that distinguished Christ's feelings on the Cross from ours.

We can mortify the flesh in many ways, but in emotion it has a weapon beyond our control. Calvin states that "flesh" in Scripture has two meanings: "our depraved and sinful nature, and [second,] men are called flesh because there is nothing firm or stable in them."[122] And if flesh symbolizes inconstancy, it also explains it: "the life of men is unstable, being continually distracted by the carnality of their minds."[123] Thus are we vulnerable.

Emotions are powerful and destructive. Calvin frequently translates them into terms of gross matter: he speaks of them "swamping" and "sinking" the soul.[124] Emotions represent danger and are the voice of evil for Calvin. "The flesh is ever ready to suggest to our minds that God has forgotten us."[125] Calvin portrayed the character of evil variously, in his own words and often those of Saint Paul and Saint Augustine. One can weigh the different portrayals against each other, step back, and reflect upon the intensity of different images, groups of words, and moods. And when one does this the prevailing impression is of the direct equivalency of evil and sexuality. The dominant words and their associations in Calvin seem to me to give to evil the character that sin has at the center of Leviticus. Human beings must be protected from contamination by human sexuality. And for evil the *Institutes*, like Leviticus, uses primarily a vocabulary of apprehensiveness, offense, and aversion.

Thus Calvin's Satan is less a wily, audacious troublemaker and sower of contention than he is for Luther. Satan is less the loss of God, Christ, faith, and hope than he was when Luther portrayed his *Anfechtungen* as the assaults of the devil.[126] Luther's evil is Augustinian; it is the privation of good, the general cause of specific troubles and sorrows, though, as with Augustine, concupiscence is the foremost manifestation of evil in human life. And evil for Calvin is less any and all ungodliness than it was for Paul; while Paul traces our enslavement to ungodliness, in his metaphor of the life of the flesh, to carnality, he is not transfixed by a specific horror of the flesh as Calvin so often seems to be.

Calvin will readily paraphrase the Old Testament dispensation: "Baptisms and purifications disclose to them their own uncleanness, foulness, and pollution, with which they were defiled in their own nature; but these rites promised another cleansing by which all their filth would be removed and washed away (Heb. 9:10–14)."[127] Here he is, in fact, translating Saint Paul's own paraphrase of Leviticus back into its original terms, and the persistence of that language in Calvin suggests that he felt the presence of what he understood to be sin unremittingly.

In an interesting statement about Augustine's conception of evil, Calvin confronts the nature of good and evil in his frequently oblique way: "I shall not say with Augustine, although I willingly embrace his statement as true, that in sin as in evil there is nothing positive. It is, however, an argument which does not satisfy many people."[128] I have suggested that the thought and sensibilities in Calvin's conception of good and evil may be closer to Plato's than to Augustine's. The image of the body as prison is originally Platonic. And the body for Calvin is experienced as an adversary, the adversary of the spiritual and the good; thereby it is lowliness and evil. Life is not mind *and* matter (as it was for Luther) but mind *versus* matter; insofar as mind is on the defensive, it would be more accurate to say that life is matter versus mind. This sense in Calvin is dualism outright.

The hypothetical reconstruction by a psychiatrist and classicist of a basis in experience for Plato's dualism recalls very strikingly the aspect of Calvin with which we are dealing. The biographical hypothesis itself does not matter here; Bennett Simon's analysis of its psychological connotations does:

> the core unconscious meaning of madness in the Platonic dialogues is the wild, confused and combative scene of parental intercourse as perceived by the child. We may take this inference from the imagery and total context of the dialogues in which madness is discussed. The equation embraces the two main aspects of madness in Plato, unbridled impulse and ignorance. The wildness of the primal scene is associated with lack of restraint of impulse and appetite, and the frightening yet fascinating aspect of the scene is associated with blindness and ignorance. The appetite cannot be controlled or the veil of ignorance lifted unless the primal scene can be controlled or abolished. Philosophy provides new ways of looking and new objects of contemplation and thereby liberates men from their blindness and madness.[129]

The sexual connotations of matter, which is unconsciously identified with evil, and the horror of it, and belief in its complete and violent opposition to mind are very much shared by Calvin and Plato.

The strong sense of creaturely guilt in Calvinist theology is expressed frequently as the impingement of flesh upon spirit; the flesh threatens to alienate the believer from God just as it alienates the believer from himself. The temptation of the *vita contemplativa* was not merely a way to avoid the interpersonal relations that the life of Christian love discomfortingly would entail for Calvin. It was a temptation to escape from body into mind, and into an extraordinarily powerful mind that could serve to rationalize that temptation by letting itself be used in the service of divine truths. It seems of the highest likelihood that guilt in Calvin was intensified by the fact that he had to be at least subliminally aware that his dualistic tendency approached the heretical as he knew it to be defined.

The extent of Calvin's distrust of matter may be measurably reflected in the extent of his concept of accommodation. First, he construes the whole of the visible church as an accommodation. Since

in our ignorance and sloth (to which I add fickleness of disposition) we need outward helps to beget and increase faith within us . . . God has also added these aids that he may provide for our weakness. And in order that the preaching of the gospel might flourish, he deposited this treasure in the church. He instituted "pastors and teachers" (Eph. 4:11) through whose lips he might reach his own; he furnished them with authority; finally he omitted nothing that might make for holy agreement of faith and right order.[130]

There is, further, a hint that all of Scripture is allegorical — a concretization and hence vivification of truth to its carnal perceivers. This is certainly true of the Old Testament dispensation. It is a necessary accommodation to our physical conceptualization that the law "under the prohibition of fornication, murder, and theft, forbids lust, anger, coveting a neighbor's possessions, deceit, and the like . . . murder that is of the soul consists in anger and hatred; theft, in evil covetousness and avarice; fornication in lust."[131] And so the spiritual gospel is opposed to the carnal law. But even the Gospel itself may be an allegorical accommodation. A man can be taught, Calvin writes, about sin, judgment, and faith, and he may gain some sense of God's mercy.

> On the other hand, suppose he learns, as Scripture teaches, that he was estranged from God through sin, is an heir of wrath, subject to the curse of eternal death, excluded from all hope of salvation, beyond every blessing of God, the slave of Satan, captive under the yoke of sin, destined finally for a dreadful destruction and already involved in it; and that at this point Christ interceded as his advocate, took upon himself and suffered the punishment that, from God's righteous judgment, threatened all sinners; that he purged with his blood those evils which had rendered sinners hateful to God; that by this expiation he made satisfaction and sacrifice duly to God the Father; that as intercessor he has appeased God's wrath; that on this foundation rests the peace of God with men; that by this bond his benevolence is maintained toward them. Will the man not then be even more moved by all these things which so vividly portray the greatness of the calamity from which he has been rescued?
>
> To sum up: since our hearts cannot, in God's mercy, either seize upon life ardently enough or accept it with the gratefulness we owe, unless our minds are first struck and overwhelmed by fear of God's wrath and by dread of eternal death, we are taught by Scripture to perceive that apart from Christ, God is, so to speak, hostile to us, and his hand is armed for our destruction; to embrace his benevolence and fatherly love in Christ alone.[132]

EARLY CHILDHOOD

Calvin's psychic life reflects, of course, its own history. A sequence of events in his early childhood, seen in the light of psychoanalytic theory, seems to have been immediately important for him and to have affected his experience of a relatively ordinary pattern that followed in later childhood, the consequences of which he perpetuated and vastly extended, probably in resignation. The first events were the death of his mother in 1514 or 1515, when he was five or six years old, and shortly thereafter, the remarriage of his father. Both occurred in the late oedipal phase of child development and the years in which ambivalence is most sharply experienced — and will be decisively important in the formation of object relations — and also the years when morality becomes internalized through the formation of the superego. The precipitant of the latter is considered to be the child's need to repudiate the oedipal feelings about which his parents have given enough information for him to be feeling the highest degree of guilt: the child's superego (identifying with and modeled on a parental superego) protects him by projecting his guilt.[133]

The later environmental pattern that also seems crucial is one that echoes the structure of loss and replacement in the death of Calvin's mother: an arbitrarily decided shuttling around of the child, and then youth, from one situation to another. And the replacements were relatively congenial; within them, as through his father's remarriage, many real human needs were met and Jean Calvin could be content, consciously. This is another kind of almost all rightness, and one that could be devastating.

The feelings Calvin can be certain to have felt at the death of his mother were both intense and inadmissible. The inadmissible feelings were those of the oedipal complex, the reality of which, Charles Brenner states, is only barely conveyed as "a tempest of passions of love and hate, of yearning and jealousy, of fury and fear that rages within the child."[134] Additionally, it can be assumed that he felt sheer anger with his mother for dying.[135] His father then replaced important parts of Jean's loss — human warmth, care, and the appearance of motherhood. Yet his father, who had been his rival, also became, by remarriage, the betrayer of his mother's memory. The sense of betrayal was probably preconscious; the oedipal rivalry was, of course, repressed. Consciously, Jean could only be grateful to his father and remember his mother with love; he would have been, for various reasons and among other things, furious with both. But the contents of the id do not know the law of contradiction: all of these feelings would have been major constituents of the child's ambivalence and decisive for him in later relationships.

Another result of this sequence — and it, too, becomes part of object relations — would have to have been a problematic attitude toward sexuality, and this may be the source of a specific sense in Calvin of sex and sexuality as sordid. His father's betrayal of his mother's memory would have appeared to be a betrayal committed for the same sexual needs he himself was strongly feeling; he would have felt at least semiconscious horror at being confronted with them in his father. The superego that formed at this phase, then, had a very sharply defined object, and it looks as if that superego was precipitated in an iron form and never relaxed sufficiently to grow flexible and mature. The child Jean, we know, had a prominent habit of censoriousness: Beza states that "even in his tender years he was in a surprising manner devoted to religion, and a stern reprover of all the vices of his companions."[136] This habit, it is well known, was also prominent in his student days.

It looks as if the intense and contradictory contents of Calvin's psychic impulses were decisively organized in later childhood and youth. At about age twelve, as the first stage in the clerical career his father had chosen for him, he was placed in the Montmor household, a branch of the family of Charles de Hangest, Bishop of Noyon.[137] Parental decisions for careers and apprenticeships were normal in the sixteenth century; we know from the grateful and respectful dedication of his first book that the household was congenial to him. Yet who was Jean Calvin in this household? He was an accepted member by the grace and at the pleasure of the family, and he already knew very well how contingent warmth, comfort, and peace were.

However, he had these things for a while, and the move to the Collège de la Marche and then the Collège de la Montaigu in Paris were progresses in one course. Then came the abrupt change of mind by his father: he was taken away from his preparation for a religious career, designated by Gérard for a civil career in law, and sent to Orléans. In itself, there is nothing extraordinary in this, either; it could have been the result of Gérard's reassessment in 1525 of the solidity of a clerical career for his son or of his own social anxieties. And of great significance, law was extremely congenial to Calvin. Though he changed his career path after Gérard's death, his mind in obvious ways remained that of a lawyer; further, it was his legal education that introduced him to the worlds of humanism and philology.

But Calvin's experience of this pattern would have been shaped by the echoing in it for him of his first object loss and its replacement. To that experience and its reinforcements, I think, one can relate several important qualities and characteristics in his life and thought. The most obvious effect would have been a very high degree of insecurity: good things don't last; they may be more or less replaced, but then the replacements don't last either. Closely related to this may have been a passive stance in regard to his personal fate, a fate, moreover, that could not be extensively explained. Calvin always knew what he wanted to do with his life and was entirely capable of taking control of it, even in difficult and dangerous circumstances: his emigration from France under persecution is evidence of this. But the result of that emigration was his encounter with Farel in Geneva. Amid the cataclysmic changes wrought in his life by this meeting was the reinforcement of personal passivity. The association of this quality with predestination is unavoidable for a historian writing after Erikson, but feels hollow. However, it seems likely that an unusually great personal passivity in Calvin found compensation in the striking activism of his church, and even more—because more distant—in his direction of the church in persecution beyond Geneva. His dogmatism may be another, parallel response, echoing for himself the pattern of arbitrariness that was part of his early experience.

Given the unstable, precarious nature of life, it would be pleasantest or most fruitful to turn one's back to the outside world while one can and lead a very concentrated existence within the nest or niche in which one is fortunate to have found one's self deposited, yet being wary and on guard against an abrupt intervention that could end it. A protective shell would certainly be a good idea, both against outside intrusion and against too much feeling—that is, against the intrusion of a weaker self.

For the purpose of expressing acutely ambivalent feelings, it is not uncommon for a child to splinter them into positive and negative parts and assign them to two distinguishable kinds of objects—the objects and everything subsequently encountered that can be made to conform to them are designated and perceived as positive or negative.[138] I think that Calvin evolved exactly this form of interpersonal emotional economy. The people whom he knew well, to whom he felt close, and whom he considered trustworthy, always quite few in number, were positive. A subset of this was people whom he knew in his pastoral role but who were totally removed from physical proximity: people at a guaranteed distance. Everyone else, or all otherness, undifferentiated, was negative. And, with the two kinds of people, he had two different relationships. With positive objects, he was trusting, open, and receptive; with negative objects, he behaved in formal roles. His persona in the formal relationships could be pleasant or unpleasant; it was always impersonal.

If this made life immediately easier, it was also a false economy that made life harder. The strong negative feelings projected onto the outside world had as their original object the people in Calvin's inner world: the original feelings included distrust and resentment. In his economy, others had no chance to be anything but negative (and Calvin, to be subject to hurt), while friends were not allowed anything but positive behavior—and that allowed, of course, for a far greater number of shocks and disappointments than needed to be the case. The latter also meant more inadmissible resentment, that also to be projected onto the other kind of object.

The disjunction between the two kinds of relationship in this economy seems to clarify an incident that has often been noted — Calvin's behavior the evening of his wife's death, and his reporting of it — and that behavior may shed more light on the disjunction.

During the evening, Calvin was called away from Idelette's bedside for some routine ministerial duty, and went; he returned, before her death and in time to pray with her. He simply mentions to Farel, in the letter describing her death, that he "had to go out at 6 o'clock that night."[139] The letter to Viret that contains the well-known tribute to the fact that his wife never in any way hindered his ministry also notes positively that "I have been bereaved of the best companion of my life."[140] But it looks as though it did not occur to him, when he left her that night — or it was not possible to conceive of it — that Idelette needed ministering: ministering was what he did in the church of Geneva. Nor, probably, did it occur to him — or it was not possible to conceive of it — that the love he felt for family and friends was related in nature to the Christian love he communicated to his congregation. There were two calls that night, and they were the same; the disjunction in Calvin made him feel that a separate and formally more important call had come. One could probably conclude that he felt very strongly that night the force and bite that the disjunction must always have had for him.

The false economy was the product of a false environment; some of the falseness in the primal situation was a child's normal reaction to parental death as desertion. The economy also matches strikingly the tendency of an introverted intellectual to divide the world into trustworthy and hostile parts and abstract them into good and evil. The prominence of sexuality as a negative and problematic area in the evolving of Calvin's economy provided the face of evil: that, too, is consistent with a tendency in introverted intellectualism. Elements in type and in environment seem to have been mutually reinforcing.

We need now to try to weigh the substance and experience of dualism in Calvin's thought, life, and writings, and we need to examine deeper levels of his *modus vivendi* in light of it.

GOD-IMAGE AND GENEVA

There is a decidedly tyrannical quality to Calvin's God, in positive as well as negative actions. Power asserting itself as control *of* something, *over* something, rather than in creative action, is both a positive attribute of God and a good in itself for Calvin.

Jung sees two psychological aspects in the derivation of an individual's God-image. The first is that it will have numinosity—that it will represent the highest values of the self and be thereby compelling. "The image of God is the symbolic expression of a certain psychological state or function, which has the character of absolute superiority to the conscious will of the subject," and which can thereby enforce "a standard of accomplishment that would be unattainable to conscious effort."[141] But God as a projected psychic value will further reflect the characteristics, not just the standards, of the self. And especially in the introvert, for whom the inner life is normative, "his God, his highest value, is the abstraction and conservation of the self."[142] It then follows that the content of the introvert's projected God will be tyrannical, for in a certain sense, seen from the viewpoint of the world that he affects, the introvert is himself tyrannical. "Since, in order to escape affectedness, the introvert cannot abstract indefinitely, he ultimately sees himself forced to shape the external world."[143] The introvert is a tyrant by virtue of being on the defensive. The world, otherness, is threatening; there is a consequent need to control, defend, even to retaliate. The introvert's God will be foremost a tyrant.

Calvin's need to control his own world—beyond the exigencies conferred by his historical situation—arose from the impulse for self-defense and, perhaps paradoxically, from self-contempt. Otherness was threatening unto annihilation; Calvin also felt that he merited annihilation. I think this is the perspective in which one must see his assertions that suffering at the hands of one's enemies was proof of righteousness and his statements that he was acting, in crusade against his enemies, as God's instrument— that it was not Calvin versus his opponents, but absolute good versus evil; that, if he wielded a heavy and active sword, he could properly speak of "the actions that the Lord has placed in my hands."[144] These are not sublimated delusions of grandeur, as they have sometimes been taken to be; they are, rather, adaptive depersonalizations for a self with an extreme sense of unworthiness and in sometimes desperately uncongenial psychological situations. It is of the greatest importance to recall that Calvin never enjoyed his role as God's instrument and always felt that it was alien to his nature. "There is nothing I dread more than returning to the charge from which I have been set free." His letters show him to be weary and disgusted with contention. Power itself, and all that it entailed, were simply not gratifying to Calvin.

The thwarting of his nature that his calling represented was paralleled by his personal asceticism. In this light, the strict disciplinarian of the Genevan church is consistent. As God subdued Calvin, and as Calvin sought to subdue his own flesh, he would pit the Genevans against evil. Intellectually, the Augustinian world view taught that we are living amid evil, that the earthly city always was and would be evil. But Calvin's antagonistic world view and the psychic experience in which it was rooted posited an active, assertive character to evil. Despite his insights into the equivalency of act and impulse, he repeatedly states that there is a need to rein, check, and bridle excesses. Although we cannot get at the root, we can control some of the externalizations. The consideration that evil is contagious is a justification for this.[145] Yet we know that the faithful cannot be fatally swayed. Rather, our duty in our calling and as regenerated Christians is to take an active stance against evil because it actively opposes the good and because faith can defend itself only in a struggle with its opposite.

Calvin's governance of the church was internally consistent. It could be less than humanly wise. Between gentleness and harshness, he preferred the latter. While the magistrate should avoid "excessive severity," he should also take care lest "by superstitious affectation of clemency [he] falls into the cruelest gentleness, if he should (with a soft and dissolute kindness) abandon many to their destruction."[146] Calvin was also personally consistent, but in contradiction to theological commitment, on the matter of excommunication; here, his ability to accept an inconsistency can only be understood as an inability to see it. While he will sometimes state that there are sure signs of election (he defined them variously as calling or the combination of profession of faith, partaking of the sacraments, and leading an upright life), his basic position is that we do not know the elect. He is in agreement with Luther; they both maintained a distinction between the invisible church of the elect and the visible church. Since regenerate man was *simul iustus et peccator*, there was no way to distinguish among men, and God's decrees were secret. But against this conviction Calvin did judge, condemn, and excommunicate from the church, "that they who lead a filthy and infamous life may not be called Christian, to the dishonor of God, as if his holy church was a conspiracy of wicked and abandoned men."[147]

Following God's calling was a form of self-abnegation for Calvin. He was always detached from his calling. He typically wrote, "I speak, but I must listen to myself, being taught by God's spirit."[148] He followed God's calling because he distrusted himself—he distrusted the assertions of his unconscious that made him feel like a prisoner of carnality and he distrusted the temptation that his intellectualism presented to save him from carnality. Confidence is his more usual note. But the very great tension in the *Institutes* is the evidence of a self in conflict and frustrated by its inescapability. The resentment that his dogmatism and absolutism provoked despite his confidence that they were in the service of God would not have been a mirror of positive reinforcement for anyone, and for realistic reasons Calvin had further to be on the defensive. Self-distrust and self-doubt are essential ingredients in Calvin the despot.

A further observation can be made. Calvin did not hesitate to talk about his unworthiness. That sentiment, I think, is part of what sometimes seems in him a certainty that he is of the elect in a sense outside the measure of the tests for election and distinct from the faith that sustained him in his trials of despair. A curious but lawful contingency seems to exist between self-loathing and selfishness: one demands, and thinks one has a right to demand, affirmation from without, precisely because it is not forthcoming from within.

It is in a similar way that Calvin's sense of persecution and his right-eousness in face of it are, to a great extent, his sense of conflict and internal struggle projected into the world. We must always remember that Calvin engaged in a continuous argument with himself. If he had an answer to his doubts, either theologically in faith or psychologically in the conviction of election, the question could never be finally resolved, any more than the conflict between mind and body that he experienced, to which the doubts were related, could be ended.

METHOD, STYLE, AND MENTALITY

Calvin considered himself variously as student and teacher. He could say that reason was from the spirit of God, in sharpest emotional contrast to Luther's characterizations of reason as whore and beast. Calvin was self-consciously an intellectual. He was also an introverted intellectual, and a highly characteristic sign of his psychological type was his use and preference for the *a priori*.

Emotions that are unconvincing because they are logically, not ex-perientially, derived abound in Calvin. The joy of the elect is a motif: in suffering, while "our minds are constrained by the natural feeling of bitterness, they are as much diffused with spiritual joy."[149] The life of the damned is characterized as misery. "With full cellars and storehouses, men would faint with thirst and hunger unless they enjoyed their bread through his grace."[150] It is "wretched. . . to be cut off from all fellowship with God," and it was thus correct for the prophets to say that the damned experience all the horrors and torments of hell; though they spoke "through physical metaphor" — of God's fire, of his crushing hand — they "employ no exaggeration."[151]

The *a priori* is strongest in Calvin's derivation of definitions, and his very pronounced tendency toward thinking in mutually exclusive contrasts is most evident in these definitions: his logic is also dialectical. If God is everything, we are as nothing; if God is good, we are evil; if Christ saves, we need salvation and would otherwise merit damnation. Faith is the belief in God's promise, and God is all powerful: accordingly, "what is more consonant with faith than to recognize that we are naked of all virtue, in order to be clothed by God? That we are empty of all good, to be filled by him? That we are slaves of sin, to be freed by him? Blind to be illumined by him? Lame, to be made straight by him? Weak, to be sustained by him?"[152] Again, more rhapsodically and demonstrating a habit of mutually reinforcing thought and expression, the suffering of the innocent is read from (and rationalized as the occasion of) God's graceful nature. "If we are cast out of our house, then we will be the more intimately received into God's family. If we are vexed and despised, we but take all the firmer root in Christ. If we are branded with disgrace and ignominy, we but have a fuller place in the Kingdom of God. If we are slain, entrance into the blessed life will thus be open to us."[153] Succinctly, "if the death of Christ be our redemption, then we were captives; if it be satisfaction, we were debtors; if it be atonement, we were guilty; if it be cleansing, we were unclean."[154] This distinctive mode of thought ranges beyond theology. To support his conviction that slavery to sin is, though slavery, nevertheless voluntary and not in contradiction to God's goodness, Calvin notes that "men are despoiled of freedom unless they recover it from elsewhere."[155]

A priori knowledge conceives of unknowns in terms of what is known: progress in knowing is made by working and being impelled forward from within, rather than responding to what is outside. It is very likely that it will proceed negatively: a thing that is other than this will be construed as not-this. It is philosophically viable to maintain that intelligible discourse depends upon, and consists in, the making of such distinctions — in the specifying of what things are not, of the way in which they differ from other things, in order to identify them.[156] Sixteenth-century rhetoric theory made teaching subject to speech. Rhetoric theory also prescribed the use of mutually exclusive viewpoints to render arguments incontrovertible. Calvin was subject to its influence and also to that of the forensic discipline of law, and they form a reinforcing background for a strong intellectual tendency. It could be noted that his adoption of Saint Augustine's characterization of the way he worked may be still more appropriate for his own work: "I count myself one of the number of those who write as they learn and learn as they write."[157] Ford Lewis Battles has described Calvin's basic thought process as a honing out of truth, progressively, inside the bounds of opposing extremes.[158] I suspect that Calvin generally did this honing as he wrote — that he followed his words as they expressed the movement of his mind.

The bipolarity of the derivations in Calvin consistently echoes and seems certainly to emerge from a conviction of the radical difference between human and divine, of their mutual exclusivity: "The Spirit is so contrasted with the flesh that no intermediate thing is left."[159] More precisely, the derivations match Calvin's antagonistic conception of reality: reality consists of polarities, of radical opposites, in contrast and in conflict with each other. This dialectical conception of reality seems rooted in Calvin's emotional experience and projected into a dominating presupposition about all of life.

Calvin's style is as significant and symptomatic as his logic. It is above all a formal rhetoric, yet emotions do break through, and, when this happens, they seem more powerful for having been checked. These emotions are reflected in a characteristic vocabulary that links doctrine and polemic and uses to advantage the emphatic nature of rhetorical convention. One can extract clusters of key words. First, there are the characteristic words for the flesh: it is pollution, filth, foulness. We are mired in it; it is a stinking swamp. Opponents' doctrines are associated with the flesh; opponents are typically characterized as animals — as dogs or swine, both filthy and mindless — and the characterizations depict both the spirit versus the flesh and mind versus matter. The opponents are also characterized by madness or insanity and drunkenness: they are out of control — like the emotions. There is a cluster of words to describe their stupidity: they are mindless, they prattle, they babble.

The same vocabulary substantiates the conventions of exhortation, question, and exclamation. These techniques are conspicuously employed by Calvin in ridicule of opponents. Absurdities are attributed and made total, to be implicitly contrasted to his own normal and moderate sanity or insight or goodness, and the substance of the attributed qualities consistently reflects his values and feelings. Both feeling and opinion are often conveyed by a common device in sixteenth-century rhetoric: the metaphoric use of exaggerated violence. Calvin will refer to "tearing Christ apart" or "tearing Scripture to pieces." Of the Roman clergy he writes, "For, as thieves slit men's throats and divide the spoils among themselves, so these men, after putting on the light of God's Word, as if slitting the church's throat, supposed that everything dedicated to holy uses was laid out for booty and spoils."[160] He uses absolutes such as "entirely," "altogether," "in every way" for emphasis. There is "not even the slightest taste of right and sound doctrine"; "not one man in a hundred knows how to worship God." Exhortation can confer urgency upon his values: "But because, as we said, they assail us with still other devices, come, let us keep beating them back!"[161]

As typically, Calvin's style is characterized by an elaborately measured formality. Rhetoric itself is a device of artificiality and manipulation. Renaissance humanists claimed as a major achievement the rediscovery of ancient rhetoric, displaced in the Middle Ages by an overvaluation, to its exclusion, of grammar and logic. Rhetoric was again considered important in the Renaissance because it was appropriate to human nature. It involved the will and emotions; it was a tool of persuasion through its appeal to these powers; thus (in contrast to mere didacticism) it could effectively move men toward the good. Truth was moral, and teaching had to use methods that were morally effective. Rhetoric was, in this sense, a method of deliberate control. While it coordinates itself to human nature, it is as nonnaturalistic as it is nonspontaneous: it plots an attack and deploys its forces. A rhetorical technique of particular usefulness to Calvin was the anticipatory disarming of negative reaction through countercharge of the expected criticism.[162] But rhetoric was also a psychological strategy for Calvin, and its manipulativeness was part of that strategy. Ill at ease with his own feelings and those of others, control through manipulation and the method of artifice itself must have had the highest appeal for him.

Calvin's rhetoric is strikingly exceptional to a central prescription of rhetoric theory followed in the Italian Renaissance and most eminently in northern Europe by Erasmus: that of adjustment and adaptation of message to individual audience. Yet the difference lies within crucial agreement about the involvement of will and feeling, as well as mind, in persuasion. Calvin's rhetoric was written and published for unknown and unlimited readers; it was also written by an intellectual whose abstractive perception did not construe accidental and circumstantial differences as the determinants of will and feeling: the human soul had its own dramatic life.[163]

Calvin chose to persuade by the stately, serious, and formalistically elegant high style of classical rhetoric. I think his choice included the intuitive awareness that this style would be empowered by his temperament and mentality, the dualistic aspects of which he considered to constitute man's nature. Many of his treatises are throughout in the unmistakable voice of the *Institutes*. In his scriptural commentaries, there are intermittent versions of that rhetoric—they are also linked by the controlled sincerity and intensity of the personality so closely related to it.

Emphatically parallel constructions abound in the *Institutes*, as does *conduplicatio*—the repetition of words or phrasing in successive clauses. The *Institutes* contains repeated, consecutive "if. . .then" clauses. Calvin typically writes of Christ that "He, he alone deserved to be preached; he alone set forth; he alone named; he alone looked to when there was a question of obtaining forgiveness of sins, expiation, sanctification."[164] Or of the Catholic church, a whole page of parallel constructions begins with this series of questions:

> But how could they excuse themselves, since among them it is far more wicked to have skipped auricular confession at the turn of the year than to have led an utterly wicked life the whole year through? to have infected their tongue with a slight taste of meat on Friday than to have fouled the whole body with fornication every day? to have moved the hand to honest work on a day consecrated to some saintlet or other than religiously to have exercised all the bodily members in the worst crimes?[165]

The rhythmic effect of the constructions is hypnotic, and the quality of bombardment is manipulative. The *conduplicatio* is also a controlled way of expressing strong emotion.

The polarities of the parallel constructions, like Calvin's logic, seem also to be expressions of an inner sense of conflict—and it is a commonplace in psychology that the expression of conflict will to some extent depotentiate it. The conflict seems implicit where the constructions appear, and sometimes it is explicit:

> The godly heart, therefore, feels in itself a division because it is partly imbued with sweetness from its recognition of the divine goodness, partly grieves in bitterness from an awareness of its calamity; partly rests upon the promise of the gospel, partly trembles at the evidence of its own iniquity; partly rejoices at the expectation of life, partly shudders at death.[166]

DIMENSIONS OF DUALISM IN CALVIN'S PERSONALITY

ANOTHER EMOTIONAL ECONOMY

I am maintaining that sexuality and emotion *per se* presented significant problems for Calvin. It is entirely possible to find a positive Christian position on sexuality in his writings, expressed at some length and with obvious conviction. It is impossible not to see example after example of open and strong emotional expression, not just of despair and pain, but of hope and happiness. Notably absent, however, are some key emotions, and the distribution of the ones that are present tends to locate happiness either in close personal friendships or in the solitary religious life, while unhappy, negative feelings characterize Calvin's everyday life in the world—apart from formal worship and the execution of his pastoral duties. We have seen that Calvin's mode of expressing emotion suggests a discomfort with it—indeed the singularity of expression may sometimes obscure the reality and intensity of emotions he did experience, and such instances seem to capture a picture of Calvin against himself most sharply.

Of the greatest significance is a structural peculiarity that emerges when one examines together his attitudes toward sexuality and toward emotionality. For both, we can find a negative theoretical position or classification on the one hand, and, on the other, positive commentary on instances of the actual phenomenon. But the two sets of statements are strikingly asymmetrical. Statements of Calvin on sexuality *per se* that are emphatically negative abound; statements on sexuality in the life of the Christian, the positive position worked out in reference to the negative, are very rare. The treatment of nonsexual emotion presents a strong contrast. Despite Calvin's conception of emotions as instances of human weakness, included, as we have seen, at the outset of his most extended treatment of them, the *Commentary on Psalms*, he goes on to encourage and present a succession of examples of emotional experience as part of the Christian life. However, negative references and usages of sexual metaphor are interwoven with these undisparaged depictions of nonsexual emotions: at the least, we are not likely to forget the core of our infirmity.

With Paul, Calvin believes that those who do not have the gift of continency are better to marry than to fall into the sin of fornication. Marriage has been provided by God, in accommodation, as "a necessary remedy to keep us from plunging into unbridled lust."[167] More positively, and with Augustine, he believes that the incorporation of sexual intercourse into the bonds of marriage forms an honorable institution of God and a dignified institution. The generation of man "is not unclean and vicious, but is so as an accidental quality arising from the Fall."[168]

However, the emphasis in Calvin's thought on marriage is upon the power of God over sin through something very much like justification; it is the implication of sin that is transformed, for marriage is an intervention, like Christ's, to save mankind despite man's nature. It is a major example of man's total dependence upon God in his postfall condition. "The uncontrolled passion with which men are aflame is a vice springing from the corruption of human nature; but for believers, marriage is a veil which covers that fault, so that God sees it no longer."[169] Calvin urges his readers not to forget the weakness of human nature, not to forget that continency is a special and untypical gift. He states and repeats the need to be certain, should one think he or she has received this gift, that "the power to see it through" has also been given.[170] He is neither didactic nor dogmatic when he does this: his insistence seems deliberately restrained and soft edged; he is earnest and concerned, and one construes this to be the result of a personal sense of danger in sexual feeling. Thus it is an area for special pastoral care.

Calvin's skepticism about celibacy and his positive valuation of marriage are also matters of anti-Catholic strategy; the indissolubility of the bonds of marriage clearly appeals to his sense of order; he likes the stability implied in the idea of mutual help and obligation.[171] But he manifestly and sometimes avowedly feels awkward when talking about sexual relations and expresses disgust with intercourse even in marriage.[172] The only extended and particularized statement he makes about intercourse is that it is as necessary as, and is therefore like (he tells us he is offering an analogy), food, drink, and sleep.[173] The only particularized advice he gives about marriage is not to allow it to assert its capacity to interfere, through its rather trivial distractions, with prayer—indeed, that we not be distracted from prayer by temptation is a reason *for* marriage.[174] The problem is body versus soul. Perhaps the most characteristic note in Calvin on marriage is the combination of resignation, sincere acquiescence, and personal detachment which also characterizes his discussions of his calling.

In contrast to his endorsements of marriage and threading like a leitmotiv through the tracts of the *Institutes* between these endorsements is the idiom and metaphor for sin of the life of the flesh. The attitude manifest in this idiom is not qualified by the positive possibilities of marriage; it is evidence of the reality to Calvin of his theoretical position on postfall man as distinct from prefall man and of the primacy of this condition for both theologian and minister.

Human emotion is defined in such a way that positive emotional experience is excluded. The positive emotions of the religious life—hope, trust, and the love of God and righteousness—are simply defined as non-human: they are God-granted.[175] Love of one's neighbor is also a gift of God, a capacity we do not naturally have.[176] Of course descriptively and not analytically, Calvin felt hope, trust, and love of God, and, if derivatively, love of his neighbor, and he certainly felt love for his friends. But these feelings are disavowed. The emotions that Calvin construes as both human and licit are negative: they are pain, suffering, and unhappiness. These, like other emotions, are evidence of our weakness, "the feelings of the flesh,"[177] and, because of that weakness, we may give utterance to them.

The significance of the sphere of legitimate feeling may lie not only in its exceptional classification but in a compensatory function that it could serve. Emotion at a distance from its actual center, as other feeling was in relation to sexuality for Calvin, was not just less tainted and therefore less unacceptable: it may have represented a peculiarly important outlet in a psychological economy that probably contained a great deal of unwanted feeling. One senses that that feeling was consciously and determinedly suppressed.[178]

In this light, the strong motif of self-punishment in Calvin can be looked at further. Not inconsistently in view of the strength of his sense of sin, the feeling of pain would have been the emotion with which he felt most comfortable psychologically. One could additionally postulate that self-punishment served the function Freud assigned to the phenomenon: it could have been sexually compensatory, and it seems plausible to see this possibility in Calvin's attraction to contrariety and to being overpowered. His dialectical conception of knowledge and experience of reality could partially explain his conviction that one cannot experience the happiness of God's favor without first having been exercised in adversity or first having thoroughly felt, through inner temptations, the terrible anger of God.[179] But psychologically the polarities, along with the mechanism of sharp release from deprivation and the argument that fulfillment is enhanced, that grace is made all the more remarkable, by the prolongation

of deprivation, have a sexual quality.[180] Calvin himself seems well aware
of (and doesn't regret for a moment) a more general but probably related
quality of perverseness in many of his statements. With some seeming
defensiveness, and provocatively, he asserts that

> the Lord daily proves, in his own people, that the punishments
> he lays upon them, although they occasion shame and disgrace,
> are so far from opposing their happiness, that they rather pro-
> mote it. Unless they were purified in this manner, it were to be
> feared lest they should become more and more hardened in their
> vices. . . . [When] we, after having been reproved for our sins,
> repent, this result not only absorbs the curse which was felt at
> the beginning, but also proves that the Lord blesses us more by
> punishing us than he would have done by sparing us.[181]

It should be recalled that Lutheran theology contained many a paradox,
and it should be noted that the world of letters in the sixteenth century
was highly conscious of the phenomenon of contrariety in love: its contradictory aspects were literary commonplaces.[182] Paradox and perversity
would have reached ears attuned to associating both with human love and
able to accept as plausible a common psychology of human love and love
of God.

Calvin also used the metaphor of the raising of the dead to describe
the impact of God's grace upon man, and here, as so often, he used Paul's
words. But like his use of paradox, his version is a little more extreme
than the norm. For Calvin seems to mean something besides the positive
use of the condemnation of the law. He also seems to want to experience
pain tantamount to death rather than merely accept the fact, beyond our
understanding, that it may sometimes be necessary. And the peculiarity
of many of Calvin's paradoxes is that they are not such in analytical retrospect; rather, the contradiction itself is experienced and is as strong as
the two sets of feelings that simultaneously form it. Thus, discussing not
qualified feelings or mixed feelings, but insisting on the simultaneity of
two pervasive and mutually exclusive feelings, he can maintain that

> [The Lord] would have us ever to bear in mind the miserable
> condition of our nature; and this can produce nothing but dread,
> weariness, anxiety, and despair; and it is indeed expedient that
> we should thus be thoroughly laid prostrate and broken down,
> that we may at length groan to him; but this dread, derived from
> the knowledge of ourselves, keeps not our minds while relying
> on his goodness from continuing calm; this weariness hinders
> us not from enjoying full consolation in him; this anxiety, this

despair does not prevent us from obtaining in him real joy and hope.[183]

Calvin's writing is at work here. The second procession of longer and lyrical clauses perfectly balances the first somber and concentrated procession; it also belies the absolute nature of the feelings in the first by claiming a simultaneous absoluteness. The reading of the idea is wrenching. Or, succinctly and now peremptorily, Calvin will state that, in order that "we may indeed be in a suitable state to hear the call of God, we must be altogether dead in ourselves. The character of the divine calling is that they who are dead are raised by the Lord."[184]

To live means to be battered even by grace; death is the way toward life. Calvin believed in the willful suppression of feeling because "the fact that men live and breathe and are endowed with sense, understanding, and will tends to their destruction."[185] Alienation from God is succinctly defined as death;[186] the suppression of feeling thus mitigates against a living death.

One always senses both the effect of Calvin's thinking upon his feelings and an unusual quality in these feelings themselves, the two in interplay. One has to believe that some of the suffering that he encountered had been relished: he does not merely illustrate and urge a pious attitude from which one could draw strength in trial. Just this additional note could have more effectively elicited that strength than straightforward exhortations to bear the cross. It seems an example *par excellence* of rhetorical communication—however, this functional equivalent of hyperbole relied on the force of manifest conviction. You would have thought you were listening either to a good orator or to a saint.

It is characteristic that Calvin wrote most extensively and specifically of human feelings of sorrow, pain, and despair, and of the God-given emotions exercised in piety and worship, in others rather than himself. The prominent writerliness of his scriptural commentaries may have provided the comfort of additional distancing mechanisms. Such phrases as "in short," "as I have said," and "in summary" emphasize his role as commentator, while the explicit and untypically frequent "I" of these writings is that of an editor and philologist. It is within the framework of this presence that Calvin can also make clear his empathy with the trials of the Lord's people as he ferrets out unvoiced sorrows, delineates unconscious psychological dimensions, and articulates the resistance and incapacity that all must sometimes feel before the positive prescripts of their religion.[187]

Such a twofold presence is most marked in the *Commentary on Psalms*. Here, Calvin's personal and human presence seems to amount to identification with the principal subject of the commentary, David. The closeness Calvin feels to him is evidenced in his delineation of David's office, the course of his life, and the particular dilemmas and difficulties he faced in that life. David is of course a model of faith for all believers and one whose faith is all the more credible for the discouragement and pain to which he, too, gave voice. As much as he delighted in the law he knew himself to be mortal and acknowledged, specifically, his personal sins. But for Calvin, David was also the servant of God chosen suddenly, sustaining daily the most formidable tests and sometimes defeats, and persevering despite being "forsaken by almost all men."[188]

David is also the Old Testament prefiguring of Christ and may have been an unconscious way for Calvin to express a sense of pride and martyrdom. More important and consistently, David, as the Old Testament type of Christ, may have provided Calvin with a way to see, hear, and believe in Christ's full humanity. As Calvin points out, "other parts of Scripture [in contrast] celebrate the meekness, the mercy, and the gentleness of our Lord."[189] Thus it probably was very helpful in thwarting his reserve about Christ Incarnate to witness David as "rigorous, austere, and full of terror" in defense of the Lord's purpose, and to be able to say that this was "not at all inconsistent with the kindness with which Christ tenderly and sweetly cherishes his own people."[190] God's inscrutable wrath was always more acceptable to Calvin than Christ's humanness: David's entirely scrutable and all too human, and probably all too familiar, wrath, like his consciousness of sin and his inability not to weep and protest his suffering in situations Calvin saw as very much analogous to his own, seem, in the commentary, to make the union of the two natures of Christ more convincing to him.

Along with the emotions appropriate to the religious life, all other emotions tended to claim their power; that these included preeminently the emotions of carnality made Calvin continuously suspicious of all feeling and guarded against it. At the farthest remove from the determining source of feeling he does not lose sight of that source; he enjoyed dwelling far from it; there, he seems to be interestedly considering the ways in which one might be able to give voice to one's humanness even to the glory of God.

JOY, HARSHNESS, AND CONDESCENSION

Calvin did accept, endorse, and himself enjoy a delimited cheerfulness in everyday life in Christian society, a cheerfulness in the service of the Lord, a mutually supportive joy in executing and wondering at God's commandment to love one's neighbor, and a shared and thus amplifying expression of admiring worship. But the enjoyment of the Lord's goodness to us, as Calvin understood us to be, did not make for our spontaneous enjoyment of each other, and his fearful and suspicious conception of sin made him react to impulses toward enjoying each other, or anything else that was not of and for God, as dangers greater than any cost of suppressing them. This attitude was sometimes expressed with sarcasm and condescension: for example, before the Reformers brought back the Word of God, the Schoolmen delivered sermons composed of bedazzling "misty questions" and "smooth stories, or not unamusing speculations, by which the people might be excited to cheerfulness."[191]

The Genevan opposition resented both the imposition of Calvin's will and its content—it was thought and felt to be repressive, censorious, and hostile. An anonymous letter to the *Seigneurie* in 1547 concluded:

> Do not be ruled by the voice or the will of one man. For you see that men have many and divers opinions in them. Each individual would wish to be ruled as he liked. A drunkard would wish to go around with drunkards, idlers likewise. Wise men would want everyone to be like themselves. But this is not possible and often the opinions of one single man will cause much evil.... If there is a personage who is saturnine by nature, he desires, if he has power, that everyone be saturnine like himself and he will hate everything contrary to his nature. And if he has this preeminence and authority, he wants what is natural to him to be put into effect.... On the contrary one who is joyful will ask for pleasure and fun.... Therefore it seems to me that a *seigneurie* should establish a state in which there is no discord of making a people subject to something against their nature. There is no king or government of a republic that allows a man to do what he does not wish to be done to himself.... But suppose I am a man who wants to eat his meals as he pleases, what affair is that of others? Or if I want to dance, or have a good time, what is that to do with the law? Nothing.[192]

Homo ludens, nothing but that, was an image to the pastor of Geneva of man's self-incurred plight. That which was not for God was against God; if you're not part of the solution, you're part of the problem. His harshness had the form of dour and rigid severity, provoking reactions that made it worse because they proved to him his assessment of human nature.

LOVE AND FRIENDSHIP

There are passages in the *Institutes* that confront the gentleness and sweetness and beauty of God's and Christ's love for man, though they are most typically cut off by quotations from the church fathers or deflected into didacticism. The faithful feel "utterly ravished" by God's "abundant sweetness"; therefore, "it is no wonder if a perverse and wicked heart never experiences that emotion by which, borne up to heaven itself, we are admitted to the most hidden treasure of God and to the most hallowed precincts of his Kingdom, which should not be defiled by the entrance of an impure heart."[193] Despite the deflections, Calvin is manifestly describing something he has felt wholeheartedly. Similarly, one cannot doubt the unreservedness of his love of God; Parker aptly speaks of Calvin's "burning sincerity."[194] In his own accent, Calvin firmly believed that "the word of God is not received by faith if it flits about in the top of the brain" but is, rather, received "when it takes root in the depth of the heart," thus becoming "an invincible defense to withstand and drive off all the strategems of temptation."[195] The love that Calvin felt and expressed for his fellow believers, however, is less clear cut, for it involved emotional interchange.

Wielding the formulas of rhetoric, Calvin has no trouble venting anger and indignation in the *Institutes* or any other writings. He talks of the "utterly foul imposture," not just impiety, of the papists on confirmation (a matter of relatively minor significance), for

> they determine that this sacred anointing ought to be held in higher veneration than baptism, because it is exclusively administered by the hands of the prelates, while baptism is commonly dispensed by all priests. What can you say here but that they are plainly mad who are so fond of their own inventions that by comparison they carelessly despise God's most holy institution? O sacrilegious mouth, do you dare oppose to Christ's sacrament a grease befouled only with the stench of your own breath, and under the spell of mumbled words, and to compare it with water sanctified by God's Word?[196]

It is typical of him to assert, in regard to the Catholic church, "that this, this very doctrine itself whereby they claim to be the church, is a deadly butchery of souls, a fire-brand, a ruin, and a destruction of the church."[197] But it should be observed that in these expressions of anger, and especially of sarcasm (and ridicule, too), Calvin feels superior, and his principal technique is further to belittle, rather than merely refute, his opponent. It is emotional interchange with equals that is problematic for him, insofar as it involves a positive, receptive, nonfearing evaluation of otherness, and this is paradigmatically the case in love. Neighbors and brothers are equals.

Jung noted that "the Christian principle of love is extroverted and absolutely demands the outer object."[198] Luther had much to teach Calvin here, and it is a measure of his influence that he did teach him the social dimension of a christologically centered theology. Calvin was proud of his teachability. But he measured it in terms of the extent to which it ran counter to his natural inclinations, and these inclinations are evident in the doctrine of love that he learned from Luther. Luther's true Christian "lives and labors on earth not for himself but for his neighbor, therefore the whole spirit of his life impels him to do even that which he need not do, but which is profitable and necessary for his neighbor."[199] He also brings this love with him into the civic sphere, where he hopes it can find further reinforcement. In contrast, Calvin situates the love of mankind, indeed all feelings of humanity, only within the civic sphere: it is enjoined in and for that sphere; it is unnatural even in regenerate man. It is also, in one real sense, extraneous:

> Yet civil government has as its appointed end, so long as we live among men, to cherish and protect the outward worship of God, to defend sound doctrine of piety and the position of the church, to adjust our life to the society of men, to form our social behavior to civil righteousness, to reconcile us with one another, and to promote general peace and tranquillity. All of these I admit to be superfluous, if God's kingdom, such as it is now among us, wipes out the present life. But if it is God's will that we go as pilgrims upon the earth while we aspire to the true fatherland, and if the pilgrimage requires such helps, those who take these from man deprive him of his very humanity.[200]

Society could not exist without love. Of 1 Corinthians 13:5 ("Love seeketh not its own"), Calvin writes, "It can be inferred from this that love is not innate in us, for we all have a natural tendency to love and care for ourselves. . . . Love is the only cure for such a perverted tendency."[201]

Love for Luther is the content of the Christian servitude that is freedom. God so loved man that he gave his only begotten son; Christian love can be *imitatio*. To Calvin, love is the second table of the law; it supports the "true worship of God," the first table, by honoring God through the honoring of his image in man. It is very difficult to love one's enemies, but we are commanded to do so. And this we do, as men and women, not in compassion for their weakness and suffering, but "it is that we remember not to consider men's evil intentions but to look upon the image of God in them, which cancels and effaces their transgressions, and with its beauty and its dignity allures us to love and embrace them."[202] Love is part of Calvin's theology of glory.

Sometimes Calvin can sound Lutheran: "Our freedom is not given against our feeble neighbors, for love makes us their servants in all things." But it is primarily negative: "rather [this freedom] is given that, having peace with God in our hearts, we may also live at peace with men."[203] Said with extremism, but, as an abstraction in metaphor, accurately for Calvin, "doubtless it is the fear of God alone, which unites us together in the bonds of our common humanity, which keeps us within the bounds of moderation, and represses cruelty; otherwise we should devour each other like wild beasts."[204]

Love is always subordinate to faith; "love itself [ought] to abide under purity of faith."[205] If both lay claims, we must not give in to pity.[206] This was a general policy in his governance in Geneva, and was sometimes expressed in his writings with that frequent note of superiority and self-righteousness that Calvin the servant of God thought nothing of sounding: "when by our devotedness to the cause of religion we cannot avoid exciting the displeasure of our brethren against us, it is our duty simply to follow God, and not to confer with flesh and blood."[207] Yet Calvin considered such a conflict of priorities exceptional. Love is perhaps most characteristically defined by this introvert and intellectual as "mutual edification." Paul stresses "this one point: that we should edify one another in the Lord with mutual love."[208] Calvin accepted the point thoroughly and turned it by analysis into his own: "*justice* is the name given to the rectitude and humanity which we cultivate with our brethren, when we endeavor to do good to all and when we abstain from all wrong, fraud, and violence. But *judgment* is to stretch forth the hand to the miserable and the oppressed, to vindicate righteous causes, and to guard the weak from being unjustly injured. These are the lawful exercises in which the Lord commands his people to be employed."[209]

There is still a personal reserve about love here, and it is supported by Calvin's general (and theologically grounded) suspicion about all human relations. "If," he wrote, "not content with having to do with God only, we turn our eyes to men, it is almost impossible to prevent pride from insinuating itself into the room of faith."[210] Love, therefore, had to be both enjoined and controlled. Luther taught Calvin the Christian dimension of love, and Geneva, and probably Bucer, gave it practicable and manageable form. It was formalized and institutionalized. It was a duty, and the models for its performance were the four offices of the church. Like the calling, and in fact part of the calling, it was part of a role—the impersonal opposite of Luther's emotional spontaneity. Playing a role predetermined the quality of relationships: responses in the other were controlled, and responses in the self rendered easy.

The serenity and warmth that characterize Calvin's letters to his close friends, with some of whom he corresponded over a span of decades, contrast strongly with the tone of his published writings or the record of his public office. Also distinct is the fact that the friends are individualized—a point only surprising of one whose inclination was to stereotype. That inclination would seem to follow from his abstractive modes of thought and of perception and from his sense of otherness as preeminently hostile. For Calvin, the citizens of Geneva, outside of church worship where they formed a congregation, were, in small or large groups, pretty much an undifferentiated mass that had to be controlled. For someone to be a friend, that person had first to be removed from that otherness by individualization. It seems not to have been recognition of personal similarities that enabled Calvin to do this, but the presentation of strong grounds for trust. The trust was not extended beyond these friendships: the most striking note in Calvin's close relationships is their enclaved nature.

In his small but stable number of intimate friendships, Calvin did not have to be on the defensive. One of the themes in letters to his friends is the danger of the world outside their small circle, and these letters also convey a sense of enjoyment of the shared separation; another theme is the need for mutual support and strategic planning for surviving in the world. Calvin certainly argued with friends when they disagreed or when there were miscommunications. His flaring temper seems to express fear that a friend was really part of the outside (as distinct from being mistaken on a particular point); when reassured of trustworthiness by basic intellectual agreement, the quarrel was over. In practical terms, the issue, always made into a test, was loyalty. Calvin was both stronger and more fragile when he let down his guard. He may have served his friends better than he let them serve him.

Geneva was, of course, an enclave. Persecuted Calvinists outside Geneva formed small cells that were also enclaves, with what was almost a private language (the Psalms set to music) expressing their sense of separateness from an actively hostile environment. It should be remembered that all of Calvin's writings would have explicated their historical experience.

TENSION AND DEFENSIVENESS

Corresponding to the tension in the *Institutes*, Calvin the person was extremely tense, and the tenseness was a perceptible presence in his formal interactions in everyday life. In his farewell to the Petit Conseil, he regretted and asked pardon for his impatience and bad temper, that irritability that so frequently sent off sparks or exploded.[211] It seems not unusual for an intent intellectual to feel driven and, if interrupted or questioned about his course, annoyed and upset, and it seems not unnatural for someone who is certain he is doing God's work to be impatient with demands for explanations of instances of that work. Both considerations apply to Calvin, yet his tenseness seems most of all an internal stance of defensiveness. Rather than criticism or vilification of others, it was self-defense that most usually characterized his outbursts of temper in personal interactions. And his most usual defense of decisions or actions was that they were not his, but God's. Calvin should be trusted to have studied matters carefully: "What is more, I say only what is well known, what none can contradict without blatantly denying the Word of God."[212]

In introspective moods, Calvin could be aware that his personality caused trouble: as he lost patience with the people of Geneva, he realized that he himself gave them much to bear.[213] His statements about his inclination to retreat from public life are a negative form of awareness of interpersonal unease. He almost stated it positively, but was, somewhat paradoxically, too precise, and thus limited the implications of the problem. Speaking to his congregation of marriage after the death of Idelette, he noted that "it would rather be a fault in me, if I could serve God better in marriage, [to remain] as I am. . . . But I know my infirmity, that perhaps a woman might not be happy with me."[214] It was probably correct intuition to see the sexual relationship as a peculiar problem. But it seems to have been sexuality that made all otherness charged for him; conversely, that was the most extreme instance of the more general problem inherent in his psychological type. Thus Calvin could have entirely good relations with women physically removed from Geneva, corresponding at length and with involvement over years; in Geneva, aside from his close friends (male) and his congregation *as* congregation, otherness was experienced as discomforting and hostile, and he had to defend himself both to and from it. Perseverance helped him greatly in his public life — a healthy way to override hesitation and fear. He preferred to write with bravura or nonchalance about outbursts of hostility against decisions which he initiated or supported. Of a riot during the Perrin affairs, he wrote to Viret:

> Everything looks terrible. I throw myself into the thickest of the crowds, to the amazement of everyone. The whole mob makes a rush towards me; they seize me and drag me hither and thither. . . . I called God and men to witness that I had come to present my body to their swords. I bade them, if they wanted to shed blood, to start with me. Even the worthless, but especially the more respectable, at once cooled down. I was at length dragged through the midst of them to the Council. There new fights started, and I threw myself between them. . . . I succeeded in getting everyone to sit down quietly, and then delivered a long and vehement speech, which they say moved all of them.[215]

But looking back in later years, Calvin gives us an internal perspective: "I have lived here amid continual strifes. I have been saluted in derision of an evening before my door with forty or fifty arquebus shots. Just imagine how that frightened a poor scholar, timid as I am, and as I confess I have always been."[216] I so strongly feel an undercurrent of tension in virtually all that Calvin said or did that I take moderation to be for him an aesthetic rather than an expression of temperament. Its verbal form is closer to the latter: he strongly needed to discipline himself, and he felt a need as well as a duty to control others.

Physical riots could have been written off as expressions of the vola-

tility and savagery in human nature had they not fit so neatly into a
continuous situation in which Calvin lived in Geneva: an awareness of
being widely disliked and of being needed, and also tolerated, for his
intellectual and political abilities. He was needed to defend the faith and
to keep order in Geneva, and in this respect, he, Jean Calvin, lived there
at the sufferance of the citizens. His preference for the *vita contemplativa*
does not sufficiently account for the anguish he recorded at the prospect
of returning from Strasbourg, where his life had had the quality of release.
The abyss of which he now spoke was a specific and known situation,
different from merely the idea of public life. As hell was rejection by God,
the abyss he now was facing was rejection by the Genevans. Part of the
prolonged and agonizing decision whether to return was the question
whether he could live with that rejection; part of it was whether he could
do anything about it. He seems to have had impulses to try, though with
doubts as to whether he really could change or behave differently (the two
not clearly distinguished by him). Perhaps decisively compounding the
doubts was his defensive position that it was totally irrational to care about
the feelings of the Genevans toward him as a person.

Evidence that their feelings did matter precedes the actual decision
to return, as part of the preface to recall. It was not Calvin but Viret who
was first asked to respond to Sadoleto's challenge to the heresy of Protestantism in Geneva. When Viret declined, Calvin was asked, and he
accepted.[217] The task was a natural one for him, and his response one
of the most important concise statements of Reformation faith—it may
have been this work that won Luther's commendation of Calvin.[218] Unmistakably in the style of the theologian and writer of the *Institutes*, it
is also a highly individual document written with conviction, confidence,
and power. Finally, it contains many personal emphases that would be
gratuitous (even in the perspective of rhetoric) had they not been responses
to someone or something other than Sadoleto's challenge. At his strongest,
Calvin was also suggesting to his audience in Geneva that he would be
able to amend his faults, and was perhaps experimenting for himself with
that possibility.

Thus Calvin asserts his paternal affection for the church in Geneva,
proclaims his sincerity, and gives assurance that sincerity is more important
to him than all his erudition and industry. He then indirectly addresses
the central personal issue between him and the Genevans. He considers
his behavior, in this response, to be important, and he informs Sadoleto
that it will consist in continual moderation of harshness so that it will be
clear to all "that I have not only much the advantage of you in the goodness
and justice of the cause, in conscious rectitude, heartfelt sincerity, and
candor of speech, but have also been considerably more successful in
maintaining gentleness and moderation."[219] Interestingly, one of Calvin's

rare autobiographical statements occurs toward the end of the treatise. Not self-consciously a message to the Genevans, and totally unapologetic, it seems to be a sincere offering of some of his experience, despite personal diffidence, because it would be useful reinforcement for his answer to Sadoleto's charges of superficiality and impulsiveness in the Reformers' rejection of the Catholic church. It does strengthen that answer, and its earnestness also strengthens his earlier assertion of his intention to temper himself.

The past problems in Geneva were more vivid and his optimism lessened as recall seemed really to be forthcoming. He remembered that his awareness of the opposition to his governance had had the effect of making him "perish daily a thousand times over."[220] Recalling "the wretchedness of [his] life there" and contrasting it to his release from that life, he implored of Farel, "Who will not excuse me if I am unwilling to plunge again into the gulf and whirlpool which I knew to be so dangerous and destructive?"[221] His own wish would be rather to be beyond the seas than there. He broke down in tears during the negotiations.[222] He finally would not make the decision that was as death, but did make it by letting his friends voice it: "But in that cause I am suspicious of myself and will not admit myself to counsel, and I have decided to consult those who are of good judgment and upright spirit."[223] Farel reinforced the decision with insistent, vehement, violent reminders that it was God's will. But then Viret, for strategic reasons and because he knew Calvin well, tried further to convince him that the hostilities he dreaded might not be resumed if he returned *now*, at the right moment, *in ipso articulo temporis*.[224] Farel, in impatient exasperation at the loss of that possibility and the triumph of the obstacle impeding their cause, shouted threats: Calvin could indeed now count on the love inherent in the prayers of the Genevans for his return, but it happened to be now or never; those prayers would cease if he made the Genevans doubt his commitment by lingering.[225] There were always two levels of issues in the Geneva question—one, theological, strategic, and licit; the other, delicate and not licit.

The Geneva to which Calvin returned was the same he had left. At the end of his life, in his farewell to his fellow ministers, he summarized his life there, proclaiming it to have been one of faith and commitment to the good of the church despite the failure of his efforts, despite the ferocity of the continual strife amid which he lived, and despite his infirmities which he knew to be trying. His summation ends with a charge curiously skewed, from a theological and psychological viewpoint, and sounding like a legal accusation. "The Church of Bern has betrayed this Church, and they have always feared me more than they loved me. I want them to know that I died in the opinion that they feared rather than loved me."[226] Calvin also lived with this opinion. Representing an acute form of creatureliness to him, it is part of both his personal and public life.

THE WEIGHTING OF DUALISM
IN CALVIN'S THEOLOGY

Had Calvin's personal preference been a Zwinglian-like spiritualism, it is difficult to see how he could have been the convincing and successful proponent of Protestantism that he was. His Protestantism consisted not merely in intellectual consent, but in approval. It represented a commitment based upon feeling as well as upon will and agreement, though the vector of feeling was, in contrast to spontaneous overflow, compounded of attraction, want, and admiration from somewhat afar. However, Calvin accepted the Protestant faith in the most difficult aspect it entailed for him—the acceptance of his full humanity, not only through searching introspection but in sharing his love of the God of faith with the community of faith in open expression, and by worshipping this God as the theologian of his glory deemed it proper, as a member of the community in an essentially undifferentiated way. That this did not come easily made the wish not less, but more sincere. That constancy matched sincerity in his hierarchy of personal values was a natural concomitant of its purpose: to enable him to proceed as he wished to proceed, able to thwart impulses to the contrary.

Thus we can find, believe, and be further taught by sections of the *Institutes* on those issues that would have been the most greatly charged for Calvin: he was not merely paraphrasing, and his teaching is sometimes at its best in these instances because he is his own student as well. This seems eminently the case in a major section on the dual natures of Christ, proceeding from the concept of the *communicatio idiomatum*. Calvin is far more sympathetic to the concept than later Calvinists: while he dissociates himself from the use made of it in the eucharistic doctrine of Lutheranism, he does not disavow it even in discussion of the Eucharist— the term was "long ago invented to some purpose by the holy fathers."[227] His affirmation of the dual natures constituting the one Christ is followed by the most deliberative confrontation—and the contrast between the deliberative mode and the more usual didactic one is again significant— with the problem of dualism and its Christian solution. Of John 1:14, "the Word was made flesh," he writes:

> If anything like this very great mystery can be found in human affairs, the most apposite parallel seems to be that of man, whom we see to consist of two substances. Yet neither is so mingled with the other as not to retain its own distinctive nature. For the soul is not the body, and the body is not the soul. Therefore,

some things are said exclusively of the soul that can in no wise apply to the body; and of the body, again, that in no way fit the soul; of the whole man, that cannot refer—except inappropriately—to either soul or body separately. Finally, the characteristics of the mind are [sometimes] transferred to the body and those of the body to the soul. Yet he who consists of these parts is one man, not many. Such expressions signify both that there is one person in man composed of two elements joined together, and that there are two diverse underlying natures that make up this person. Thus, also, the Scriptures speak of Christ: they sometimes attribute to him what must be referred solely to his humanity, sometimes what belongs uniquely to his divinity; and sometimes what embraces both natures but fits neither alone. And they so earnestly express this union of the two natures that is in Christ as sometimes to interchange them. This figure of speech [*tropus*] is called by the ancient writers "the communicating of properties."[228]

He is quietly and obliquely acquiescing in the theology of the *communicatio* here. He also uses one of his key words, "mingled," which, in the previous paragraph, he had typically coupled with the adverb "confusedly"—it generally means that without stipulation. That he confronts that which horrifies him in the context of an argument opposing the horror seems counterphobic. Another key word, "earnestly" (*religione*) is further indication of deep respect. I think it very significant that the perspective that enables him to acquiesce in the concept is that which construes it as purposeful speech; he is also demonstrating the effect this speech is having upon him. However, I think it can also be said that the effect doesn't hold; it has always to be renewed because of an inner voice to the contrary of commitment.

A similarly deliberative statement on the humanity of Christ appears in the discussion of the descent into hell. Calvin's formal, anti-Castellian position on this subject is well known. The discussion of the idea in the *Institutes*, however, is restrained, and it seems to serve more as the occasion for a statement on Christ's full humanity even in regard to the nature of his feelings—a position that elsewhere is denied. As we have seen, Christ's emotions were different from ours in their steadiness—the opposite of an extremely painful aspect of human feeling, to Calvin. But in his suffering on the Cross (Calvin's understanding of the descent), Christ

had, therefore, to conquer that fear which by nature continually torments and oppresses all mortals. This he could do only by fighting it. Now it will soon be more apparent that his was no common sorrow or one engendered by a light cause. Therefore, by his wrestling hand to hand with the devil's power, with the dread of death, with the pains of hell, he was victorious and triumphed over them, that in death we may not now fear those things which our Prince has swallowed up. . . . [Calvin briefly polemicizes against an interpretation denying the reality of the feelings, then resumes his analysis.] And surely, unless his soul shared in the punishment, he would have been the Redeemer of bodies alone. . . . His goodness—never sufficiently praised— shines in this: he did not shrink from taking our weaknesses upon himself. Hence it in nowise detracts from his heavenly glory. . . . this Mediator has experienced our weaknesses the better to succor us in our miseries."[229]

This is a familiarly awesome Calvin, maintaining distinctions without obliterating their context. The statement is also in his characteristic language of reserve and empowered by his characteristic logic. However, the theology is unexceptionably and genuinely Lutheran. But not only the counterstatements on the distinctness of Christ's feelings from ours, but the weighting of ideas throughout the *Institutes* related to that distinctness, suggest very strongly that Calvin needed to hear himself say this. The statement is of additional interest for its evidence of awareness of the counter-phobic mechanism. Like the polemic, the phrase "nowise detracts" sounds like negation as Freud defined it. Another apparent instance of negation in regard to the same subject occurs in the commentary on John: "For none will ever come to Christ-God who neglects the man. Wherefore, if you want to have anything in common with Christ you must especially take care not to despise the flesh."[230]

Thus we are dealing with a Lutheran Christian, though one different from Luther. Calvin always seems to have meant his positive as well as negative statements about human existence in this world, and they are consistent: the complexity and basic tension in life consists not in dualistic conflict, but in living with it. And from this viewpoint, it is extremely important to note that Calvin's argument with himself seems above all to have been a one-way argument, and in a sense always the same argument. Here, his theology, distinct from Lutheranism, also stands close to, but separate from, the strong current of ambivalence in Italian Renaissance thought.

I suggest that there are two sets of closely and necessarily related arguments in Calvin, one addressed to all Christian believers and one to the particular believer Jean Calvin. The first does conform to the pattern of ambivalence, and, as evidence of that pattern, Nicole Malet's inter-pretation of the polarized groups of words that emerge from an analysis of Calvin's vocabulary is important.[231] Similarly subsumable within that psychological concept, Calvin's exhortations to his readers and listeners are absolutely symmetrical in content and intensity: the believer's primary allegiance and basic and ultimate concern is for God, through Christ; through Christ and for God, however, each must labor for his fellow Christians and form a fitting community of worship with them. As often as not, Calvin will say "we" rather than "you" or "believers." But there is another mode of address than the communal: there is a purely personal mode. Here, that symmetry does not pertain. And it is not that a counterpart of the twofold exhortation to believers is merely less balanced and more heavily weighted to what would be called his weaker side, the temptation to withdraw from the *vita activa*. It is rather that there is no counterpart at all to the exhortations not to forget the primacy of God and Christ and the state of the human soul, for which they are the remedy. Calvin simply seems never to have had to pull himself back from the world; all of his writings, formal and informal, indicate that his internal argument was unchanging.

Calvin accepted the Lutheran and Renaissance rehabilitation of the realm of the physical, but accepted it as more inescapable than desirable. He believed with his heart as well as his mind in the full communal Christian life that was linked to that realm and tried to live it, but this seems to have come so uneasily that one feels a continuous undercurrent of strain in his writings. More specifically, he very often seems tired. He does not find in the active life the quietness he so clearly likes. One never senses in him enjoyment of the buzz and hum of the world; perhaps this is why, in contrast to Luther, there is no real humor (other than the sardonic) in even his personal writings. There also seems to be no spontaneous response to the world of nature that is emphatically the world of matter. He can include argument from design, but the examples that demonstrate it are certainly not from the French countryside or the Swiss Alps. A response like Luther's to an animal even comelier than the sow is, for Calvin, impossible to imagine.

The cluster of words for peace that balances the cluster for immoderation in Calvin's writings contains more that are closer to stillness than to harmony. An interesting aesthetic argument within the society of worship, and part of the history of music in Calvinist churches, seems to reveal Calvin the person within his formal role. Louis Bourgeois, whose hymns have been considered an important sustaining force for the Huguenots in persecution, had to have a harmonized psalter printed outside Geneva. Calvin opposed unison to harmony in church singing with the opinion that harmonized singing was distracting: "All that is needed in the praise of God is a pure and simple modulation of the voice."[232]

Calvin the person as well as the theologian very much liked the mutual reciprocity that he considered to provide stability in Christian society.

However, his personal admiration seems to be for the idea within that reciprocity — for "this most beautiful order and as it were symmetry" which preserves the safety of the church.[233] Calvin's concern to insure the peace of mind necessary for prayer, in his writings about marriage, convey the feeling that prayer is also a lull, a refreshment of silence, enabling him to touch base with his real strength before returning to the ferment of the church of God in sixteenth-century Geneva. His calling, like justification, had to be experienced ever anew and also depended upon the practice of his idea of persistence.

I think it is beyond doubt that Calvin was sensible of his dualistic inclination, and I suggest that it pushed him to a doubt beyond and different from the fallings away from faith that were an accepted part of Protestant experience. Luther and Calvin each doubted whether one so sinful as himself could be saved; Calvin seems also to have sometimes doubted whether one so sinful should be saved. He agreed with and gave powerful expression to a primary Reformation concept — that, despite all its dreadfulness and its incomprehensibility, God's allowing of evil to exist (and men to be damned for it) was part of his benevolent purpose toward mankind. To agree with heart as well as mind, however, is not necessarily to agree completely. Parallel to the fear and pain of incomprehension was, I think, a measure of skeptical disagreement about what *was* benevolent. It is against this disbelief that Calvin often seems to be taking a leap of faith.

The rhetoric in which he gave expression to a very strong sense of conflict can be further considered in this light. We have seen that part of the polarized vocabulary and structure of his prose consists in a recurrent idiom of dualism, which seems to explain the polarity and suggest that its expression, in its unconscious relation to his theology, was a therapeutic self-confrontation. However, the exact mode of reality of the struggle of spirit against flesh is indefinite: the reader cannot really know whether it is meant metaphorically or literally, whether it is part of a long tradition of Pauline rhetoric (among other Pauline voices) or an independent description of experience that could avail itself of a familiar phraseology for its own purposes. I suggest that this indefiniteness was purposeful and essential in Calvin's use of rhetoric.

To say "I am dead" means "I am as if dead"; to say "I loathe myself," and to say it without qualification, could mean just that. Had Calvin been constrained to answer the question whether his expressions of self-hatred or his clearly related expressions of conflict between spirit and flesh were meant literally, he would have said that they were not — as he occasionally did in regard to other phraseology in other places.[234] During the actual process of writing in the idiom of dualism, however, I think Calvin suspended — through an intuitive but real choice — the question of mode of reality. In suspending the question, the expression of experience could be literal insofar as it was not specifically metaphoric. In being tentatively literal—and that would mean temporarily larger than life, for it would have been temporarily unchecked by its wider orthodox context—it could be the better seen, scrutinized, analyzed, and grappled with. This seems to be another and major instance of the counterphobic. It was living dangerously, playing with fire, in an entirely purposeful way. But it could only have been done within controlled circumstances, and the conditioning of Calvin's audiences in the first half of the sixteenth century provided such circumstances: a rhetoric of dualism would be read *as* rhetoric; it *would* be read as metaphor. This seems especially likely for his self-vilifications: he applies to himself, or uses in general characterizations of the nature of man, the almost monotonously familiar language of religious polemic, that language being an adaptation of the conventions for mocking or debasing and for the expression of indignation in classical and Italian Renaissance civic rhetoric.

In a somewhat cathartic way, others may have been able to identify with Calvin's voice by virtue of sharing, in varying degrees of intensity, the same psychic experience. Even to accept something as a valid metaphor is to see plausibility in the metaphor.[235] Rosalie Colie's idea of the possible transition in poetry from figures of speech to figures of thought, for which the poet depends upon the familiarity of metaphoric tradition as he extends it in unconventional ways,[236] seems applicable here. Such an analysis applied specifically to Calvin's speech about the disjunction between the physical and the nonphysical could be carried a step further—for, as twentieth-century theorists of language would stress, that speech also physically embodies the conflict with matter that the words explicate. Thus one could see as an epitome of Calvin's mentality his use of the language of dualism in the discipline of rhetoric.

LUTHER, CALVIN, AND THE EUCHARIST: A SUMMATION

The one clear and important doctrinal difference that involved Calvin in polemics with Lutherans was that of the Eucharist. Yet even here, it should be observed, there are very great areas of agreement, and the disparities can again be analyzed as psychologically engendered facts rather than theological tenets. Calvin always considered himself to be in basic agreement with Luther and believed that only heated temperaments and historical circumstances had prevented this agreement from being acknowledged.

If Luther, that distinguished servant of God and faithful doctor of the church, were alive today, he would not be so harsh and unyielding as not willingly to allow this confession: that what the sacraments figure is truly offered to us, and that therefore in the sacred Supper we become participants in the Body and Blood of Christ. For how often did he declare that he was contending for no other cause than to establish that the Lord does not mock us with empty signs, but accomplishes inwardly what He sets before our eyes, and that the effect is therefore conjoined with the signs.[237]

First, and in distinction from the Roman conception, the Eucharist is special but not different in nature, and not separate from, the substance of the Christian life. It is the divine promise, the Word, made efficacious through faith, through the power of "that inward teacher," the Holy Spirit. It is the Spirit

by whose power alone hearts are penetrated and affections moved and our souls are opened for the sacraments to enter in. If the Spirit be lacking the sacraments can accomplish nothing more in our minds than the splendour of the sun shining upon blind eyes, or a voice sounding in dead ears. Therefore I make such a division between Spirit and sacraments that the power to act rests with the former, and the ministry alone is life to the latter—a ministry empty and trifling, apart from the action of the Spirit, but charged with great effect when the Spirit works within and manifests his power.[238]

From this perspective, the Eucharist is no different from the experience of faith throughout the Christian life. The sacrament "assures us that all that Christ did or suffered was done to quicken us, and again, that this quickening is eternal, we being ceaselessly nourished, sustained, and preserved throughout life by it."[239] The concomitant of the sacrament, and one that can exist very much apart from it, is the Word. "Whatever benefit may come to us from the Supper requires the Word: whether we are to be confirmed in faith, or exercised in confession, or aroused to duty, there is need of preaching."[240]

Still, the sacraments are special. In accommodated form, they render the Word convincing and vital. They also serve the function of actually rendering the Word efficacious "in the fulfillment of what it promises." The fulfillment is actual partaking of the body and blood of Christ: the literal rendering of the Substitution. To use one of Calvin's words, the sacrament is preeminently useful.

Both Luther and Calvin proceed from a rejection of transubstantiation. Yet it is not because the body and blood are not there. Rather, it is because the clergy, who are mortal, have no special power to produce the body and blood, and because the claims of reenactment of the sacrifice (by the power of the priest) threaten the historicity and uniqueness of the Passion. Yet there is a real presence, for Luther and Calvin alike. There is a true communion — "a marvelous communion of his body and blood."[241] For "that sacred partaking of his flesh and blood, by which Christ pours his life into us, as if penetrated into our bones and marrow," is testified and sealed in the Supper. Thus communion occurs. Communion, however, is not salvation, but a witness to salvation. It is assuredly "not by presenting a vain and empty sign, but by manifesting there the effectiveness of the Spirit to fulfill what he promises. And truly he offers and shows the reality there signified to all who sit at that spiritual banquet, although it is received with benefit by believers alone, who accept such great generosity with true faith and gratefulness of heart."[242] The real presence of the body and blood is distinct from both a local presence, which would rival and vitiate the uniqueness of the Cross, and from a merely spiritual presence. Accordingly, Calvin takes on as his first opponents the Zwinglians.

> Such is the presence of the body (I say) that the nature of the sacraments requires a presence which we say manifests itself here with a power and effectiveness so great that it not only brings an undoubted assurance of eternal life to our minds, but also assures us of the immortality of our flesh. Indeed it is now quickened by his immortal flesh, and in a sense partakes of his immortality.[243]

The eucharistic communion is a form of *unio*. Calvin writes that, in the sacrament, we have "a witness to our growth into one body with Christ such that whatever is his may be called ours. . . [we are reminded] that we cannot be condemned for our sins, from whose guilt he has absolved us, since he willed to take them upon himself as if they were his own. This is the wonderful exchange which, out of his measureless benevolence, he has made with us."[244] Not magically made sinless, but graciously having righteousness imputed to us as if it were our own: that is the *unio* that evoked Luther's bride and bridegroom image.

Still, Calvin disagreed with Luther: the real presence was not physical; it was a spiritual presence. "The body of Christ is really, to use the usual word, i.e., truly given to us in the Supper. . . a life-giving power from the flesh of Christ is poured into us through the medium of the Spirit, even although it is at a great distance from us and is not mixed with us."[245] Inherent in his position are his conviction of absolute divine transcendence and of the sinfulness of the physical: "Let nothing be withdrawn from Christ's heavenly glory — as happens when he is brought under the corruptible elements of this world, or bound to any earthly creatures."[246] The real presence is both efficacious and spiritual.

Insofar as Calvin's conception of the Eucharist is theologically solid, it is the logical conclusion of the unique historicity of the Passion. Insofar as it is contradictory, it results from the combination of doctrine—Lutheran doctrine—which draws him in one direction, and his unconscious, which draws him in another. It has been noted that the sacramentalism of Lutheran orthodoxy itself has a distinctive psychological dimension. Jung, writing of the dispute between Luther and Zwingli, maintains that for Luther "the religious meaning of the immediate objective experience was so great that his imagination was spellbound by the concreteness of the material presence of the sacred body. It was surely not just the power of tradition that made Luther cling to this dogma. It was acknowledgment, demanded by Luther's psychology, of the fact of feeling, grounded upon the immediate sense-experience."[247] But, whatever its psychological foundation, Lutheran orthodoxy won out. Calvin learned from Luther despite resistance. The Lutheran victory was expressed in Calvin's designation of Christ's presence in the Eucharist as a real presence, but a presence characterized as a mystery totally beyond human comprehension and even fathoming. This is also an assertion of incongruity.

> Even though it seems unbelievable that Christ's flesh, separated from us by such great distance, penetrates to us, so that it becomes our food, let us remember how far the secret power of the Holy Spirit towers above all our senses, and how foolish it is to wish to measure his immeasurableness by our measure. What, then, our mind does not comprehend, let faith conceive: that the Spirit truly unites things separated in faith.[248]

Or concisely, "I rather experience than understand it."[249] Calvin's mind was subdued into orthodoxy—and perhaps gained satisfaction in letting its capitulation be known. The maximum sign of the influence is in Calvin's acceptance of a social element in the Eucharist: as we are united with Christ so, too, the whole church, partaking of the sacrament, is one body.

> We shall benefit very much from the sacrament if this thought is impressed and engraved upon our minds: that none of the brethren can be injured, despised, rejected, abused, or in any way -offended by us, without at the same time injuring, despising, and abusing Christ by the wrongs we do; that we cannot disagree with the brethren without at the same time disagreeing with Christ; that we cannot love Christ without loving him in the brethren. . . . Accordingly, Augustine with good reason frequently calls this sacrament "the bond of love."[250]

What Calvin specifically and clearly rejected in Luther's doctrine was the concept of the ubiquity of Christ, from which Luther derived the real presence in a physical sense. Yet Calvin's arguments indicate that his reasoning in the rejection of the concept may have been eminently Lutheran. His perception of the Lutheran concept is crucial. To Calvin, Luther was impugning the true humanity of Christ by attributing ubiquity to even his ascended body. "Let nothing inappropriate to human nature be ascribed to his body, as happens when it is said either to be infinite or to be put in a number of places at once."[251] He asks, "where is the very nature of a body, which exists in its own dimensions, and where its unity?"[252] Again, "firm and clear testimonies of Scripture [teach that] Christ's body was circumscribed by the measure of a human body."[253] Thus the ascension renders a physical presence on earth impossible. There is a parallel to the extra-Calvinisticum in that Calvin wants here to maintain the essential distinction of the two natures.[254] But it is essential to note that he perceived the Lutherans as attributing a divine quality, ubiquity, to something in Christ which rendered him human, equivalent to, and thereby efficacious for, man — his body. Calvin may be arguing with Luther in Luther's spirit here. He certainly rejects not the "what" but the "how" in Luther's eucharistic doctrine: how does the true communion take place? Given its actuality, what is the physical basis for it? His answer is not that there is no physical basis for it, but that it is a mystery beyond and contrary to all human understanding, and human hypotheses, such as the ubiquity hypothesis, can only be wrong.

On one other and peripheral eucharistic matter Calvin and Luther disagree: the communion of the unworthy. Calvin maintained that the unworthy did not eat the body and blood of Christ, and (the position that caused difficulties in Geneva) that it was positively harmful for them to partake of the sacrament. They dishonored God; they profaned and corrupted the elements, as they did everything they touched; they brought condemnation upon themselves.[255] But that the elements were distinct from the body and blood he maintained throughout: faith enabled the communicant to perceive not what they were but what they showed forth. The issue was that the lack of faith of the unworthy rendered their participation impious and thereby sacrilegious. Herein, on the centrality of faith, Calvin demonstrates his affinities with Luther.

Calvin misunderstood Luther on the Eucharist, and his misunderstanding obscures a real difference. Calvin considered himself to be preserving the true and necessary humanity of Christ. Rather, he missed Luther's orthodox argument that the union of persons in Incarnate Christ was such that each nature participated in the qualities of the other. Had Calvin focused upon this, he probably would have disagreed more broadly in the dispute. Calvin's understanding of the *communicatio idiomatum* required an existence in which the properties of one nature were received by the other, but not to their transformation: "Each [nature] nevertheless retains unimpaired its own distinctive character."[256] The formal possibility of the separate existence of the two distinct natures had always to be maintained.[257]

The need for separation was psychologically rooted in Calvin's aversion to the mingling of heaven and earth, just as his rejection — a rejection with the character of resistance — of physical presence had psychological roots. His vocabulary, always a good sign, opposed "spiritual" to "carnal" eating.[258] But he was decisively influenced by Luther, and what we have in the end is neither Lutheranism nor Calvinism, but, once again, Calvin's Luther — even on the Eucharist. The Lutheran anthropology and the Lutheran doctrine of Christian love and the Calvinist horror of the flesh and the Calvinist *a priori* come together when he tells us to offer, in the Supper,

> our vileness and (so to speak) our unworthiness to him so that his mercy may make us worthy of him; to despair in ourselves so that we may be comforted in him; to abase ourselves so that we may be lifted by him; to accuse ourselves so that we may be justified by him; moreover, to aspire to that unity which he commends to us in this Supper; and, as he makes all of us one in himself, to desire one soul, one heart, one tongue for us all. If we have weighed and considered these things well, these thoughts, though they may stagger us, will never lay us low. How could we, needy and bare of all good, befouled with sins, half-dead, eat the Lord's body worthily? Rather, we shall think that we, as being poor, come to a kindly giver; as sick, to a physician; as sinners, to the Author of righteousness; finally, as dead, to him who gives us life.[259]

FORMALISM IN LIFE, THOUGHT, AND STYLE: A SUMMATION

A character trait will manifest itself as the stamp of an individual's personality and behavior; it will be predictable to others and experienced as a normal part of the self by the individual. Differing from character neuroses in its nondiscomforting nature, it is still, like the neurosis, a compromise between impulses and inhibitions and forces of the ego that try to direct and organize an appropriate satisfaction for them.[260] The formalism that is so striking a continuum in Calvin the person and theologian appears to be his dominant character trait and one that served as the bridge between his least and most successful personal responses to the conditions of his life. It seems reasonably certain, too, that the pronounced formalism in the organization of communal life in Calvinist churches, recognized as a positive and historically important reflection of Calvin's political and legal capabilities, owes something to the phenomenon of overdetermination—the psychological terms "design" and "style" have absolutely literal application in Calvin. He *had* to legislate communal life for himself.

The concept of calling can have two emphases. In one, the individual is a Christian and his life a priesthood in a form and in ways appropriate to his individuality. In the other, the form confers the Christian life upon an individual; it enables him to live as a Christian, executing his Christian duties. Calvin's life was organized into the social roles dictated by his position in Geneva. He was pastor, preacher, administrator of church polity, coordinator of church and municipal government, and advisor to Protestants outside Geneva. These roles enabled him to do things that would otherwise have been forbidding; the roles probably enabled him to do some things for which he regretted not having a natural bent. The roles were probably sometimes welcome and at other times experienced as grim necessity. But they reliably provided him his responses to otherness. Lutheranism is continued, but it is as if frozen. The formalization of the Christian life into roles was a devitalization as well as an abstraction of Lutheranism; the dynamism of compulsion presents the strongest contrast to the Lutheran outflowing of spontaneous expression.

The frozen quality of life in major parts of his personal world is typical of the Calvin known to history. The quality is paralleled by the rigidity in his dogmatic theology—and typically (as well as with theological consistency) he will end his discussions of truths that surpass human understanding with the curt admonition not to be further curious. The expression of his thought is frequently apodictic. The context of the rigidity is a formal logic and literary style. This formalism was not just an effective means of presentation or an aesthetically grounded order: it was part of a pervasive stance of guardedness made of defense and self-discipline. The *Institutes* is as fraught with personal tension as it is with the background of predestination.

It is beyond question that one of the major reasons for the success of Calvinism was the order and systematic nature of the *Institutes*. The movement had a textbook, and it was eminently communicable and teachable. The order and systematization have been in several ways exaggerated. Objectively, the interdependency and interwovenness of doctrine would have defeated anyone seeking a perfect scheme of presentation, and subjectively, psychological concerns (usually manifested in polemics) and political strategy—for example, the need to annul any identification with Anabaptism—repeatedly break the order. Book II, on Christ the Redeemer, cannot be kept out of Book I, on God as Creator. Scripture is needed to reveal creation as God's work, blinded as our eyes are by sin. Sin requires redemption; Scripture is the promise of redemption. The church of the elect exists within the society of man, and this brings in the matter of God's special concern for the elect.

Irrational and illogical personal judgments abound. Calvin's interpretations of Paul on love and James on works are forced and strained. The judgments that the papacy is not a papacy, that the whole Roman church is not a church, are based on the "objective" rhetorical question, "Surely a church is recognized by its own clear merits.... Where in their church is there a ministry such as Christ's institution requires?"[261]

Calvin's style is often responsible for a greater impression of systematization than the content of a passage may warrant—but this is also to say that systematization is a constant value. His didacticism is conveyed in sentence patterns that work to emphasize his logicalness. Sentences begin, unnecessarily, with "for," "therefore," and "thus." *Porro* is a recurrent beginning. While these are fairly frequent usages in Latin, Calvin uses them with more than usual frequency, and the same stylistic tendency is reflected in his French writings—for example, *c'est à dire* is recurrent in the commentaries. Indeed the potential in Latin for more than usual conciseness and impersonality, for emphasis through sentence structure rather than elaboration, may be part of Calvin's manifest enjoyment of the language.

Calvin's didacticism is part of a general impersonality in his presence as writer. When emotions threaten to break through, things do not get out of hand. Indignation and rapture can be expressed in controlled parallels; another technique, especially when an emotion is positive and approaches love, is the indirect and oblique use of quotations to express feelings. Luther paraphrased Scripture; Calvin will fill a page with quotations: "Thus spoke Daniel,..." "He eloquently declares,..." "In such a form Isaiah prays...."[262] A very characteristic pattern in his writing is a sharp deflection toward the end of an eloquent statement of a doctrine or idea that is of obvious personal importance: he will move suddenly into a didactic mode to end the sentence. Feelings are controlled; a perhaps unintentional result is to highlight, as an impressive feat, the clauses preceding the deflection.

If not realized everywhere, order and systematization remain eminently characteristic of Calvin, and they are a reason for the impact of the *Institutes*. So too are the immediate qualities of its logic and style. The complexity of the *Institutes* consists in its rich and subtle theology, and Calvin, thoroughly in command, conveys these qualities positively. His logic combines subtlety and clarity in sustained analyses of such matters as the joined but distinct natures of Christ; the simultaneity and equal necessity, but radical distinction, of faith and works; the paradox that man, subject to God's plan, is still responsible for sin. His language further conveys his mastery of complexity and his ability to render it communicable. It is above all precise: his rich vocabulary is always the right vocabulary. He claims to love brevity, but he also has a passion for thoroughness. They combine in the use of painstakingly chosen words that convey distinguishable facets of a thing or mutually supportive approaches. He can astonishingly analyze the Incarnation in one sentence: "Since neither as God alone could [Christ] feel death, nor as man alone could he overcome it, he coupled human nature with divine that to atone for sin he might submit the weakness of the one to death; and that, wrestling with death by the power of the other nature, he might win victory for us."[263] His thoroughness through precision, moreover, is embodied in a prose that, continuously dealing with death, sin, pain, and ugliness, is supremely elegant, and its elegance is persuasive. Calvin the rhetorician and Calvin the theologian are rarely separate; the objectivity of truths felt to be absolute is not incompatible with, and is sustained by, a highly self-conscious choice of words and sentence patterns:

> But if there is anything in the whole of religion that we should most certainly know, we ought most closely to grasp by what reason, with what law, under what condition, with what ease or difficulty, forgiveness of sins may be obtained: Unless this knowledge remains clear and sure, the conscience can have no rest at all, no peace with God, no assurance or security; but it continually trembles, wavers, tosses, is tormented and vexed, shakes, hates, and flees the sight of God.[264]

Calvin also exploits, and seems to love, the possibilities in single words or pairs of words. His reply to Sadoleto, in the form of a legal brief and as a contained oratory, includes single showpiece sentences that are more appropriate here than such sentences would be in the *Institutes*. Summing up his responses to the major charge against the Reformers, that of kindling strife by breaking with Rome and further splitting into sects after the break, he reminds Sadoleto of the ignorance and indolence among pastors and the people, on the one hand, and the brawling of the Schoolmen before the Reformers came, on the other, and states, "You cannot take credit for peace; that was caused by no other reason than that Christ was still."[265]

The beauty of Calvin's prose consists in its precision, richness, and deliberate elegance. The long, stately periodic sentences of the *Institutes* are also complex and crafted. Clauses are intricately arranged and balanced or counterbalanced, either through the replication of length and tonal and rhythmic elements or through a complementary equivalent composed (for example) of units of different length but equal weight, or with reversed tonal interrelations. His sentences very frequently follow the pattern of suspended syntax, and a crucial part of their sense progressively emerges in their structure—his prose is an exemplar of the pointed style.

Above all, Calvin was a master of the incantatory—the stylistic mode that is not admired from without, that does not just impress, but hypnotically pulls the reader into its orbit. Here the aesthetic power, the technical contrivance, and the manipulativeness of rhetoric to which we have referred, are one. Calvin can combine parallel constructions, condensed antitheses, and artfully controlled variation in rhythm, as in the following passage whose elaborate and intricate literary form is typical:

> If we seek salvation, we are taught by the very name of Jesus that it is "of him." If we seek any other gifts of the Spirit, they will be found in his anointing. If we seek strength, it lies in his dominion; if purity, in his conception; if gentleness, it appears in his birth. For by his birth he was made like us in all respects that he might learn to feel our pain. If we seek redemption, it lies in his passion; if acquittal, in his condemnation; if remission of the curse, in his cross; if satisfaction, in his sacrifice; if purification, in his blood; if reconciliation, in his descent into hell; if mortification of the flesh, in his tomb; if newness of life, in his resurrection; if immortality, in the same; if inheritance of the heavenly kingdom, in his entrance into heaven; if protection, if security, if abundant supply of all blessings, in his kingdom; if untroubled expectation of judgment, in the power given to him to judge. In short, since rich store of every kind of good abounds in him, let us drink our fill from this fountain and from no other.[266]

The qualities of Calvin's prose would find an affective response in any time—a response that the Renaissance rhetoricians deemed essential for the spread of moral truths, and for which they would have conditioned a receptive audience.

TIME-CONSCIOUSNESS IN CALVIN'S THEOLOGY

THE WEBER THESIS

The Weber thesis presupposes the facts that people do not respond to beauty alone and that they more typically respond to self-interest. Weber maintained that Calvin not only endorsed certain highly controversial practices of early capitalism (notably the taking of interest), but endorsed the secular world in general and created the psychology of capitalist man. I have noted Ozment's argument with Weber on anxiety: the Reformation decisively reduced, rather than enhanced, this characteristic. While anxiety was part of the regenerate life, it was an anxiety under control and lived with—lives were lived despite it; it did not serve as a driving force in these lives.[267]

There is, however, no explicit condemnation of early capitalism in Calvin. But endorsement and condemnation are not the only possible responses to historical developments. One can accept a development such as early capitalism as a fact, one of such significance that it cannot be ignored; because of its significance, one can feel both able and constrained to use it for one's own extraneous purposes. At the same time, one can feel entirely indifferent to it and simultaneously disapprove of it, because one can do nothing about it and because there is no intellectual or moral reason to single it out and condemn it specifically. This was Calvin's attitude.

In his treatises and commentaries more than in the *Institutes*, in his French writings more than in his Latin, Calvin made a deliberate effort to render his theology relevant. Abstraction was real enough to him; palpability and familiarity were more real for his popular audience. And the metaphor he would choose as often as another was money: "In fact, since those who have money are so careful to guard it, it was very right that this inestimable treasure, the Gospel, when God enriched us with it, was as it were enclosed in good conscience, which is, so to speak, the true coffer, to hold it safe and secure, so that it wouldn't be stolen by Satan."[268] Similarly, lack of charity could be characterized as theft—the metaphor of private property. Speaking of the sin of theft, he writes

> And such injustice occurs not only in matters of money or in merchandise or land, but in the right of each one; for we defraud our neighbors of their property if we repudiate the duties by which we are obligated to them. If a shiftless steward or overseer devours his master's substance, and fails to attend to household business; if he either unjustly spends or wantonly wastes the properties entrusted to him; . . . if the master, on the other hand, savagely harasses his household—all these are deemed theft in God's sight.[269]

Thus Calvin could use a vocabulary becoming, in the sixteenth century, the language of capitalism. But it was not an endorsement; rather it was a detached recognition of an externally caused inevitability, and a pragmatic and strategic use of that inevitability for entirely separate purposes. The recognition was an instance of the Pauline doctrine of the use that was not use—a favorite text of Calvin's. Assuredly, Calvin did not like capitalism: where your treasure is, there is your heart. The hearts of the faithful were given over wholly to rendering glory unto God; moreover, in Calvin's dialectical universe, glory to God meant positive rejection of that which was not of God. To be faithful was to damn as well as to praise. But it was not necessary to damn capitalism specifically. For it was merely the earthly city in another manifestation, and as such, it was meaningless and valueless. There is no rejection of early capitalism in Calvin because, in his Augustinian world view, an apparently new phenomenon was not new. It was abstracted, deindividualized, into the sin of the earthly city through which we are passing, as on a pilgrimage, to something good and meaningful beyond. Like Paul, Calvin could use the things of this world; Calvin could recognize them as God's gifts. But we use them with total indifference—paradoxically, an all-consuming indifference, for we are thereby asserting our faith.

UTILITARIANISM

"Use" is a key word for Calvin. As Harbison has observed, the motif of usefulness runs "like a red thread" through his writings:[270] he speaks repeatedly of "advantage," "utility," "profit," "fruit," and "benefit." He could say, "I do not demand at all that people agree with me or my opinion or whatever I say, except upon condition that they first recognize that what I teach is useful."[271]

Harbison points out that the justification of doctrine as useful was a psychological need for Calvin. In his resistance to God's calling, in his desire always to remain in a quiet corner in scholarly activity, he had to rationalize the attention that he did manage to give to scholarship by making it part of his calling: it was "useful" in his role as church leader to produce scholarly theology. Impersonally and pragmatically, "when I consider how important this corner of the world is for the spread of God's Kingdom, I have reason to be concerned about protecting it."[272] Self-indulgence became strategy. It was also extremely shrewd strategy—or, at least, Calvin's instinct in his rationalization was very good. Utilitarianism was one of the highest ideals of the Renaissance, one of its typical themes. Medieval thought was perceived as intellectualist and ineffective: it did not change lives. Scholarship must be effective; it must have a use beyond the uncovering of truth, and the use was moral betterment—impact was measured not by appreciation but by change. Erasmus intended his philosophy of Christ to be revolutionary; Ignatius of Loyola subordinated the need for theoretical correctness to the need for religious results in the *Constitutions* of the Society of Jesus in 1550. Melanchthon refuted Pico's defense of philosophy over rhetoric: wisdom enjoyed merely in contemplation was useless. His practical conclusion was that a writer's main concern is to make his language correspond and thus speak to his audience.[273] A personal solution of Calvin's could thus find a strong and widespread echo.

POLITICAL IDEAS AND POLITICAL THINKING

Luther regarded church order as a theological *adiaphoron*, not, as Calvin did, as a necessity grounded in the New Testament. Accordingly, he left the dismantling of the Roman Catholic churches and the substitution of reform to the German territorial rulers. Calvin of course involved the clergy far more, both in establishing the churches and in making judgments that were the basis for discipline. Still, he carried Luther a step further in legitimizing civil authority. The civil authority was given a positive role in religion, at the expense of the clergy, by virtue of its calling—first as the power of all coercion, and second as the power of order, sustaining existing institutions against attack and creating the very means of providing order. Negatively, "since the church does not have the power to coerce and ought not to seek it (I am speaking of civil coercion), it is the duty of godly kings and princes to sustain religion by laws, edicts, and judgments."[274] Positively, and expressed with significantly natural and compelling metaphor, the function of civil government

> is no less than that of bread, water, sun, and air; indeed its place of honor is far more excellent. For it does not merely see to it, as all these serve to do, that men breathe, eat, drink, and are kept warm, even though it surely embraces all these activities when it provides for their living together. It does not, I repeat, look to this only, but also prevents idolatry, sacrilege against God's name, blasphemies against his truth, and other public offenses against religion from arising and spreading among the people; it prevents the public peace from being disturbed; it provides that each man may keep his property safe and sound; that men may carry on blameless intercourse among themselves; that honesty and modesty may be preserved among men. In short, it provides that a public manifestation of religion may exist among Christians, and that humanity be maintained among men.[275]

This is a strikingly positive attribution of real power, because it is power over souls, to secular authority. It is also significant that Calvin discriminated among governments. He specifically felt that "aristocracy, or a system of aristocracy and democracy," was best.[276] Thus there were qualitative distinctions to be maintained in the earthly city, in addition to positive interaction between the earthly and heavenly. There was also the possibility of benefit within earthly institutions that, despite its unrelatedness to spiritual good, was worthy of pursuit and only potentially, but not necessarily, harmful. Certainly, Calvin writes, "Christians ought indeed so to conduct themselves that they always prefer to yield their own right, rather than go into a court, from which they can scarcely get away without a heart stirred and kindled to hatred of their brother." However, "when any man sees that without loss of love he can defend his own property, the loss of which would be a heavy expense to him, he does not offend against this statement of Paul, if he has recourse to law."[277]

The context of these quite significant opinions is a world view in which they are not significant. Calvin will often talk of God's gifts—of talents, attributes, and blessings. "These are the benefits that are daily conferred on us by [God]. Since, therefore, this life serves us in understanding God's goodness, should we despise it as if it had no grain of good in itself?"[278] The precise answer, in the end, is yes. For the gifts of God must be weighed against "the most unhappy condition" of the earthly life.

> For, if heaven is our homeland, what else is the earth but our place of exile? If departure from the world is entry into life, what else is the world but a sepulchre? And what else is it for us to remain in life but to be immersed in death.... If to enjoy the presence of God is the summit of happiness, is not to be without this misery? But until we leave the world "we are away from the Lord" [2 Cor. 5:6]. Therefore, if the earthly life be compared with the heavenly, it is doubtless to be at once despised and trampled under foot.[279]

Here again is the Augustinian world view, reinforced by Calvin's dualistic temper and made dogmatic by his logic. But it is also made necessary by them—and the world in this statement is constructed by logic. There are two kinds of commentary in Calvin's writings. One, the predominant kind, is about a twofold set of things or one part of a set: what is said about one part has reference to the other, its opposite; it also may be totally determined by it. That is to say, it may not be about itself at all, but about its opposite. The other kind is descriptive—though, insofar as Calvin is certainly registering a perception in the first kind, it would be more exact to say that he has two different ways of seeing. One must always question what the purpose of a statement is when one encounters a contradiction in Calvin. It will often be the case that one of the contradictory statements is independent and the other is not. In this typical and succinct statement, Calvin is not talking about the world, though his experience in the world is part of it: "Indeed, there is no middle ground between these two: either the world must become worthless to us or hold us bound by intemperate love of it. Accordingly, if we have any concern for eternity, we must strive diligently to strike off these evil fetters."[280]

It is also the case that the sets Calvin posits are "closed"—one part of a set can be part of a different set, and its function in that new context will define its nature differently. In such cases, one must refer to the weighting of the different views or to the larger context in which a set appears — and the latter is often the answer to the problem of discrepancy, for Calvin's world view is rarely long in the background. Both kinds of perception have significance for Calvin's historical impact.

Calvin's statements about democracy are similarly dependent upon context. The *Institutes* contains a positive endorsement of rebellion with a democratic basis and even a condemnation of its absence when circumstances warrant it, and this position was put to use by others in theory and practice of resistance. If there are, Calvin wrote,

> any magistrates of the people, appointed to restrain the willfulness of kings (as in ancient times the ephors were set up against the Spartan kings, or the tribunes of the people against the Roman consuls, or the demarchs against the senate of the Athenians; and perhaps, as things now are, such power as the three estates exercise in every realm when they hold their chief assemblies), I am so far from forbidding them to withstand, in accordance with their duty, the fierce licentiousness of kings, that, if they wink at kings who violently fall upon and assault the lowly common folk, I declare that their dissimulation involves nefarious perfidy, because they dishonestly betray the freedom of the people, of which they know that they have been appointed protectors by God's ordinance.[281]

The support that the *Institutes* lent to rebellion, however, was there despite its author. It is stated as a logical concomitant of his appraisal of kings vis-à-vis their religious duties, and that is a closed set. The wider textual setting of this famous passage is an argument that private individuals, as citizens, should obey existing authority, whatever its particular nature, because it has been ordained by God. Even the evil of defective government serves a positive purpose: to chastise us for our sins and to try our patience. So much is obedience to existing authorities a tenet and positive part of religion that we must treat the evil rulers not only with obedience but "with reverence and esteem" — the constituents of our worship of God. "All equally have been endowed with that holy majesty with which he has invested lawful power."[282] God's judgment awaits those who resist: "God is armed to avenge mightily this contempt toward himself."[283] Calvin was also personally quietistic, disgusted by contention, and endowed with an aristocratic contempt for the inconstant masses — a motif in his writings. His objections to rebellion were as strong as God's wrath.

The use of metaphors particularly appropriate in his economic environment and the presence of incipiently democratic proclamations does not indicate endorsement, nor does outright and unequivocal condemnation in more traditionally expressed theology indicate rejection. What is significant here is that, as the secular could not be discussed without consideration of the spiritual, the reverse is true; when Calvin considers the secular directly, that consideration is newly attentive. This time-consciousness suggests further development of Harbison's methodological presupposition that there was an unusually close and historically decisive relation between Calvin the person and the times in which he lived.

Toward the Historical Significance of Calvin's Medievalism

Like the dualism that is part of his theology, Calvin's intellectualism and tendency toward abstraction correspond to equivalents in medieval thinking, the thinking that found its formal and dominant expression in scholasticism: it was the questions the Schoolmen asked, not their approach to them, that Calvin disliked. Renaissance humanists from Petrarch onward perceived just these qualities of abstraction and dualism as the core of the medievalism that they rejected; they consciously opposed their conception of rhetoric to medieval intellectualism. We have seen that intellectualism and dualism are psychologically compatible, and the intensity of the Renaissance attack on intellectualism does indeed seem to indicate an attack as well on its psychological foundation.

Jung has formulated what seems to be a useful concept of "cultural preference," seeing a biological standpoint in antiquity, followed in the Middle Ages by a compensatory metaphysical standpoint.[284] I think the Jungian concept of persona—the mediator, created by the self, between self and environment—could be complementary to cultural preference in the organization of historical data in the early modern period. Not to the minimizing of other characteristics, the ways in which significant numbers of people present themselves and wish to be, in the world, must represent significant commitments.

There appears to have been something compelling in the view of the relation between self and world formulated by Nicholas of Cusa such that it recurs in multiple but recognizable variants and in multiple fields of expression in Italian Renaissance culture.[285] In his vision, man, the world, and God were united: nature was the book of God; man was a microcosm of his universe, yet an individual reflection of it, like the reflection of himself that he would see in God.[286] The appeal of the perception of unity could be at its highest when it was not immediate: that seems one aspect of Pico's proclamation of confidence that the hidden Pan could be found in the ever-changing Proteus and his proclamation of himself as Lord of Concord.[287] There is a common rejection of a world view in both the philosophical conviction and the programmatic idea: medieval hierarchicalism and distrust of the world and the flesh are being rejected.

The rejection constitutes a broad shift in values and sensibilities. In retrospect it seems lawful that it was accompanied by ambivalence. This is overt at its advent in Petrarch.[288] The intellectual basis for his questioning of medieval values and their implications for his life was the alternative idea that the origins of evil are external and societal, not internal—that the ills of the world neither follow from nor threaten the spiritual state of the individual living in the world.[289] Charles Trinkaus has stressed Petrarch's creative and therapeutic use of a kind of role playing for the purpose of making others aware of "the importance and difficulty of finding one's bearings."[290] Toward this end, Petrarch frequently presented himself as an individual torn by irreconcilable conflict. But in the complementary role of advocate of a life of faith in and through the resources of the earthly city, he used a technique more properly described as shock therapy. That this technique was contrived to upset the foundations of long-ingrained habits of thought seems especially evidenced in the aphoristic revaluations of will vis-à-vis knowledge in *De Ignorantia*. Just this Petrarch brings strongly to mind the Luther who would teach Reason, like the Pope, its place. And the style of Petrarch and Luther, in these very similar missions, is paralleled by the enthymemes used by Pico—the traditional figures of thought in rhetoric that rely upon bravura as well as intellectual manipulation to effect a basic change in viewpoint.[291]

These techniques, clearly responsive to long-neglected needs, seem to have resulted in an overshooting of the mark. That more was repudiated than intended or than humanly appropriate seems the implication of the work of art historians in particular. They have suggested a conception of the Lutheran and high Renaissance synthesis of inner and outer reality as, in actuality, a delicate, tenuous, and difficult balance. Panofsky has noted the paralyzing conflict in Dürer's *Melancholia*; Dürer's identification with Christ borders on blasphemy. Such jolting occurrences as the presence of a distorted black and white skull, almost unrecognizable, in Holbein's rich, lushly sensuous, and meticulously individualistic portrait *The Ambassadors*, or the vulture that Erich Neumann has convincingly found incorporated in Leonardo's *Virgin and Saint Anne*,[292] are not frequent, but they are not isolated, and they seem to record eruptions of the unconscious—to indicate subliminal uncertainty about overt commitments and conclusions that elsewhere seem total. Renaissance occultism seems to constitute further evidence of an inadequately nourished part of human existence that could eventually find more salutary a central place in cultural life and wider affirmation; its proud intellectual obscurity is also protective.

Calvin's dualistically infused and intellectualist mentality, in the total context of his theology, seems strategically related to the culture of the early and high renaissance. The techniques that impelled that culture in a monist direction were perhaps purposefully forceful enough to counteract the doubts even of some of their proponents: the techniques are dialectical in character. Against this background, Calvin's reworking of Lutheranism looks most of all like a course correction. The dualistic facet of Calvinist theology is not a rejection of Lutheranism, but amounts to a disagreement with earlier criticisms of medieval values. It might accurately be seen as a reassessment and revision of those values with the benefit of the criticism; additionally, it was affected by the changing temper of sixteenth-century history.

A historian of French Renaissance literature has noted an increasing awareness, in the course of the sixteenth century, of "the gap between man and the ways he would like to live."[293] That awareness, I think, is part of a cultural environment to which Calvinist theology spoke directly. The form and the vehicle of the course correction that I am positing was a lucent, awesome expression of an aspect of human nature that had lately been disparaged and, in Calvin, was given prominence. Contemporaneous cultural phenomena, especially Mannerist art, seem analogously related to high Renaissance culture and indicative of an audience that could find Calvin's writings, in just those aspects in which they have often seemed extremist to historians, highly congenial.[294] I think it will be worthwhile to look more closely at Mannerist art from this viewpoint.

An important human aspect of the shift we are discussing could be described as a strategic retreat. As a less abrupt break with the past than Lutheranism, it seems logical to conclude that the Calvinist form of Protestantism would have been psychologically more comfortable and acceptable in the still very conservative sixteenth century (and one could note that Lutheranism outside of Germany was Lutheran Protestantism without something quite personal—Luther's German—that eased its way at its advent). "New" and "novelty" were pejorative words not only for Calvin. Change in early modern Europe was fear provoking and guilt provoking.[295] In addition to preserving some of the old—and related to this—Calvin presented a very controlled rendition of a synthesis that had been regarded as the result of spontaneous self-expression. The schematic and formalistically depersonalized qualities in Calvin's version could have been stabilizing in a very welcome way. It may have been the case that some medievalism was needed to render modernity acceptable. Yet it is essential to note that the medievalism upon which Calvin insisted was also changed, and it became, I think, part of a modernism more comprehensive than that which the Renaissance proclaimed for itself in its historical perspectives.

The political and social contexts of Calvinist theology will shed additional light on its relation to the culture of earlier decades. The same is true of Mannerist art and its environment. Mannerism has often been depicted as a response to a spiritual crisis grounded in the insecurity and flux of Italy's political life from about 1530 onward. The Italian crisis, however, is part of a broader European crisis in the perspective of which

Calvin as well as the Mannerists can be seen and qualities in their work considerably explained.

Against all these contexts my concern with Calvin's historical significance leads me to try to define more exactly the nature of his secularism. The desacralization of the Reformation is an obvious part of all his life and thought. Here the Reformation reinforced, and was supported by, a broader trend that includes the development of science and the early history of nation-states — the most familiar characteristics of modern secularism. But a major concomitant of this secularism, to which rhetoricians in the Renaissance and Reformation made a decisive contribution, was an understanding of the way in which human beings in the most basic sense shape their experience of the world. The possibility of both inner and outer change became a defensible part of people's mentalities. The extent to which and the ways in which the possibility could be realized required definition. Here Calvin and the Renaissance rhetoricians offered two different answers.

Calvin's psychological make-up is reflected in his answer, as it is in his whole reading of Luther. We will look more closely at Mannerist art because, in a somewhat literal way and by its very limits, it sheds further light on the theologian's mentality and his historical success. Mannerism seems to me to share and to state with clarity and comprehensiveness a concern central in Calvinism. Calvinism further addresses it in a positive, practical way.

Calvin's writings found immediate resonance far from Geneva and outside the sphere of religion. In great measure, his apparent responsiveness to realities both tangible and intangible seems to be the key to his ability to affect these realities in turn.

3

From Church History to Intellectual History

Part One
Mannerism, Calvin, and Their Times

MANNERIST ART

SPIRITUALISM

Although Mannerism, and especially Italian Mannerism, is a highly controversial art style, historians agree that one of its primary and universal characteristics is a very strong spiritualism or other-worldiness. The late Michelangelo is perhaps the clearest representative of this quality. The motif of a desire for release from imprisonment in the body dominates his sonnets as well as the unfinished statue of a bound slave, in which inner form seems to be struggling against sheer matter (plate 1). Always characterized as neoplatonic, this manifestly dualistic quality has led Max Dvorak to speak of the medievalism of Michelangelo's late work.[1]

Mannerism was a well-observed phenomenon in its time and aroused much criticism as a deviation from the Renaissance norm. Typically, it was regarded as a new medievalism, linked to the northern, "Gothic" influence. Vasari notes the change in Pontormo that led him to become the acknowledged epitome of Mannerism:

> For Pontormo to have imitated Dürer in his motifs is not in itself reprehensible. Many painters have done so and still do. In this he certainly did not go astray. However, it is extremely regrettable

that he took over the German manner lock, stock, and barrel, down to the facial expression and even in movement. For, through this infiltration of the German manner, his original early manner, which was full of beauty and grace and which, with his innate feeling for beauty, he had completely mastered, was transformed from the ground up and utterly wiped out. In all his works under the influence of the German manner, only slight traces are recognizable of the high quality and the grace which had previously belonged to his figures.[2]

The spiritualism of Mannerist art, its apparent medievalism, most notably took the form of nonnaturalism. There are purely disembodied figures, as in Pontormo's *Pietà* (plate 2). There are also juxtapositions in the same paintings — which are surely making a point — of exaggeratedly disembodied figures with contrasting, exaggeratedly muscular, physical bodies, as in the same Pontormo's *Christ before Pilate* (plate 3) and *Resurrection* (plate 4). Rosso's *Transfiguration* (plate 5) consists of the clashing, unintegrated juxtaposition of the purely physical in its lower half and the spiritual in the upper half. But Rosso could spiritualize in a variety of ways: in his *Deposition from the Cross* (plate 6), the forms of the figures are elongated, unnatural S-curves, and the air of unreality they produce is further conveyed by the exaggerated emotions of the mourner. Often, entirely physical figures are desensualized with unnatural, unreal light. El Greco epitomizes the nonnaturalistic figures and unreal light combined.

The physical is retained; in fact, the unreal light accents its sharp contours. The light merely serves to desensualize it: the physical is frozen. Two worlds, the physical and spiritual, frozen in juxtaposition, have equal facticity and make equal claims. But they are not integrated with each other, and there is a preference for the spiritual: the physical has the facticity of relentlessness.

ABSTRACTION

Mannerism became the focus of serious attention by art historians, after several centuries of disdain, in the 1920s, coinciding with the advent of modern abstract art — and it is often noted that a renewed sensitivity to nonnaturalistic art was a major stimulus to the rehabilitation of the art of the late Renaissance.[3] Art theory matched practice. In contrast to its scarcity in the early and high Renaissance, theory flourished in the Mannerist period. Art is intellectualized in the flourishing of the systematic spirit; the theorizing is systematic consideration of the irrational.[4] The content of the theory is still more significant. Its foremost characteristic is abstraction; it is *a priori* as well as metaphysical. Its most common concept is the internal idea according to which the artist creates — rather than recording the perception of nature or classical models based on nature, as in the Renaissance. The concept is characteristic of both Aristotelians and Platonists. Writing of "this ideal concept, this intellectual Design," the Aristotelian Zuccari interposes it decisively between the artist and nature:

> The reason, then, that art imitates Nature is that the inner artificial Design, and therefore Art, proceeds to bring forth artificial objects in the manner that Nature itself proceeds. And if we wish to know why Nature can be imitated, it is because Nature is guided toward its own goal and toward its own procedures by an intellective principle. Therefore her work is the work of an unerring intelligence, as the philosophers say; for she reaches her goal by orderly and infallible means. And since art, chiefly with the aid of the above-named design, observes precisely the same [method] in its procedure, therefore Nature can be imitated by art, and art is able to imitate Nature.[5]

A connection with the natural is maintained, but it is mediated. Transposed into the Platonic language and thought of Lomazzo, the central concept of *a priori* mediation remains:

> Where matter, conforming with the divine power and with the Idea of the Angel, is also combined with reason and with the divine stamp, which is in the spirit, where it approves this facility of adaptability in which beauty consists, the latter, due to such diverse disposition of matter diversely in all bodies, appears to be more or less discordant or in harmony with the shape which the spirit possesses from its origin.[6]

The split between inner and outer, between the artist's spirit and his physical subject, is dualistic to an extreme.

> The spirit, created as it is, surrounded by an earthly body, stoops from its corporeal ministry. Weighed down by this propensity, it forgets the beauty that is hidden within it, and insofar as it is enveloped in a terrestrial body, it proceeds to use this body, accommodating to it the senses and sometimes also reason. Hence it does not behold this beauty which radiates within it, until the body has matured and reason has awakened, with which it observes the beauty that shines in the sight of the whole world and there abides. Finally, the beauty of the body is nothing more than a certain demeanor, vivacity, and grace, which radiate within it from the infusion of its Idea; and the latter does not descend into matter unless it is most properly prepared. This preparation of the living body is accomplished in three particulars, which are order, mode, and form.[7]

GOD'S POWER

In face of the split between inner and outer worlds, the art theorist draws a connection between the inner idea or inner design and God, the creator of the outer world—a reconciliation that both validates and consecrates the inner idea. It is an appeal to an authoritarian and all-powerful, effectualizing God, and, moreover, an appeal that proclaims man's inferiority vis-à-vis God—this in sharp contrast to the high Renaissance concept of genius, of which it seems to be a deliberate reworking. "I say, therefore," Zuccari writes,

> that God, all-bountiful and almighty, and first cause of everything, in order to act externally necessarily looks at and regards the internal Design in which He perceives all things that He has made, is making, will make, and can make with a single glance; and that this concept by which He internally purposes, is of the same substance as He, because in Him there is not nor can there be any accident, He being the purest act. In a similar way, because of His goodness and to show in a small replica the excellence of His divine art, having created man in His image and likeness with respect to the soul, endowing it with an immaterial, incorruptible substance and the powers of thinking and willing, with which man could rise above and command all the other creatures of the World except the Angel and he almost a second God, He wished to grant him the ability to form in himself an inner intellectual Design; so that by means of it he could know all the creatures and could form in himself a new world, and internally could have and enjoy in a spiritual state that which externally he enjoys and commands in a natural state; and, moreover, so that with this Design, almost imitating God and vying with Nature, he could produce an infinite number of artificial things resembling natural ones, and by means of painting and sculpture make new Paradises visible on Earth. But in forming this internal Design, man is very different from God: God has one single Design, most perfect in substance, containing all things, which is not different from Him because all that which is in God is God; man, however forms within himself various designs corresponding to the different things he conceives. Therefore his Design is an accident, and moreover it has a lower origin, namely in the senses. [8]

Both the objective physical and the subjective spiritual realm remain, but there is now felt to be a gap between them—the subject-object problem which Panofsky sees as characteristic of Mannerism. [9] The accomplishment and ideals of the Renaissance are retained and transformed: the appeal to God is the metaphysical resolution of a gap now felt between subject and object.

TENSION

There is an extremely great amount of tension in Mannerist art, a fact that has been noted by many art historians; Wylie Sypher observes it in his comparison of Mannerism and late Renaissance and seventeenth-century literature in England.[10] The medievalism of Mannerism was tantamount to a retreat within; its counterpart was the expression of doubt about the Renaissance synthesis of inner and outer realms, of the spiritual and physical. While the synthesis is retained as a *fait accompli*, there is a crisis of confidence. Could the artist convey the delicate balance? And was it, in fact, dependent upon the artist's conveying of it? That is, there were inner doubts about artistic ability, and doubts about the ultimate truth of that which one was nevertheless committed to believe. The doubts led to withdrawal and alienation from the outer world. The result was a dualistic conviction of the incompatibility of self and outer world, just as suspicion of the mutual exclusivity and irreconcilability of mind and matter seems the initial impulse to the doubts.

The tension was the result of the coexistence of doubt and conviction. Panofsky has characterized the mood of Mannerist art as "at once triumphant and insecure"—he sees it epitomized in "the sad yet proud faces and gestures of Mannerist portraits." In the Mannerist period, "the artistic mind began to react to reality with simultaneous arrogance and insecurity."[11] The medievalism may reflect a feeling that the cultural shift in the Renaissance was too radical; the old was still present within and strong and was now manifesting itself. But both the medievalism and the tension that characterized it may be, as well, a response to the material world—a logical reflex in the historical environment from the second third of the century onward.

DISCOMFORT, DISTRACTION, AND DISTORTION

The tension in Mannerism is variously but unmistakably expressed. Figures can be radically, exaggeratedly physical, but their poses are unbalanced, contorted, and strained. Rosso's *Moses and the Daughters of Jethro* (plate 7) is typical, and is additionally characterized by the violence of diametrically opposing, exaggeratedly conflicting movements.

The unnatural, elongated figures we have seen were rationalized positively in Mannerist art theory as reflections of "grace" or "elegance"—an assertion of the internal idea or design. But the internal design is not the whole of the paintings. In Pontormo's *Madonna and Child with Saints* (plate 8), the expressions of the figures which form the design—and they are locked into it—are curiously at odds with each other. Although the figures are in repose, there is a simultaneous movement of attention by some into the center of the grouping and by others outward, to something beyond the frame: we do not know what that object is. The emotions range from devotion, directed toward the Madonna and Child at the center, to distraction, alarm, and distress, directed outward. The Madonna at the center (and the thematic center of the painting) also gazes outward. Parmigianino's *Madonna dal Collo Lungo* (plate 9) is another example of such design and ambiguous context. In addition to an extreme degree of distortion, the painting contains an isolated classical scribe, who is strikingly disproportionate to the figures, and an isolated classical column, which does not bear anything. The quotational classical motifs are authoritarian; they are also part of a contrast between the physical as constituent of reality and the physical *qua* physical, as a mere abstraction. The curves and elongations in the painting form an exaggeratedly patterned surface design. The artist expresses his noninvolvement with the physical (which he nevertheless painstakingly portrays) through an exaggerated involvement with the artificial and inner.

It is common to find in Mannerist art figures uneasily, uncomfortably compressed and crowded at the surface. The mood is tense, and the figures seem separated from the space surrounding them. And they are exaggeratedly *posed*: art, when naturalistic, is at the same time removed from nature. The posing, moreover, is an immobilization, as in Rosso's *Marriage of the Virgin* (plate 10).

CONTRIVANCE

Mannerist art is characterized by the use of flat light. It produces sharp, exaggerated contrasts that intensify the drama of its often very worldly subjects—the same subject matter as Renaissance art. But it is now unnatural, contrived, and exaggerated drama. It is, rather, melodrama—the equivalent in art of rhetoric.

Frozenness in Art and the Unfree Will

The painterly quality throughout Mannerism is frozenness. It is not nonphysical, but is is nonspontaneous and nonvital. And, uncomfortably confined in physical bodies, separate from the outer world and thus impotent in regard to it, the psychological quality to which the figures in Mannerist art correspond, and which permeates all the examples above, is the absence and denial of free will.[12] It seems above all the experience of unfreedom despite all the impulses that lead one to think one acts with deliberation and freedom: unfreedom is always "unfreedom despite." All of the qualities of Mannerist art that we have seen are reminiscent of Calvin, and especially this quality.

MANNERISM AND BAROQUE

Ignatius of Loyola also spoke of the abdication of personal freedom, of the obedience, "like a corpse," that the Jesuits owed to the papacy, and Pevsner has correlated Mannerist art with the Catholic Reformation.[13] Yet the corpse-like self-abdication of the Jesuits has as its counterpart a more fundamental assertion of the determinative role of the will in the attainment of salvation. Indeed, the abdication to a higher will in Saint Ignatius itself sounds a note of triumph that differentiates it in nature and tone from Calvin's submission to a will beyond his understanding. "He who aims at an entire and perfect oblation of himself, in addition to his will must offer his understanding which is the highest degree of obedience. He must not only will, but also think the same as the superior, submitting his own judgment to the superior as far as a devout will can bend the understanding."[14] In the course of the century, the Jesuits emphasized free will even more than did Thomists.[15]

The tension in Mannerist art is not matched by a corresponding tension in Jesuit theology, and there is further contrast in the positive involvement of the senses in the spiritual exercises. Jesuitism corresponds, more accurately, to the Baroque in its combination of dogmatism with aggressive, extroverted self-assertion and its thoroughly internalized integration of the spiritual and physical. Arnold Hauser has contrasted Mannerism as the expression of "the conflict between the spiritual and sensual impulses of the age" and the Baroque as "the resolution of that conflict on the basis of spontaneous emotion"[16]; the expansive energies and triumphant mood of the Jesuit crusade can be linked to the later stylistic movement.

THE PSYCHOLOGY OF MANNERISM

Mannerist art expresses a mentality that seems to correspond very closely to the psychology of introverted intellectualism. It is abstract and dualistic. Hauser, a Marxist and Freudian, has characterized the psychology of Mannerism as narcissistic. He finds the narcissism expressed in the inner inertia and tension in the art, its taste for the nonnaturalistic, its intellectualism, and its concentration on the human form to the neglect of environment. Where it does have to cope with environment, as in painting, it typically creates what Hauser calls "fictitious space," in which "the easy and comfortable relationship between object and environment [characterizing Renaissance art] was lost"—this is the disintegration that Sypher sees in Mannerist art, paralleled in poetry by what he terms the power of the isolated phrase.[17] Hauser's fictitious space is constructed through figures "packed together in a corner or lost in a vast, vague, unlimited area," conveying a sense of rootlessness and having gone astray.[18] It is in relation to such phenomena that Hauser construes the psychology of Mannerism as that of an alienated society, experiencing "a crisis of the sense of reality" in which "the loss of object-love involves the loss of the whole of the external world...[having] the paralyzing effect of an illness."[19]

To Hauser, Mannerist art inclined toward narcissism as a consequence not only of the emphasis upon the self, with which the artist compensated for his shaken sense of tradition, but also of his discovery of and preoccupation with spontaneity, with the creative power of mind: this now familiar aesthetic stance has its origins in Mannerism.[20] Mannerist spontaneity consisted in "the revolutionary idea that the mind could watch itself at work"; the "totally new idea of fictitious space" further expresses this, for it represents art "as an autonomous creative activity" and reminds the spectator of "the self-deception necessary to the artistic experience."[21]

There is indeed self-consciousness in Mannerist art. But the self-consciousness that Hauser presents as spontaneity does not comprise either the quality of frozenness that pervades this art or the tension in it that seems always rooted in self-doubt. It is closer to Calvin's self-consciously rhetorical expressions of self-abnegation. The psychology here may be of a self felt to be so strong that it needs to be abnegated; the impulse to do that is as much guilt as fear. Mannerist self-consciousness seems also mirrored in a pervasive sense of entrapment—entrapment within a self from which the conscious mind is estranged. This could properly be called self-alienation with no need for reference to the Marxist concept.

MANNERISM IN RELATION TO
THE RENAISSANCE

Freezing the Synthesis

Mannerism is not a rejection of the physical realm: it is a freezing of a hitherto living and viable synthesis of inner and outer. This is clearest in its portraiture. Bronzino, one of the leading portraitists, reveals his conception of and attitude toward physical nature even in his allegories. *Venus, Cupid, Time, and Folly* (plate 11) is a painting of and statement about pure eroticism, utterly depersonalized. It is first a painting of nakedness—the nakedness of the two central figures is contrasted with the lush cloth backdrop on which they rest and made striking by the eery white light shining on their intercoiled bodies, frontalized across the picture plane. Cupid's body is preeminently undignified: he is contorted by animallike passion; the human is obliterated. Secondly, the eroticism is frozen—it is sterile and lifeless. The white light turns the bodies to marble; they are in strong contrast to the flesh tones of the horrified onlooker (and of the two eery masks on the floor). The physical is deathlike in quality. And finally, eroticism is in the most direct sense deadly. The painting shows Venus seducing her son Cupid in order that, out of the love that she arouses in him, he will destroy Psyche, the soul. Here is the dualism of mind versus matter, the pure sexuality of matter, and its seeming relentlessness.

Bronzino's portraits, such as *Ugolino Martelli* (plate 12), are highly and deliberately formal. The figures are immobilized and are cool and emotionless. Martelli's body is, additionally, unnaturally elongated. The whole is inscrutable, and there is an air of mystery about it: Hauser feels in the mystery of Mannerist portraiture a sense of alienation of creator from his object.[22]

A RETREAT WITHIN

The psychological quality of the retreat within, and its dualistic implication, are seen by Otto Benesch in a contemporaneous northern manifestation in the art of Breughel. The "mask" quality of his faces intensely expresses "the enigmatic inner life" of his subjects in all its unpredictability, inscrutability, and anonymity in the face of the relentless, vast mechanism of the universe. Human nature, like the universe, obeys its own laws. Benesch interestingly draws a parallel with Bosch and the late medievalists. One could note, in regard to Mannerism as in regard to Calvin, that self-containedness seems wary and protective vis-à-vis both outer and inner reality, both seeming now to elicit a new sense of complexity.[23]

DISTANCING

Parmigianino's *Self-Portrait with Mirror* (plate 13) is a paradigm of Mannerism. On one level a distortion, it is also a statement of obliqueness, indirectness, and distancing from reality. The Renaissance was a *fait accompli*; its appreciation of individualism was maintained. But that individualism is either dead, as in Bronzino, or, as here, removed from direct access. There is an impediment between the artist and his subject, between inner and outer reality. Even when the outer reality is his own physical self—especially when it is his own physical self—the psychologically engendered force of dualism manifests its strength.

A NEW AUTHORITARIANISM

Prescriptions for artistic creation in Mannerist art were highly authoritarian, and this is clearly seen in the contemporaneous art academy—both in its numbers and in its nature. While academies had existed in the high Renaissance, they were an expression of enthusiasm for antiquity, and their atmosphere was "free and bold" and typically informal.[24] But in the Mannerist period they strikingly increased in number, and they were characterized primarily by the teaching of elaborate and highly schematic rules as the foundation for an absolutely normative imitation of antiquity—at the expense of the imitation of nature, which, for Renaissance artists, had vied with antiquity as a model or had served to justify the imitation of antiquity.[25] Pevsner rightly implies that it was no coincidence that the proliferation of academies and their transformation occurred under the auspices of Mannerism, "the most schematic and the most 'totalitarian' of all modern styles and the one most devoted to taking over compositions and details from the works of the great classical masters."[26] He plausibly correlates the authoritarian stance of Mannerism with the Medici court of the second half of the sixteenth century, "one of the foremost representatives of the early phase of absolutism" — the academy was "its equivalent in art."[27] But an endorsement of power and a love of imposed order may not be the only characteristics of authoritarianism.

Pevsner points out that Vasari played a decisive role in the transformation of the academy from an unorganized group to a "regulated enterprise and soon a governmental institution." It was at his suggestion that Cosimo founded in Florence what was to become the leading exponent of the new type, the Accademia del Desegno.[28] Vasari's organizational formality finds a parallel in his own architecture and art theory, which together shed much light on Mannerist authoritarianism.

Vasari, who is of primary importance for the earliest historiographical images of the Renaissance, maintained that the modern masters (above all, Michelangelo) indeed superseded antiquity, but only by virtue of closely studying and thereby truly understanding the ancients. While nature is normative, "those most famous ancients . . . without a doubt did gloriously surpass her." Thus progress always has consisted (if manifested as greater truth to nature) in a return to ancient models — models based upon, and then surpassing, nature.[29] Vasari was extremely proud of his own "correct" use of antiquity. He pointed out that in his colonnade for the Uffizi Palace (plate 14) he broke the architrave above the pillars, extending it outward to underline the importance of antique motifs and to demonstrate his own classical orthodoxy. But just this break in the architrave undermines the classical mood of the building. The details and the proportions may be correct in the most exemplary manner, but the proportional schemes of the ancient orders were based not only upon the proportions in nature but on the conviction that nature was orderly and harmonious. These qualities were conveyed in the serenity of uninterrupted evenness of surface and the ease and comfort of spatial adequacy. The surface of Vasari's building is, in contrast, crowded and agitated: classical details are overabundant, and they are exaggerated by physical devices that break up the spatial flow. Hauser describes the Uffizi aptly:

> Instead of a sense of elevation to a higher, more even, more peaceful level of existence, one feels bewildered, uprooted, insecure, removed to an artificial spatial structure that seems abstract in relation to ordinary experience. It is neither a part

or continuation of empirical reality, nor is it an artifact felt to be a sublimation or summary or quintessence of that reality; the impression it creates is that the order of things that applies elsewhere has been displaced by another, fictitious order.[30]

At the least, such authoritarianism is an expression of insecurity: a capitulation to powers that know better, to rules that can do what one cannot count on one's self to do. But there is a hint in the feeling Hauser describes that the classicism of the Uffizi also is tantamount to a dualistic comment upon the relation between the spiritual and the physical, between subject and object in artistic creation, and between mind and matter itself. In his painstakingly correct quoting of antiquity, Vasari has disrupted the ancients' basic statement about nature and thereby created a counterstatement of his own.

A New Feeling about the Fact of Matter

That Vasari's counterstatement to ancient architecture may have positive significance is further suggested by the use of antiquity in Michelangelo's Laurentian Library (plate 15). It is a most curious room. One feels uncomfortably crowded from the start: it has sometimes been noted that the centrally curved stairs flow downward, like lava, pushing one away. But the classical details that dominate the surface are still more curious. The pilasters on either side of the niches are tapered from the wide top to the narrower bottom—a radical and jarring reversal of classical proportions—and the moldings at each end are narrower than the shaft, and so do not have character of capitals or bases: they are just quotations of details. The room is dominated by the enormous columns separating the niches. But the columns are paired, not evenly spaced as in ancient buildings; and not only are they not carrying evenly distributed weight, they are in fact carrying no weight at all, for they are recessed behind the plane of the wall they flank. They are thus stripped of meaning at the same time that their doubled nature, and the large (and equally functionless) volutes beneath them, assert their presence and intensify the sense of crowdedness through clutter. The conviction seems to be asserting itself that matter is both relentlessly oppressive and potentially meaningless.

MANNERISM AND CALVINISM:
THEIR HISTORICAL BACKGROUND

Disillusionment in Florence

Mannerism has sometimes been seen as a reaction to the sack of Rome in 1527. The shock of the invasion was followed by strong statements of insecurity and guilt. Peace and stability were shattered; there would be no end to Italy's troubles; and the situation was due to God's vengeance on the Italians for their sins.[31] We will return to this thesis; first, we will focus on Florence, the other center of Mannerism. Here, equally contributing to the mood of tension and the heightened presence of dualist thought, the predominant note is of disillusionment.

Guicciardini, the Florentine who chronicled his city's history, also reacted to Italian history at large. What is manifested in his comments is a striking lack of idealism. Writing in 1536 of the invasion of Italy, he is preoccupied with the fact of instability. But the instability is a manifestation of the unreliability of human nature: not concerned with God's vengeance, he certainly is concerned with human corruption. The invasions make apparent "to what great instability human affairs are subject, not unlike a sea stirred by the winds." And this leads to the consideration of

> how destructive, almost always to themselves but always to the people, are the poorly considered counsels of rulers when, bearing only in mind either vain errors or current greed, they do not remember the frequent changes of fortune, and, turning to the harm of others the power granted them for the common welfare, make themselves the authors of new commotions either from insufficient prudence or excessive ambition.[32]

Will peace never be possible? It had been achieved in the celebrated balance of power in Italy. However, there was irony in that balance. Its mechanism was the very imperfection in human nature that had created the need for it.

> This alliance easily held in check the cupidity of the Venetian Senate, but it did not unite the allies in sincere and faithful friendship, inasmuch as, full of competition and jealousy among themselves, they did not cease to watch carefully one another's movements, mutually undermining all the plans by which any one of them might grow in power and reputation. This, however, did not make the peace less stable; on the contrary, it aroused in all of them the greater readiness to try to extinguish carefully all the sparks which might prove to be the origin of a new fire.[33]

Guicciardini could admire Lorenzo de Medici as a great man, a man of "renown and wisdom," but disillusionment was always the stronger strain. The reason why Lorenzo's death was a tragedy was that he had come to function as "the mediator and almost like a brake" in the affairs of Italy.[34] Most Florentines were disillusioned even with the older Medici after the restoration. The disillusionment was a collapse of idealism with psychological and philosophical implications.

The restoration of the Medici in Florence was traumatic because it marked the failure of civic humanism. As Hans Baron has pointed out, from the late fourteenth century, humanists in Florence had asserted and dramatized the conviction that a state, in all its historicity and materiality, could be decisively affected by the intangible force of commitment to an ideal.[35] Moreover, the ideal was specific: it was commitment to the republican constitution. Discrimination among the things of the world was possible; absolutes could exist in the earthly city. There was a meaningful link between inner and outer life. The Renaissance synthesis in art had a parallel in politics.

When the political ideal collapsed, more than republicanism came to an end. Disillusionment with the now overtly absolutist rule of the Medici resulted in a retreat within. The broader ideal of the state as a work of art, mirrored in princely patronage, also became untenable. Ideals were to be realized in an inner realm. And no more than the republican spirit could assert itself decisively in the historical world could the artistic spirit find a positive relation to physical reality. Once having been realized with striking success, the synthesis of spirit and matter was an established and desirable possibility. But so widespread and deep were doubts about its realization that disillusionment was dominant. Tension was a presence, too, because the ideal stubbornly lived on to challenge self-abdication and spiritualism as satisfactory solutions, and because the spiritualism itself had the reactive character of dualism.

The Mannerist retreat within was a preservation within. Disillusionment takes the form of resignation. Perhaps the symbol of Mannerist inwardness is the profound sadness of so many of its portraits. It seems a sadness of regret.

ANXIETY, IMPOTENCE, AND POLITICS IN EUROPE

In addition to disillusionment and tension, Mannerism reflects discomfort and insecurity, as, certainly, does Calvinist theology. The wider political and socioeconomic contexts of Mannerism and Calvinism considerably explicate the intensity of these qualities. In the last decade, demographic change has been targeted as the key to what seems the most basic problem in the sixteenth-century environment: a problem of adjustment, the problem of too few goods and, now, too many people.[36] And, in light of the population rise, the most prominent aspect of the responses of rulers to the rapid and far-reaching changes in sixteenth-century Europe is their short-sightedness and inadequacy. At the same time, government at all levels was newly felt to be impersonal—either suddenly depersonalized, as in Italy, or finally recognized as such as long-standing trends coalesced and were further shaped by their environment. To a cultural historian, the impersonality and dubious reliability of government evoke the unease behind and within sixteenth-century sources.

Members of all classes would have been, to varying degrees and in different ways, aware of and worried about the nature of the solution their rulers seemed to be taking for economic problems. The solution was war, and it was not only felt as an ever increasing physical threat but as a direct financial burden and the apparent cause of a freezing of economic and social change. From the mid-sixteenth to the mid-seventeenth century, war constituted what has been called "an economy of non-productivity."[37] Its auxiliaries were administrative bureaucracies, professionally staffed armies, and large-scale intervention by the state in economic life.[38] It has been suggested that the policy of war may have had as one of its purposes social control. Large numbers of commercially successful burghers, upon acquiring sufficient funds to make major investments, chose to buy public office. This meant also the renouncing of commercial activity and the assumption of the life style of the nobility, for public office was as much an enhancement of social position as a more secure income. Thus a potentially seditious class accepted a regular code of public behavior.[39]

The policy of rulers was emphatically antiurban.[40] The entrepreneurial class was increasingly transformed into an administrative class; the new nobility also freed the old nobility for war. The war economy seems most immediately the result of the temptation of an easy solution. The Price Revolution that was more and more sharply felt was more feared than analyzed. War, as a self-financing institution through armed extortion, was logically defensible. Part of the institution was the image of royalty prevailing in the minds of both subjects and rulers: "the divinely anointed monarch of the Middle Ages became the secular divinity of the absolutist state"; he appropriately withdrew to remote quarters and delegated the management of affairs to his appointed ministers and army staff.[41]

The new nobility accepted the eagerness of rulers to incorporate new sources of wealth in their government. And by participating in these governments, they were also participating in immoral government. The sale of crown property by monarchs came increasingly to include the sale of government offices, and this practice was permeated with corruption. In France, offices were created specifically for the purpose of being sold: the corruption was overt.[42]

The connotation of illegitimacy may have been already attached to the public sphere in the minds of these former burghers.[43] Urban government itself was antithetical to the traditional idea of the body social. The egalitarian status of all citizens was irrelevant to the concept of differentiated functionalism of which that body was made. It would have been logical for a sixteenth-century town dweller to wonder whether the municipal institutions expanding around him could be effective and whether a citizen—this new role that had so little identity—might exert any control over his environment.

The influx of new nobility was threatening to the old. The latter went to war willingly, though some perhaps went gingerly, worrying about what they were leaving behind. In general, however, they seem to have thrown themselves into the dynastic and religious wars with the full enthusiasm of converts, not to a new religion, but to a new way out. It was also a traditionally grounded way for them: they had been the fighters in the body social. But the tenuousness of their new loyalties as fighters, and the quality of desperation, are manifested in the fact that they were quite willing to serve foreign kings—and the kings were understandably willing to have them insofar as the nobles would not challenge their domestic power.[44]

The peasants may have suffered most, for their discomfort was as much physical as psychological. They either lost the promise of an urban market where cities declined or (particularly in England) were increasingly the victims of the agrarian specialization through which the landed nobility tried to recoup their financial losses, taking advantage of what urban market there was. The peasantry were also the victims of the coming into existence of large numbers of new nobility who were constrained to invest in landed estates for social status: the heightened demand for land resulted in sharp increases in rents.[45]

The background to this situation was the inflation that was as conspicuous as it was puzzling. Contrasts between rich and poor became more extreme, and they were exacerbated by the population rise. Population growth quickened the move from countryside to town, a pattern dating from the late Middle Ages but now intensified. The incentive of the old belief that "city air means freedom" was belied by living conditions that deepened and emphasized the miseries of the poor. The move from the countryside was also quickened by agrarian specialization. Finally, the state took more and more money in taxes, just as the armies, in which much of the taxes were invested, plundered the land.

Among some there doubtless was conscious distrust of the soundness of policy and the character of society. Many must have felt the impotence of bafflement: action was being taken at a distance, by legitimate sovereigns, without explanation. It is likely that some had preconscious doubts about the meaning, now, of individual personhood. A very circumscribed reflection of this situation, and part of the lives of Mannerist artists, was the new relation between artist and society in Italy. Breaking away from patronage, the mid-sixteenth century saw the real birth of the art trade. Thereby, Hauser remarks, the artist's works "become commodities."[46]

Religious protest had a particularly fertile field by virtue of its

correspondence to prevailing feelings and impulses. Calvinism has been
called a peculiarly urban theology.[47] It is that, and more than that, because
the emphatically communal form of Protestant church life, given sharper,
stronger lines by Calvin, could serve to offset with exactness the experience
of an increasingly impersonal environment.

IMPERSONAL AND PERSONAL FEELINGS ABOUT THE TIMES

The feelings and impulses engendered by this environment were given
expression in a very characteristic form that rendered openness to religious
protest all the more understandable. The expression was a polarity of
extreme impersonality and generality, on one hand, and of extreme
subjectivism and particularity, on the other – one beyond and the other
far within the political horizon, and, as such, each was as distanced from
this horizon as it was a reaction to it.

The intertwining of political and religious protest was overt in the
Peasants' War in 1525. The results were disastrous. As conditions got
worse and apparently hopeless, the targeting of political, social, and
economic policy became less precise. A motif in Calvin newly
complementary to the motif of pilgrimage through the earthly city is the
misery of life in "this our age of iron," our "worse than iron age." This
bespeaks a mood, and, in speaking of his age of iron, Calvin was using
an extremely popular convention. Henry Kamen has pointed out that the
concept of the Iron Age was far more prevalent in sixteenth-century
literature than was the concept of the Golden Age; the latter was actually
widely used as a medieval literary theme, while the Iron Age theme was
selected from antiquity as peculiarly characteristic of the sixteenth century.
By 1529 the phrase "Iron Age" was well known.[48]

The Iron Age was generally seen as the context of the glorious
achievements of the new age in arts and letters, a context that threatened
these achievements.[49] But if Renaissance writers had a more balanced sense
of progress than their heirs in the seventeenth and eighteenth centuries,
they were equally prone to generalizations. A definite association was made
between ironness and the spread of the profit motive in the sixteenth
century. The Iron Age was iron precisely because of gold. The new God
gold displaced an economy seen to be "natural"; virtue and morality were
devalued to the benefit of wealth; virtue and morality in fact declined.
The lamented coldness of the Iron Age consisted in the decrease of charity,
a direct concomitant of the new worship of money.[50] While moralistic
and not class-specific, this is tantamount to a critique of the beginnings
of capitalism. However, it is not the whole of the meaning of the Iron
Age. Personal love also was seen to have decayed: this was associated with
an inner withdrawal that Kamen sees as self-alienation, in the face of the
extremely rapid nature of change in the sixteenth century that seemed to
outpace human capacities for adjustment.[51] Rather desperate explanations

1. Michelangelo: Unfinished Bound Slave. Florence, Accademia.

2. Jacopo Pontormo: Pietà. Florence, Certosa del Galluzzo.

3. Jacopo Pontormo: Christ Before Pilate. Florence, Certosa del Galluzzo.

4. Jacopo Pontormo: Resurrection. Florence, Certosa del Galluzzo.

5. Rosso Fiorentino: Transfiguration, Città di Castello, Cathedral.

6. Rosso Fiorentino: Deposition from the Cross. Volterra, Pinacoteca.

7. Rosso Fiorentino: Moses and the Daughters of Jethro. Florence, Uffizi.

8. Jacopo Pontormo: Madonna and Child with Saints. Florence, S. Michele Visdomini.

9. Parmigianino: Madonna dal Collo Lungo. Florence, Pitti.

10. Rosso Fiorentino: Marriage of the Virgin. Florence, S. Lorenzo.

11. Bronzino: An Allegory: Venus, Cupid, Time, and Folly. London, The
National Gallery.

12. Bronzino: Ugolino Martelli. Berlin, Staatliche Museen.

13. Parmigianino: Self-Portrait in Round Mirror. Vienna, Kunsthistorisches Museum.

14. Vasari: Screen from the Uffizi. Florence.

15. Michelangelo: The Laurentian Library Vestibule. Florence.

were given for the multiple evils of the time: Estienne attributed them to the increase in geographical mobility and the expansion of educational opportunity.[52] But among the most frequent associations was the one of iron and war. This was of course an old association, but it now had new meaning, both in regard to the frequency and the civilian encroachments with which war was waged. Nevertheless it was a moral critique, not a critique of social and economic policy: war promoted vice and desolation.[53]

The most spectacular military event of the age, in the eyes of contemporaries, was the sack of Rome in 1527. Yet this was experienced neither as the result of dynastic rivalry between the Hapsburgs and the Valois nor as the universal evil of the age. It seems, rather, to have elicited the most subjective experience possible of a still completely impersonal force.

The violence and sadism of the sack were horrifyingly noted afar, as were the direction of the worst tortures and most obscene mockeries by Catholic Spaniards against Roman ecclesiastics. Hartt writes of it that "it was as if some of the deepest and blindest forces in the collective id of sixteenth-century Christendom had been let loose, and as if Christianity were doing to the Church what they had wanted to do for a long time."[54] Working toward a correlation with Mannerism, he abstracts four themes from sources contemporaneous with the sack: "a sense of deep collective guilt; a desire for punishment; a need for the healing of the wounds inflicted by punishment; a longing for a restored order in which the individual was no longer free to seek his own destruction."[55] But there are sexual connotations to all these themes, and to the nature of the violence in the sack. If it was experienced as God's merited judgment, it is also clear that it was experienced as rape — as pure sexuality, completely depersonalized and completely out of control. Impersonal and intrusive, engaged in violent wars, sixteenth-century government may have had a sexual connotation, and so, too, may the widespread feeling of impotence vis-à-vis the new powers.

The alternative to the polar opposites of impersonal and personal reactions to sixteenth-century events was not a blend or synthesis, but, rather, an equally informative insane reaction. In 1575, Loys Le Roy, who was generally both eminently sane and extremely optimistic, ended his enthusiastic and detailed description of "the excellence of this age" with a bizarre but symptomatic vision of impending disaster:

> I foresee already in my mind certain peoples, strange in form, colour, and habits, pouring in upon Europe, as did formerly the Goths, Huns, Lombards, Vandals, and Saracens, who destroyed our towns, cities, castles, palaces, and churches. They will change our customs, laws, languages, and religion; they will burn our libraries, ruining everything noble they find in the countries they

occupy in order to destroy their honour and virtue. I foresee wars springing up in all parts, civil and foreign; factions and heresies arising which will profane all that they touch, human and divine; famine and pestilence menacing mortals.[56]

THE SPECIAL SIGNIFICANCE OF DISCIPLINE IN CALVINISM

For those who became Calvinists, another intangible quality may have directly answered their unease. Michael Walzer has drawn an interesting corollary between discipline as a mental stance in Calvin's religiosity and in both the religiosity and political activities of the Calvinist revolutionaries—the revolutionary "saints"—of the sixteenth century. He notes that Calvinism was the "product of an extraordinarily successful effort to resist the religious compulsion of the personal and the emotional," and relates it to Calvin's strong sense of the estrangement of man from God.[57] Reconciliation was impossible; man's estranged plight was reflected in "fearfulness, anxiety, distrust and war." The solution was obedience—first to God, then to the state.[58] Walzer sees as semblances of the earthly chaos which Calvin associated with fallen man not only the wars of the sixteenth century but the anxiety-provoking status confusion and status panic that the bourgeoisie and lower nobility experienced so strongly.[59] Discipline, as mental outlook and lifestyle, as it was for Calvin, became a possible solution. "The pious and rigorous routine of the saints' lives brought them a sense of self-assurance, which was the end of alienation and which in politics often looked very much like fanaticism."[60] It initially took the form of absolute obedience to the state. For the state, as an order of repression, promised control—control of the confusing and conflicting forces in society, these corresponding to and reflecting conflict within the self. The magistrate was not considered paternalistic; one did not revere him but deliberately obeyed him. And the order resulting from this obedience (and, implicitly, self-abnegation) alleviated anxiety.[61] Calvinism thus confirmed an existing mental state, and sainthood offered a way out of it, in personal life through the exercise of self-control, in political life through the establishment of the holy commonwealth, first through the existing magistracy—and then through revolution.[62]

Psychologically, discipline was stabilizing. A formalized role in society created a sense of security. Its earliest effect in the political sphere was a holding pattern rather than a transformation, then a means to transform that guaranteed control of conflicting forces rather than a natural reconciliation. Walzer notes that the French Huguenots—the intellectuals, the new or newly educated gentlemen, lawyers, and merchants—had both the anxiety and capacity for sainthood.[63] He sees as parallel to the appeal of Calvinism to them the contemporaneous revival of Stoicism among the Catholic nobility: "the need for some new ideological brace was widely felt."[64] Similarly, men in England in the sixteenth century "were extraordinarily preoccupied with the historical fact of social mutability," and this preoccupation was reflected alike in their questioning of the assumption of a great chain of being and their ultimate adoption of Calvinism, a new solution to assuage new doubts.

The dominance in theology of predestination, Walzer implies, was the ultimate solution. The implication is plausible because the theology of predestination presupposes the believer's feeling that he deserves damnation and because it had the positive connotations of control. It could have represented an escape from specific changes regarded as threatening and from an exhilerating but terrifying release from the constraints of a past order. It was the abdication of idealism because there were both fears and doubts about worldly reform and worldly well-being. In the end, God alone had the power to effectuate his decisions and thereby reconcile the two realms that had now sharply reemerged in consciousness.

SUMMARY

I have spoken also of the discipline of rhetoric and want to move now toward a personal discipline, in both Calvin and a less circumscribed Calvinism, that comprises the transformative as well as the protective and defensive. Mannerism counterpoints this aspect of Calvinism.

The contingency in Calvin and the Mannerists of a dualism (which had earlier been disparaged) and of a highly formal rhetoric in one and a formalized melodrama in the other is striking. Calvin's most characteristic doctrine, the unfree will, is strongly reflected in Mannerist art. The frozen sensuality in Mannerism which conveys the sense of unfreedom suggests that its basis lies in an acceptance of the facticity of matter, quintessentially the body, and a horror of it. This attitude is also present in Calvin. In both, there is an emphasis on clashing antitheses which seems to reflect consciousness of an inner struggle between spirit and flesh.

Calvin and the Mannerists, however, make the points on which they agree in different ways. The relaxed and open sensuality of the Renaissance is absent in both, but while the sensuous is frozen in Mannerism, it is, rather, controlled in Calvin. For he does not only comment on its problematic nature, but in his writing uses it positively and, I think, with positive intention. The physical does not have to be deadly. Dualism is not only a problematic reality but a problem to be dealt with.

Part Two
Calvin's Rhetoric and His Secularism

A DOCTRINE OF THE WORLD AND ONE *MODUS VIVENDI*

The doctrine of the priesthood of all believers is an important link between Calvin and Luther, and herein they may both be heirs of the nominalist rejection of metaphysical hierarchicalism. The two were also in agreement that the monastic ideals that inspired late medieval protest and reform movements were mistaken in both analysis of moral problems and estimation of human capacities. Their consequent rejection of asceticism and penitentialism as ways of life was a step toward positive reform of the world simply in removing a traditional alternative.[65] But the question remains how much, if anything, could concretely be done about the world besides the restoring of true doctrine within it.

Luther did not evolve anything that constituted a doctrine specifically of and for the world. He was more and less optimistic about the world than Calvin. Theoretically, total integration of the secular and spiritual was possible, just as the flesh could be spiritualized and just as sin was a matter of heart and mind as well as flesh. But the beneficent integration of the secular and the spiritual was highly unlikely: Luther left external things, as well as the defense of religious truths, in the hands of territorial rulers, with more resignation than hope. Being equally skeptical about the social behavior of man, a bad ruler was a necessary evil.

Luther also had a pragmatic skepticism about the moral effects of the Reformation itself, though no doubt of its inherent worth and possibly of its increasing worth.[66] It seems to be the internal peace of the individual believer for which he reserves his real hope, based upon awareness of the peace of conscience that justification implied and which, for him, was grounded in the overwhelming experience of the dawning of that peace in the *Thurmerlebnis*: that was a memory that could persist when the state of mind to which it had led did not. One could add that daily life in the world could be both comfortable and cheering for Luther, and a dimension of the differences between Luther and Calvin is that living in society *per se* was not a specifically delineated personal challenge for the one, as it was for the other.

The organization of church and state in Geneva, reflecting Calvin's legal and political abilities and the kind of thinking he enjoyed, reflects, from another perspective, a significant personal variation upon the possibility opened up in the Reformation period for the organization of temporal life in a way different from the medieval organization of life. Both Luther's and Calvin's conceptions of reorganization involved church and state with spiritual and temporal matters alike, at the same time clearly differentiating their functions and *raisons d'être* and separating them administratively. However, there is more of the temporal life and more for it formally incorporated into Calvin's polity for the church, from involvement of the councils in moral discipline by choice of the elders from their numbers, through the content and reach of education at the Genevan Academy. Its primary school served all of Geneva; the Academy itself, existing to train a ministry in and beyond Geneva, assimilated for its purposes the best of humanist education in undisguised form.

Calvin never thought the secular and spiritual could be one, but he continuously labored in and for the world. It was more exactly for God's glory, but the world could serve that positively. The distinctions in his organization of life were of basic importance, and his secularism was tantamount to a nonhierarchical dualism. In its Augustinian framework, it is akin to the nominalist emphasis on the sphere established by God's *potentia ordinata* in which the *viator* comes into his own.[67] It is not surprising that Gabriel Biel anticipated the idea of the calling; further, Biel's "own understanding of the indomitable and abiding power of sin [was] an important aspect of his democratization of the ideal of perfection."[68]

In Calvin, the idea of an active life in this world for God's purposes was both theoretically grounded and of the greatest personal importance. Against his own preferences, he accepted the facticity of his world, lived the life it seemed to dictate, and made it part of his theology. If the political theory and ethics in the *Institutes* are not always consistent or devoid of strain, their presence alone states, as does Calvin's church polity with more coherence and less strain, that we must think about the world and plan our lives in it—the implication of having a body.

The most significant personal realization of Calvin's secularism may be his use of rhetoric; his rhetoric also makes his theology an integral part of the intellectual and cultural world of the sixteenth century. It is of the greatest importance that it is rhetoric for a theology tempered by dualism. In this perspective, it is also, I think, a *modus vivendi*.

As we have seen, the rhetoric that Calvin consistently used was a kind of self-expression—the expression of a self whose mind worked very much the way rhetorical conventions did and whose polarized and discordant sense of reality could be mirrored in and empower those conventions. In expressing an internal conflict, Calvin may have been giving voice to something similar in others with similar psychic lives, and he may have been giving voice to an experience inherent in human nature in generally less extreme forms but with an unusual need for assertion in its particular cultural environment.

Rhetoric may be further integral in Calvin's mind in the perspective of a tradition that, I think, substantiates and defines more exactly his link to Saint Augustine—in this tradition, rhetoric had specific theological significance. Moreover, in the sixteenth century, rhetoric existed in a context that makes it intriguing as well as interesting to a historian. It existed in a world as conscious and self-conscious about language as, I think, only the last decade of the twentieth century has been: it was a world of discourse about the significance of discourse, one in which attention to discourse was a conceptual lingua franca.

Reformation scripturalism was part of this world; the fundamental importance of philological criticism links Renaissance humanism, Erasmian humanism, and Reformation theology. But the historical treatment of words (with which treatment the *Institutes* and other writings of Calvin's are replete) is by no means the whole of this world. Words have a history; especially in their deployment they have also a present, sensory reality. Attention to this aspect of language is fundamental to Augustine's conception of Christian rhetoric. In a sixteenth-century context it would have been both intensified and modulated. I think this aspect is the key to the personal and theological significance of rhetoric for Calvin, and I think its understanding is necessary in defining and tracking his historical success and importance.

Calvin's humanistic training and his life-long translating activity involved him directly with questions of language. He did not write about language formally and systematically, but frequently discussed aspects of it, used linguistic concepts in his theology, and commented upon Scripture from the viewpoint of mode of discourse.[69] I think it possible to establish in his thinking, not a single concept of language, but a coherent body of notions about it. It seems to me worthwhile to look further at his rhetoric— his rhetorical theology—in this light.

CALVIN AND LANGUAGE:
TOWARD ITS SIGNIFICANCE FOR HIM

Speech is at the center of the Christian economy.[70] "Word" in it has two meanings: Christ himself and Scripture. Scripture, as the revealed word of God, could be not only normative, but, in analogy to Christ the revealed Word, instrumental. John Major emphasized that we can have a truly direct experience of God (whose essence we cannot know) when we hear his Word, and Luther reinforced this idea for all the Reformers in his emphasis on the primacy of "listening" to the Word.[71] Subject to these influences, and to that of classical rhetoric, Calvin stated of the encounter between the human mind and Scripture that, "being persuaded of that which it cannot comprehend, it understands more by the certainty of persuasion than it would comprehend of any human object by exercise of its natural capacity."[72]

The concepts of faith as persuasion, of knowledge as efficacious truth, and of revelation as God's persuasive accommodation would also have been available in Augustine's writings.[73] There, they are part of a larger whole, which has been neglected in Calvin historiography. Marcia Colish has explicated the way in which Saint Augustine arrived at a conception of a specifically Christian rhetoric that would serve in God's redemptive plan.[74] Again in analogy to the Word Incarnate, the words of men could embody the truths of God, though insofar and only insofar as human eyes could see. This embodying of divine truths did not merely teach, but effectively demonstrated, the reconciliation of the human and the divine. Earthly, sensory words were fused with, informed by, and integrated with the spiritual. Augustine retrospectively considered of basic importance his realization that it is not thought, but words, which can ultimately link the believer with God. Thought fails and words succeed because God chose to reveal and link himself to us through the Word. We were created when God spoke; it was as the Word Incarnate that Christ reconciled God and man.[75] And Augustine described the assumption of human weakness by Christ, the Incarnation itself, as speech: as we were spoken by Christ, he may be spoken by us. We may approach God through speech, and through it, despite our weakness, be reconciled with him:

> Before you perceived God, you believed that thought could express God. Now you are beginning to perceive Him, and you think that you cannot express what you perceive. But having found that you cannot express what you perceive, will you be silent, will you not praise God? . . . All other things may be expressed in some way; He alone is ineffable, Who spoke and all things were made. He spoke and we were made; but we are unable to speak of Him. His Word by Whom we were spoken, is His Son. He was made weak, so that He might be spoken by us, despite our weakness.[76]

Augustine articulated this concept in works well know to Calvin.[77]

He also described personal experiences with words and analyzed their effects. In these analyses, it is clear that, through a perspective offered by classical rhetoric theory, he continued to understand the potential in human words, and valued them, as a uniting of something physical and sensible with the spiritual, a uniting that was not a juxtaposition or a clothing of the one with the other, but their integration. Hearing the sermons of Ambrose, bishop of Milan, was a crucial episode in his development as a Christian and Christian rhetorician: "At the same time with the words, which I loved, there came into my soul the very things that I wanted to refuse. Moreover, I could not separate the one from the other. And when I opened my heart to receive the eloquence of his speech, little by little the truth of what he said also entered.[78]

Augustine's epistemology relies upon the same consciousness of the physical aspect of language. The epistemology is linked with the need to express truths the believer knows (which are of the Word) in words:

> With the eye of the mind, therefore, we perceive in that eternal
> truth, from which all temporal things have been made, the form
> according to which we are, and by which we effect something
> either in ourselves or in bodies with a true and right reason. The
> true knowledge of things, thence conceived, we bear with us as
> a word, and beget by speaking from within; nor does it depart
> from us by being born. But in conversing with others we add
> the service of our voice or of some other bodily sign to the word
> that remains within, in order to produce in the mind of the
> listener, by a kind of sensible remembrance, something similar
> which does not depart from the mind of the speaker.[79]

I think Calvin came to share Augustine's perspective, and indeed was hungry for it. Always reticent about the personal role of the minister and theologian, he is more concerned to describe the improper use of rhetoric than its proper use. He rejects the use of empty, vain words without piety. Especially, we must shun those who pervert the Gospel to satisfy men's appetites, who use the Gospel to delight the spirit and surprise the imagination, who, "like serpents, please the ear but with a bastard language."[80] Yet (and he is quoting Augustine) eloquence could serve the Gospel as a servant his mistress.[81] It is significant that he considers those Sophists who misuse rhetoric to "touch neither heaven nor earth," and then he states, eloquently, that "that eloquence that is consonant with the spirit of God neither is filled with ostentation nor flies aloft in vain puffs, but is solid, filled with efficacy, and has more sincerity than elegance."[82]

In a related way, Augustine had been wary of the rhetoric of pagan poetry, which constructed a world of shadows and made "the fantastic morality of that world attractive and convincing."[83] The two were wary not of the physical but of a power misused. Therefore Augustine, like Calvin, insisted that the classical prescripts for eloquence be modified by the primacy of teaching and the willingness, for that purpose, to subordinate elegance to effectiveness.[84]

The physical, sensible properties of words were preeminent in consciousness for Calvin and Augustine. And I think that the concern they shared for the proper, positive, and effective involvement of the physical in their theology, a challenge presented by the very need to compose the theology, is the crucial link between them and identifies Calvin as part of a specifically christological tradition of rhetoric. The tradition may arise in self-consciousness about writing and consideration of writing in the perspective of the difference between redeemed and unredeemed nature. It seems to be made of writers who are more than usually preoccupied with the relation between spirit and flesh as a problem. Certainly Saint Paul was of it when he began his summation of Galatians by bidding his readers to "see with what large letters I am writing to you with my own hand."[85] And it seems to be an effective springboard to overcome doubts about the redeemability of the flesh. "For neither circumcision counts for anything, nor uncircumcision, but a new creation."[86]

The tradition that Augustine and Calvin shared was differentiated by its historical and personal contexts. The important moments for questions of language in the sixteenth century are nominalist philosophy and Renaissance humanism. These combined, most of all, to heighten consciousness of the sensory properties of language. At the same time, the restrictions which nominalist philosophy had placed on the reach of human knowledge and the relations between language and reality were accepted. Both sets of changes may have imparted more, rather than less, significance to the Augustinian tradition for Calvin.

Ockham encouraged the intensive study of language as part of a philosophy that proceeded from the limits of knowledge. He first defined the use of language negatively: it was language that did not posit and discuss essences, assigning different kinds of words to different ontological realms.[87] Language was to be dealt with logically and grammatically — and this method became more than linguistic analysis. The applicability and appropriateness of Ockham's method to every individual existent and problem renders it also a means of orientation, a unifier of experience that would otherwise be elusive. A very characteristic aspect of his own writings is the interweaving of strictly formal and strictly theological arguments that are treated in exactly the same way: How does this sentence work? In what sense are the terms of which it is composed used? What is their interrelation? Whatever substantive problems Ockham is concerned with, he is trying to resolve or prevent misunderstandings with attention to what one of his commentators has called the function of discourse.[88]

It has been suggested that his analysis of the diverse combinations in which different kinds of terms can be used "displays with the rest of his logic. . . . a sensitivity to the nuances of language which brought a new dimension to fourteenth-century philosophy."[89] And awareness of the mediating role of language in experience gave it "an active, independent power."[90]

There is evidence in Ockham's analyses of a latent awareness of the possibility that any or all of the logical and grammatical rules may be invalid and that our individual, atomistic existences may be entirely self-contained. This seems the case when he combines, with unusual frequency, jarringly unrelated and incongruous terms and descriptions to demonstrate or comment upon rules of analysis and inference. Like the reliability of our convenantal relationship with God (which is made of words),[91] it is understood that we can say no more than that clear, analytic thinking usually is reliable.

Language is human in origin. "A concept or mental impression signifies naturally whatever it does signify; a spoken or written term, on the other hand, does not signify anything except by free convention."[92] The most direct evidence of the human origins of language is the asymmetry that exists between terms and things and is the result of the changes conferred upon terms through usage (as well as of the existence of words that have a signifying function only through the terms they modify).[93] The philological studies that were so important in the Italian and French Renaissance (and biblical humanism, and Reformation scripturalism itself) may be tangible results of the significance assigned to language by nominalism—at least their emphases would have been reinforced by its work. It is basic to the historical consciousness of the Renaissance that words change in connotation; the language in which a past civilization expresses itself is the key to knowing that civilization.[94]

But nominalist philosophers did not give their attention only to language; they also focused it upon the material world, apprehended through direct experience and increasingly closely scrutinized. Both the nominalist attention and sensitivity to language and its focus upon this world may have come together to account for the peculiar attention in Renaissance rhetoric theory and literature to the physical, sensory qualities of words—called by James Winn "the Renaissance inclination to the ear."[95]

Renaissance rhetoricians maintained that their words could have an enormous impact in this world by virtue of their sensory qualities. Calls for the union of wisdom and eloquence stressed eloquence: this was the radical aspect for consciousness. As George Puttenham argued in the *Arte of English Poesie* in 1589, "the mind is not assailable unlesse it be by sensible approaches." He also described the working of an ideal rhetoric, and his specifications may bring instances of Calvin's prose to mind:

And our speech is made melodious or harmonicall, not onely by strayned tunes, as those of *Musick*, but also by choice of smoothe words: and thus, or thus, marshalling them in their comeliest construction and order, and as well by sometimes sparing, sometimes spending them more or lesse liberally, and carrying or transporting them farther off or neerer, setting them with sundry relations, and variable formes, in the ministery and vse of words, doe breede no little alteration in man.[96]

I think that Calvin was able to bring together the perspectives of the secular rhetorician and the theologian and to see with these a community in all linguistic expression. The effectiveness of a theologian's words, and of God's verbal accommodations, were, then, to be understood in the light of verbal discourse (and that means sixteenth-century ideas on language); conversely, the light shed by the Word upon speech to God's honor and reverence—the idea of redeemed speech in the tradition of Christian rhetoric—can be light for all words.

To Calvin, language had an independent existence so powerful that ignorance of it could result in deception or the prevailing of evil, while awareness of that existence could allow its enlistment in the service of the good. I think he was aware of (I use here Barbara Lewalski's formulation) the symbolic reach of language itself.[97] At the least, the psychological dimension of his rhetoric suggests an intuitive sense of it. However, there seems to be evidence that he was consciously aware of that symbolic dimension, approached discussion of it in the *Institutes*, and had it in mind a good part of the time. Further, there is some evidence that Lorenzo Valla's writings made an important contribution to his conception of language.

In his *Dialecticae disputationes*, Valla wrote of human language *per se* rather than of its literary uses or its use in Christian apologetics, and he wrote in formulations that would have had immediate personal interest to Calvin. They could and may have served as conceptual tools for the construction of a Christian rhetoric consonant with sixteenth-century intellectual suppositions and germane to Calvin's particular concern with the relation between mind and body.[98]

Valla gave attention to the relation between sound and meaning in human words. The relation that he describes is such that, precisely for its human limits, language could be analogically closer to the Incarnation than it was for Augustine. His description matches, in ideas and their formulation, a presentation in the *Institutes* of the most distinctive idea in Calvin's conception of sacramental signification: the idea of a nonverbal "exhibiting" or showing forth that both intensifies and clarifies the words of institution that accompany it.[99] Additionally, Valla's description would serve very well for a functional analysis of the most characteristic aspect of Calvin's own rhetoric: its evocative nature. Whether Calvin read the

Dialecticae we will probably never know, for he does not cite it.[100] However, positive appreciation of other writings of Valla's is recorded, most notably of the dialogue on free will. The appreciation is interestingly atypical among the many attributions of praise and blame in the *Institutes*. Neither black nor white, it may bespeak, in its relativity, an impression strong enough to have broken through some habitual and rigid disinclinations. In contrast to those who equate foreknowledge and causality, it seemed to Calvin "that Valla, a man not otherwise much versed in sacred matters, saw more clearly and wisely, for he showed this contention to be superfluous since both life and death are acts of God's will more than of his foreknowledge."[101]

Calvin had already cited the *De lingua latinae elegantia* in his Seneca commentary.[102] Valla was useful to him. We are at least confronting compatibility and commonality, and the commonality sheds light on the immediate rootedness found by the *Institutes* and may enhance our own reading of Calvin.

In a concentrated passage of the *Dialecticae*, the fundamental concepts of the continuing human creation and adaptation of language, the human transmission of meaning, and the association and nondifferentiation between human language and the speech of God are asserted. Valla's notion of "images of meanings" seems to me central and inherent in Calvin's discussion of sacramental signification, and I suggest it to be the core of his wider sense of language. The notion itself is not unique: it had been stated by earlier humanists.[103] However, it had been said of poetic language; here it is stated of all language. Valla maintains that the human voice

> is indeed natural, but its meaning descends from instruction; for men devised words which they might adjust to things known. Of whom Adam was the first, with God the creator, and they taught words with their meanings to posterity. As sounds are indeed from nature but words and meanings from a contriver, so the sounds lay hold of the ear, the meanings of the mind, the words of both. Afterwards letters are discovered as mute words or images of words, just as words themselves are as images of meanings which are now properly called names.[104]

The textual match in the *Institutes* presents sacramental signification as metonymic.[105] In the discussion, Calvin is very concerned to defend the agreement of his thinking with tradition (and with Augustine in particular). Nevertheless he is putting the term "metonymy" to his own uses; he also may be signifying to a knowledgeable audience, by use of a key term in rhetoric, an area of wider concern. Moreover, his argument is presented in graded and comparative reasoning. Like his evaluation of Valla, this is atypical, suggesting a philosophically compatible external influence.

With Augustine, Calvin wants to understand the bread and wine and the words of institution through their mode of signification. To Augustine, they function figuratively. Calvin refines this function further, calling it metonymy and likening it to that of the figures of speech used in Scripture when mysteries are under discussion. Two general points can be abstracted about metonymic signification. First, it is because of the "affinity which the things signified have with their symbols" that "the name of the thing was given to the symbol—figuratively, indeed—but not without a most fitting analogy."[106] Secondly, the figures could not be understood had not meaning been transferred to sign and the sign specifically attached to thing signified: "You could not otherwise understand [such expressions] unless you were to take them as spoken with meaning transferred. Not only is the name transferred from something higher to something lower, but, on the other hand, the name of the visible sign is also given to the thing signified."[107] Thus the symbols are dependent upon convention in a thoroughgoing way; yet their choice has reason behind it. Metonymic analogy is no mere "bare and empty token [of something higher] but also truly exhibits it."[108] The affinity that renders a symbol effective is the verisimilitude that can elicit consent; a symbol becomes referential with that consent. In terms of particular importance to himself, Calvin differentiates symbol from thing signified "in that the latter is spiritual and heavenly, while the former is physical and visible" (quod haec spiritualis est et caelestis, illud corporeum et visibile).

While Calvin can elsewhere say, in anger at quibblers, that Christ's words are not to be tested by grammar,[109] it is exactly "the common rule of words," as they are understood in humanistic rhetoric, with which he analyzes both the elements and the words of institution. Humanly devised symbols (humanitus excogitata symbola) in metonymy differ in function from the symbolic mode employed in revelation by degree rather than in nature. Though human symbols often falsely represent their objects, they "are still sometimes graced with the titles of those things. Similarly, with much greater reason, those things ordained by God borrow the names of those things of which they always bear a definite and not misleading signification, and have the reality joined with them. So great, therefore, is their similarity and closeness that transition from one to the other is easy."[110] It seems also noteworthy that Calvin does not specify the ways in which a fitting analogy may be achieved: he seems to be leaving doors open. The sacraments are distinct from each other; the scriptural examples which he offers represent a part of that which they signify or an intangible quality of it; the structure of an action also may function symbolically. It is "in this metonymy [that] they have a certain common ground with one another.[111]

It seems to be the case that a unified conception of language, and one similar to Valla's in important ways, is a functional part of Calvin's theology, and I think we shall be able to follow it also in his writing. To an expositor of Calvin's doctrine of the sacraments, Ronald Wallace, "there is no doubt that [he] sees an analogy which at least serves to regulate his thinking on this mystery of sacramental union, in the mystery of the union between God and man in Jesus Christ."[112] And Wallace observes that "in spite of his refusal to admit sacramental analogies from nature, Calvin does hazard very tentatively one illustration from nature to try to illuminate the subject [of the union of the divine and human natures in Christ]"—the analogy, for the *communicatio idiomatum*, of the real union and yet distinct individual existence of body and soul in man.[113] Indeed, I think one cannot escape the unity in Calvin's analytic standpoint—and that includes his point of departure in understanding signification—and his basic apprehension of reality, and it is a unity that might best be defined by the continuum of preoccupation with the relation between the physical and the spiritual.

Calvin probably did not come to the rhetorical use of language without ambivalence. The physical aspect of words, like anything physical, was inherently problematic for him. Rhetorical persuasion was also a matter of arousing emotions, an equally difficult area. He consistently prefers prose to poetry, which he distrusts, and in his rare positive statements about purely aesthetic power, he seems to express, equally, fear: "And actually we know by experience that [music] has a secret power, almost unbelievable, to move morals one way or another."[114] I think, however, that the positive attractions in rhetoric for Calvin included its potential usefulness in regard to the very difficulties that the emotional and the physical presented to him. First, the self-conscious and deliberative use of language was a controlled and controllable way of dealing with the experiential world and feeling. It stabilized, delineated, delimited, and defined. Second, eloquence corresponded directly and acceptably to that aspect of his Lutheran heritage with which he had the most difficulty: the idea that man was a totality, that the physical could be spiritualized and the spiritual was involved in sin. In his use of rhetoric, Calvin was working against doubts and in an important way resolving the doubts head on. He was giving himself the experience of the physical become spiritualized at his own initiative. Theology, philosophy, and psychological want come together in his rhetoric.

RHETORIC IN A
CHANGED HISTORICAL CONTEXT

In the late Italian Renaissance, commitment to the use of rhetoric beyond the strictly defined field of literature became questionable, and rhetoric receded from its position in the forefront of culture. The repudiation was in great part based on the peculiar nature of Renaissance rhetoric, as distinct from the classical rhetoric of which it was considered to be a revival.

The reason generally given for the debate and repudiation was fear of the demagogic power of language. No one had ever doubted that people were fickle and capable of evil as well as good, but it was now felt that persuasion to evil rather than good was more likely to happen. Language, which had been seen as a natural instrument for moral persuasion, came to be viewed as both deceptive and compatible with self-deception—a demagogue might not be aware of what he really intended. This idea is present in classical theory of rhetoric: the Roman historians had emphasized the disparity "between their protagonists' spoken intentions and the unwilled results."[115] Indeed, Struever points to an inherent skepticism in the linguistic self-consciousness of the rhetorician, which implied the capacity always to draw opposite conclusions.[116]

It seems unlikely, however, that the late Renaissance fear of rhetoric was a fear of radical self-deception. For the humanist rhetoricians, danger was something 'out there,' and, as such, was a problem with which rhetoric was considered capable of dealing. If eloquence was "the language of wise men in a world which disbelieves in wisdom,"[117] the wise men had a lot to teach through rhetoric, and they believed they could count on their wisdom. They also believed that any intellectual power presupposed an understanding and control of language.[118] They reiterated the idea common from Gorgias onward (and a source of confidence in the effectiveness of rhetoric) that the structure of language corresponded to the structure of the human mind—the correspondence had been extended by Cicero to include the structure of the cosmos.[119]

The optimism of the rhetoricians is reflected in their belief that the use of dialogue in their historiography was "a means of moral perfection." The historian could demonstrate through it that there is more than one side to most questions, that disparities between intention and words are common, that deceptive rationalizations can be seen to be such, and that intention is quite accessible. Integral to Renaissance rhetoric was the hermeneutical principle that "there is a coherence and integrity about the intention, about the experience of either sacred or secular author behind the literary work, which goes beyond, which transcends, literal or conventional meaning" such that one could grasp "an integral, concrete experience in the past." The historian analyzed the language of his texts to determine "the relation between expression and intention."[120]

Far more than fear of deceit, the repudiation of rhetoric was probably the result of the collapse of two ideals that the humanists had vested in rhetoric, significantly differentiating it from its classical predecessor. I have referred to the rhetoricians' belief in the autonomy of beauty as a good, indeed as the highest good. The belief was an intoxication. It also didn't exactly match theory. In theory, eloquence was neutral: wisdom imparted the good, and eloquence served it as a tool of persuasion. The Renaissance humanists removed the ancient distinction between form and substance[121] and construed beautiful form as morally good, a natural ally of wisdom and its equivalent. In fact, in the early Renaissance, the humanists "came to regard *only* the beautiful as useful."[122] The union of wisdom and eloquence tended to turn into an ends-means relationship in which eloquence was seen as "the faculty for whose perfection knowledge of all, even the greatest things, both divine and human, is necessary."[123] The humanists "came close to saying that the thought unexpressed is not worth having."[124] What they frequently did say was that knowledge was a spark brought to visibility and efficacy by eloquence; they use the vocabulary of the mystics here, and they echo the language of the Gospel miracles when they claim that eloquence could make "the transitory seem eternal, the absent present; it causes the dead to seem alive, the mute to speak, and finally the blind to see."[125]

Another intoxication ingrained in Renaissance rhetoric, and, like physical beauty, having the character of a happy discovery was with the nonintellectual parts of the human soul—the will and the passions. These seem, when the rhetoricians talk of appealing to them, quite different and disjoint from their equivalents in Scripture. From Petrarch onward, striving after the truth seemed more moral than truth attained. And a complexity and richness increased by constant change made the human soul (individual to an extreme) a subject of intense interest. Language could be endlessly creative, and that it was used in and for a world in constant flux, escaping objective comprehension, was not a problem but an opportunity to exploit.[126] The pluralism in Renaissance historical thought arose not from skepticism but from love of the richness of life and of individualism. The "permanent subjunctive mental mode" of the rhetoricians, the apprehension of the world "as mediated by expressions of thinking, feeling, wishing, willing,"[127] evoked positive pleasure, aesthetic in nature.

As the intoxication grew, the claims for rhetoric became even more extravagant. The Gospel miracles involved individuals and nature; Renaissance rhetoric included cities. Rhetoric is a social phenomenon, and "for the humanists, it is literature, not communal politics, which furnishes the primary model for freedom...creating the public space in which the conventions of political life rule."[128] Vives maintained that language is more important for society than justice itself.[129] From the German barbarians, who had no faith in public discourse, one could only expect deceit.[130]

The social nature of rhetoric, complemented by an institutionalized conviviality in Renaissance culture, is related to a basic optimism that comprises consciousness of the existence of shadow-sides in life. This optimism seems both a cause and an effect of the Renaissance inclination to monism. Rhetoricians such as Poggio could manifest cynicism and deep despair. But mood swings were more characteristic of the Renaissance, and they seem very particular sorts of mood swings. They were such that the humanists could see negative facts (for example, human limitations) and, indeed, unhappy moods, as signs of the very richness and complexity of the universe, upon which the highest goods—and the very highest was art—depended. While nominalist thinkers proceeded from a sense of the limits of knowledge, the humanists proceeded from a sense of the narrowness of intellectualism in the context of the felicitous discovery of other things besides the intellect. In humanist theory of rhetoric, richness (*facundia*) was that flexibility of form that corresponded to the infinite variety and potential in human nature to which rhetoric appealed.[131]

If will and emotion set limits to reason, they constituted a new interest for man. They also did not displace reason but redefined its context: nature and the social, civic order embodied discernible form in interesting, appealing, and challenging ways. This positive and aesthetic evaluation of complexity is as far from the principle of economy in Ockham as it is from the spirit of asceticism in Calvin. One could correlate *facundia* with that paradigmatic Renaissance idea, Melancholia, the foundation of creative genius.

It was the northerner and Lutheran Dürer, also part of the Melancholia tradition, who gave the Renaissance idea of genius the form it was to have in Mannerist art theory: the power of the artist derived ultimately from divine inspiration.[132] In contrast, a sense of power, in a world not alien to the self, predominates in the writings of Italian humanists. Their Pelagian emphasis on the importance of the will is a constant, and, in the long run, "the Italian Renaissance failed to complete its conviction of man's intellectual limitations which would lead thoroughly to grace and sense of moral impotence."[133] It is as if Ockham were Kant to a Renaissance Hegel.

Among the different facets of the human soul, the rhetoricians gave preponderance to the will, and rhetoric was important insofar as it moved the will to action through eloquence.[134] The predicted results of the actions expressed the extent to which it was believed that the will could be moved.

But then the world started looking as if it were indifferent to either the efforts of the human will or the effects of beauty. Not only unresponsive, the world in the late Renaissance seemed to be increasingly harsh and to be actually disintegrating. The result was a sense of both human impotence and the impotence of words (the opposites of which had been repeatedly identified), manifested in the repudiation of rhetoric. Self-doubts were probably the strongest accusers of the error of the rhetoricians' claims. The extremity of the claims, which had overridden awareness of the shadow-sides of language and human nature, was now duplicated in reverse. If the earlier rhetoricians had accepted the logical possibility of total anarchy and chaos, as their rejection of an objective cosmic order for a belief in a world of variety and change implied,[135] they never really believed it would happen. With the Italian invasions from 1494 onward, against the background of longstanding internal conflict, rhetoricians now believed that nothing but that could happen. For indeed it was happening, and there was nothing in humanist culture that seemed able to cope with this reality.

The union of wisdom and eloquence had not been based on either a cosmic or a religious necessity, and these were the spheres to which men now turned. As we have seen, Bouwsma suggests that "the later Renaissance seems to have been seeking to supply a defect in the culture of the earlier Renaissance."[136] The most immediate and widespread reaction was a replacement of the ideal of freedom by the ideal of order: "Society became more rigidly stratified; governments more authoritarian."[137] A resurgent papacy and now princes seemed to be reimposing medieval hierarchicalism. Divisions within society became stronger: "intellectuals became contemptuous of the masses."[138] In short, a profound conservatism, which Hay and Bouwsma both suggest to be the note of similarity necessary for the communication of the Italian Renaissance to northern Europe.[139]

The two most striking changes in the culture of the late Italian Renaissance were the emergence of Mannerist art and the repudiation of rhetoric. The pejorative connotations in the name "Mannerism" persist among historians in the idea that it is a striving for effect through "a closed list of arguments and figures."[140] It seems more valid to see Italian Mannerism as a virtuosity of despair. The purpose (and value) of art is now intellectual. Positively, it expresses what it construes as the real, not the apparent, nature of reality; negatively, it expresses a loss of faith in appearance—in physical beauty as an autonomous good and thus a natural ally of wisdom. Form and meaning are disjunct in Mannerist art because reality is disjunct. Mannerism and the humanists' questioning and repudiation of rhetoric are grounded in the same world view.

In the late Italian Renaissance, eloquence came to be seen as merely the embellishment of truth. Form and content were separate.[141] They were separate, as distinct from united, because they had earlier been seen as one. From an overshooting of the mark, as measured by classical rhetoric theory, there is now its polar opposite. The movement to the opposite extreme is manifested in qualities closely akin to those that link Calvin and Mannerism. First, the Florentine Platonists consciously turned from rhetoric to philosophy. It was philosophy both abstract and esoteric — the opposite of empirical. More broadly, man was increasingly seen, "once again, as essentially an intellectual being."[142] The rejection of the ideal of individualism was matched by a revival of the old view of the cosmos as an organized and normative unity: there was a movement toward the ideal of the One, of simplicity instead of complexity.[143] Belief in a properly ordered hierarchy was extended to man: the intellect, high and separate, ruled over the other human faculties. Optimistically believing that "to know good is to do good," the humanists were actually substituting a cosmic vision for an early Renaissance anthropology.[144] Calvin knew better about the relative power of the intellect and the nature of the cosmos, but he could sympathize with (and reflect) the desire for order and the intellectualism itself, as well as the revival of the contemplative ideal and the very strong emphasis, now, on the immortality of the soul, the vileness of the body, and the problem of the passions.[145] The word view was highly dualistic.

As logical as the humanists' repudiation of rhetoric may seem, the changed world in which it occurred is, from a different perspective, an ideal foil for rhetoric. Viewed as expression rather than implement, the polarity in so much of rhetoric — the use of antitheses, the emphasis on extremes, the images of contrasts, the parallel constructions — mirrors the nature of the clashing historical world in abstraction. In this sense, rhetoric can be, in itself, a supplementary comment upon reality. It is extremely likely that Calvin's rhetoric at least served just this purpose in his age of iron, and it was parallel to the way in which rhetoric was self-expression for him. Obsessively preoccupied with clashing antitheses, he uses them positively and artfully; the basic antitheses of heavenly and earthly and of mind and body are formulated in the abundant imagery he bases upon the contrasts of light and dark and life and death.

Always guarded in his use of rhetorical elegance, Calvin was not subject to the sudden disillusion with language that the humanists suffered. Indeed he had no reason to single out and condemn rhetorical language as dangerous: it was being human that was dangerous. Language, like the world, toward which he had never had illusions, could be regarded from the viewpoint of its potential use despite its ambivalent nature.

A more circumscribed and complementary response to such a world is contained in the history of the French Académie de Poésie et de Musique, founded in 1570. The French musical humanists proclaimed a highly self-conscious synthesis of sound and spirit with deliberate intention to soothe the chaos of the world around them, exploding and reeling in the Wars of Religion. Above all, it was the intention of Baïf, the founder of the academy, to soothe the agony of Europe's divided soul.[146] Similarly, Le Jeune compared his efforts in music, though admittedly lesser, with the pacification of France under Henri IV: "I have thought to be in fashion, at a time when so many discords are accorded, in giving Frenchmen something to unite both tones and thoughts, voices as well as hearts," and, toward this end, he now tempers his earlier lightness in music "with serious themes, tones, and measures."[147] With caution as well as awareness that they were strong competition, the psalms of the Huguenots were treated sympathetically in the Académie: hope for the religious reunion of European Christendom continued and a means might be at hand.[148]

Interest in the doctrine of the effects of the arts, always of high importance to musical theorists in the Renaissance period, was widespread in France.[149] Perhaps the doctrine was more pervasive here than in Italy because the French political environment could be seen to be calling for it, and there was in it an ear that would listen. Ronsard explained to Henri III that his reactions to pictures, as to sound, were made predictable by their creators. If the king were to hear "a well-tuned lute, the gentle harmony and sweet symphony of the strings artfully touched by a learned hand" would move him "and gently agitate the sense of hearing, so that [he would be] quite rejoiced. On the contrary, [if he were to] hear an ass braying, or a great noise of bells or of a torrent, this confusion, vehemence, and violence, which are not the friends of nature," would annoy and displease him.[150] Although a prescription for harmony, the possibility of discord is constant, and here the unpleasantness of discord is expressed in terms of sheer physicality. Ronsard's and Baïf's differences seem internecine. The French Académie cultivated its *pia filosofia* in an enclavelike atmosphere, and its work seems to constitute an ongoing meditation upon the world without.[151] And the theme of the divided soul of Europe suggests a literal dimension in the reading of Calvinist theology in the sixteenth century.

Calvin placed rhetoric in a Reformation context: a framework of inner rather than outer change. The Renaissance rhetoricians had understood the significance of language in terms of power: we shape our world through words. The thrust of humanistic rhetoric was to refer to environment the claim originally made by Gorgias that persuasive language could change lives. The Reformation also had implications for changing life. Our experience, and thus our lives in the reality of the world, could be different: this is the change Ozment calls "turning."

The inwardness of the Reformation has roots in Ockham's perception of the experiential and ultimately subjective nature of knowledge. Calvin is directly in this tradition, and he shared especially with nominalist thought the sense of human limits that followed from their investigation of the limits of knowledge. Calvin's sense of human limits is the same as his sense of unfreedom. It is as if he abstracted the core of nominalism and drew his own relentless conclusions—a movement beyond nominalist resignation, one logical and quite fruitful conclusion, to something different but equally consistent. His rhetoric may be the more significant for this consistency.

Nominalism, important for the development of empirical science, was anything but positivistic. A class of universals does not exist; a transcendent world certainly does. Yet it is the central fact about the human condition, and its tragedy, that we cannot know God: it is man's epistemological limitations that reveal his created condition.[152] Accordingly, nominalist thinkers confined themselves to the phenomenal, to one side of a dualistic world—as dualistic as that of their contemporaries, the late medieval mystics, who strove to leave behind, in their union with God, the world of the body.

To the Franciscan Ockham, in all likelihood, renunciation of mystical transcendence was supported by more than logic—it would have been supported by an appreciation of and sensibility to the natural world as evidence of God's work and glory.[153] And we have seen that this is a sensibility that links nominalism and Renaissance thought. The strain of Pelagianism in nominalism is another link with Renaissance humanism. But it is possible that the nominalists had a particularly strong psychological need to affirm power in light of their radical confrontation with limits. This possibility is further suggested by the contradictions that the affirmation of power can produce in their writings. For Biel, the power of sin was "indomitable and abiding," and he is so extreme concerning transcendence as to approach the idea of the extra-Calvinisticum. However, he emphasized equally the significance of Christ's life on earth and the imitation of Christ.[154]

Ockham and his followers may represent a humanistic viewpoint, but it is one that stands in significant contrast to Italian humanism. Ockham seems to find it important to be human, with awareness that freedom of the will does not mean power in God's eyes, with awareness that freedom may mean doing one's best as a necessary part of a salvation finally dependent upon grace. His conception of freedom also seems to imply freedom to behave responsibly in this temporal world and thereby dignify human life: he cites several times Aristotle's rejection of determinism on the grounds that we would, if denied choice and freedom, "deliberate and take trouble in vain"—Ockham wants to preserve that deliberation.[155] The dignity of man for Ockham seems not to be measured by man's power, achievements, or potential, any more than the work of the human mind results in certainties.

Ockham built the walls around the sphere to which human decisions and action were confined so strongly, and turned attention within so resolutely, that he may sometimes have lost consciousness of them: his self-confidence and manifest enjoyment in his method can suggest that. However, most typical of his intent sequestering of focus upon the rather frail lines of analytic contact that are possible between mind and outer reality is a wary equanimity not unlike that of Montaigne. They, and Calvin, are linked by the sound of distance and sense of ontological separation of subject from object. Calvinist theology and Ockhamist ideas, those ideas that are further developed in the sense of the radical precariousness of existence in late nominalism, are still more closely and specifically linked.

I have suggested that the importance of the problem of self-knowledge in Luther and Calvin could be explained by the unusually strong sense of sin in each, strong enough to overcome the usual defenses against awareness of it and enable them to realize, with Saint Paul, that what has been called our subconscious leads a life of its own. We cannot control it; we cannot even know it. Such a sense of separation and alienation within the self may be a background necessary to any new stage in awareness of the limits of knowledge. I have also suggested that Luther and Calvin might not have arrived at awareness of the centrality of the problem of self-knowledge had Ockham not had an intuitive sense of it. And Ockham may have been stimulated by a similar apprehension of the unconscious as radical separateness. Doubts about knowledge, and thus awareness of human limitations, would thereby have preceded thinking about God's absolute power. The yearning for a transcendent, nondivided God that one can see in late medieval thought may be in considerable part a projected response to a sense of inner split.

Both Ockham and Calvin could also be said to have lived a life of words. It may be the fundamental sense of disjunction that they shared that enabled Calvin, in the sixteenth century, to point to the significance of language in a wider and more systematic context than many of his contemporaries; it was also a context that corresponded strikingly to its external environment, as an earlier set of ideas and attitudes no longer did.

CALVIN AND RENAISSANCE LITERATURE

Literature, in Renaissance culture, gave particular attention to areas of dualistic conflict and to ways in which it could purposefully serve those areas. Literature was less and more radical in regard to the questioning of medieval values and assumptions than were other cultural areas. Medieval poets (such as Langland) had considered the resolution of conflict between the spiritual and secular in ways other than its purported ordering in the hierarchical thought and culture of their world. Renaissance poets could make a tacit problem in medieval poetry overt without being subversive; they could also be antimedieval by being more openly dualistic.[156]

From Dante onward, didactic literary theory focused upon what Robert Montgomery has called integrated affect.[157] The physical was a potential ally as well as problem. Theory argued for, and poets demonstrated, the use of sensory images to move an audience to moral truths. Carefully chosen images would also serve to prevent an audience from being led astray by its own imagination and the responses of its will. Hence the "visible speech" of Dante, his empathetic identification with the reader such that he is both pilgrim and spectator, his frequent shifts of perspective for the viewing of images, and the whole of what Montgomery calls "the persistent materiality of the *Commedia*" enlist the human sensibilities toward the end, not of learning the nature of divine truth, but of envisioning and thus passionately craving salvation.[158]

Italian epic poetry grappled with the conflict of spiritual and earthly. Anxiety and moral concern with the seductive power of words capable of deceiving speaker as well as listener, writer as well as reader, is often overt and deep in Renaissance literature — and expressed in equally forceful poetic language.[159] In contrast to literature and literary theory, it was a tenet of Renaissance Platonism that the potential equivalence of earthly and spiritual life permitted (and man was free to choose) total intellectual transcendence.[160] Both the unquestioned existence and unambivalent desirability of such a choice would have deprived Renaissance poetry of a great deal of its subject matter. It is an interesting commonplace in Renaissance literature to explain, and thus disclaim, the use of the concrete, vivid images of poetry, rather than philosophic discourse, as an accommodation to that human dullness that will respond only to the prodding of the senses — Spenser's preface to the *Faerie Queene* makes such an accommodation "for the use of these dayes."[161] However, the disclaimers are belied by a commitment to the poetic imagination evident in the poetry they preface, and sometimes the commitment is overt. Sidney attributes to the poet "a perfect picture," for he "yieldeth to the powers of the mind an image of that whereof the philosopher bestoweth but a wordish description, which doth neither strike, pierce nor possess the sight of the soul so much as that other doth."[162]

The formal structure of Calvin's rhetoric creates an independent and supplemental presence with, and in relation to, ideas. Calvin, like all the Reformers, scorned and inveighed against the images of the idolators. It seems quite possible that the Reformation strategy of accusing the Roman church of idolatry affected him, in turn, by requiring, and eliciting, a radically nonmimetic, nonpictorial mode of representation for religious truths: this would be another instance of the mutual reinforcement of external exigency and strong personal inclination.

It has been cogently argued by Barbara Lewalski that "Protestant poetics" was a decisive force for the evolution of seventeenth-century English poetry. It consisted in a trained sensitivity to Scripture as a text accessible through, and only through, analysis of its figurative, symbolic language, and in the expression of the Protestant sensibility, the inner life of the individual believer before God, the life described and analyzed normatively by Luther and Calvin.[163] It is a poetics to be firmly distinguished from allegory and from moralism.[164] The perception of "the symbolic dimension of the literal text" of Scripture toward which the Reformers seem to Lewalski to be groping became explicit in William Whitaker, who appealed, in her summation (of which I have availed myself above), "to the symbolic reach of language itself" when he stated, of Galatians 4:22–31:

> The sense, therefore, of that scripture is one only, namely the literal or grammatical. However the whole entire sense is not in the words taken strictly, but part in the type, part in the transaction itself. In either of these considered separately and by itself, part only of the meaning is contained; and by both taken together the full and perfect meaning is completed. . . . When we proceed from the sign to the thing signified, we bring no new sense, but only bring out into the light what was before concealed in the sign. . . . For although this sense be spiritual, yet it is not a different one, but really literal; since the letter itself affords it to us in the way of similitude or argument. . . . By expounding a similitude, we compare the sign with the thing signified, and so bring out the true and entire sense of the words.[165]

I have hypothesized that Calvin, too, extended his understanding of sacramental signification and scriptural language to all language.[166] I find a realization of the poetics derivable from that understanding in Calvin's own writings, and it is somewhat intriguing that this writing shares some highly particular stylistic marks with the poetry that, with Lewalski's work, is now demonstrably indebted to his and Luther's biblical hermeneutics. Students of George Herbert's prominently evocative poetry have drawn attention to his use of different modes of voice to convey different aspects of the same idea, and abrupt shifts in rhythm, or sudden dissonances, to stress the sheer importance of an idea or action.[167] These are especially characteristic occurrences in Calvin's writing, and such stylistic echoes cause one to wonder whether his influence upon literature may have been more direct than it has been taken to be—but it is equally plausible that these parallels are independent and spontaneous, and, as such, further define a community of which they are evidence. The very marked continuum in the heterogeneous and variously applied minds that form the community seems to be an intuitive sense, or a quiet discovery, of language as something that can be made part of one's intellectual labors.

Renaissance literature is often an emphatic statement of awareness that language mediates our experience. The point can be made by stressing the "unnatural" quality of literary language: Richard Lanham has pointed out that Rabelais, like Spenser, uses "the arcane vocabulary and repetitive syntax of incantation" toward this end.[168] Lanham has also posited for Renaissance literature a hypothesis similar to the one I am offering for Calvin's writing—that language served for many a medicinal, therapeutic purpose. Defending the commonplace Renaissance ideal of the union of wisdom and eloquence, Castiglione's Ludovico uses an analogy of uncommon force: "for to separate thoughts from words is to separate soul from body."[169] Lanham opposes to such instances of rhetorical style the serious style, which he sees as its intellectualist and introverted antithesis. Yet Calvin was an introvert who believed in the positive use of language: in the context of an extreme mind/body split, the practice of rhetoric may have been for him less easy, more deliberate, and more radical in its effect. For the sense of conflict, of unease if not pain, that rhetoric could mirror for him was a problem that was simultaneously resolved in the language in which it was expressed.

From its beginnings, the claim was made, in theory of rhetoric, that the structure of language correponded to the structure of the human mind, and therein lay its effectiveness in persuasion. However, it is striking that the specifications of the correspondence were never entirely agreed upon and often showed remarkable and elaborate arbitrariness: as it has been said in regard to the parallel theory in music of the correspondence of sound and mood, "one man's sober Dorian might be another's passionate Phrygian."[170] Yet there is a common intuition in all the claims: music or speech were being understood as expressions of something innately human that involved the way the mind worked as much as what it thought or how if felt.

All of the conventions and variants of the rhetorical style that Calvin consistently used, and that corresponded so closely to his psychological make-up, were used (along with different styles) by other Renaissance writers. But I have suggested that a psychologically engendered dualism in Calvin was a normal part of human nature, writ large. An intuitive sense of this part is probably inherent in the continuum in rhetoric of antithetical contrasts in structure, figures, and conventions. It would have been hard for the humanists to acknowledge such a part in light of the Renaissance rejection of medievalism. Calvin's sense of an antithetical aspect to reality, or, at least, to psychic reality, was sufficiently strong that he could not deny it. So his agreement with the humanists that the medieval antithesis of Jerusalem and Athens was to be rejected stopped short of their rejection of the medieval opposition of physical and spiritual: there may have been something in that opposition relevant to life even in Athens.[171]

Calvin was able to disagree effectively with Renaissance intellectual assumptions because he shared and reflected so strikingly its cultural assumptions. I am also suggesting that he may have realized just these cultural assumptions more fully than many others in the Renaissance, for reasons related to the disagreement. Literary historians have stressed the intuition in Renaissance rhetoric of the crucial relation between the sensory properties and intellectual content of literary language. Not just juxtaposed and complementary to the intellective, the sensory has semantic function itself. W. K. Wimsatt has suggested that language can be iconic, and his seminal concept of the verbal icon seems precisely applicable to Calvin's theological rhetoric.

The wonderful, artful, and highly deliberate variation in rhythm in Calvin's rhetoric is a form of orchestration. It is identical in its effect to that of enjambment in English poetry, to what Milton characterized as "the sense variously drawn out" in his "variety of pauses."[172] Both Wimsatt and John Hollander point also to Milton's associations of sound in his rhymed verse which bring, indeed force together, and thereby comment nondiscursively upon their relations, likes and contrasts in things that are otherwise discussed in the lines.[173] This phenomenon, too, occurs in Calvin's prose. While such associations of sound are most conspicuously operative in his French writings, they are scarcely less important in his Latin. A brief but now closer look at two examples far apart in the *Institutes*, each of typical rhetorical richness, should suffice. Speaking about God, Calvin writes "eius gloriam *mens nostra pro sua crassitie / concipere non poterat.*"[174] The two groups of words that I have separated and italicized juxtapose by sound an actually violent contrast, and thereby make it more violent: that of something that we desperately need to do, but cannot, and the core of that in us which causes our disability. For the emphatic association — and segregation — of like things through pure sound, we can look at the sequence "mortis aeternae maledictioni obnoxium, exclusum ab omni spe salutis."[175] The elaborate alliteration in each of the clauses is as parallel as their sense, and the parallels are made even more emphatic by the device of chiasmus: in fact, there is a cross-over not just in structure but also in the relative weightings of the *m* sounds and the *s* sounds.

Both the rhythmic and sonorous patterns in Calvin's prose constitute sensory manipulation for intellectual purposes. A related and highly effective technique is his use of pure prose poetry to orchestrate shifts in mood. Sometimes it seems both calculated and spontaneous. In preference to the analysis at length of certain doctrines, he will, rather, convey the mystery surrounding them and the awe that he feels before that mystery. And here his rhetoric seems certainly the equivalent of an independent religious statement. His discussion of the resurrection of the dead follows a summation of the doctrine of predestination and the objections that have been offered to the doctrine. The summation is throughout in his capable, confident, and adamant voice. His concluding position is to "concede to them [that God hates nothing he has made], yet what I teach stands firm: that the reprobate are hateful to God and with very good reason. For, deprived of his Spirit, they can bring forth nothing but reason for cursing."[176] Then, Calvin defers to Scripture to begin the first section on the final resurrection, constructing from scriptural passages an invocation of the risen Christ and an evocation of the joy of the fulfillment of faith: "Christ the Sun of Righteousness [Mal. 4:2] shining through the gospel and having overcome death, has, as Paul testifies, brought us the light of life [2 Tim. 1:10]. Hence we likewise by believing pass out of death into life [John 5:24], being no more strangers and sojourners, but fellow citizens of the saints and of the household of God [Eph. 2:19], who made us sit with his only begotten Son in heavenly places [Eph. 2:6], that we may lack nothing for full happiness."[177]

Then, in order that we do not despair under the burden of the cross, Calvin reminds us that we must cling to what is known concerning the nature of hope. And he explicates its nature through Paul, proceeding very gently and deliberately, offering his own awareness of its difficulty whence arises "the fact that faith is so rare in this world: nothing is harder for our slowness than to climb over innumerable obstacles in 'pressing on toward the goal of the upward call.'" And the section ends with prose poetry as emphatically such as that at its beginning, but now in Calvin's words: "Finally, above and below us, before us and behind, violent temptations besiege us, which our minds would be quite unable to sustain were they not freed of earthly things and bound to the heavenly life, so far away as it appears."[178]

The discussion of the final resurrection that follows proceeds despite what Calvin sees as human inclination not to believe it. "Even though there was no excuse for this point of view, we are nevertheless reminded by it that it is something too hard for men's minds to apprehend."[179] A little later in the same section: "I am only touching upon what could be treated more fully." He does, of course, say more; he has already cited and now gives further evidence for the helps that Scripture provides for our difficulties with the idea—the parallel of Christ's resurrection and testimony of the omnipotence of God. However, nothing is more effective than the atmosphere he has created in which to read this evidence—and which seems also a self-directed psychological preparation for a doctrine that is personally of an especially problematic nature for him.

I think that Calvin's unconscious response to the monism in Renaissance thought and Lutheran theology was disbelief, disagreement, and resistance. But he also was a student and writer. What he learned from Luther affected him, and his expression in words of a faith that was, to a considerable extent, learned, further affected him. The formal beauty of his rhetoric is often a spontaneous expression of both spiritual involvement and joy, at the same time that it can express tension, fear, and guardedness. The same is true of his descriptive and evocative vocabulary. The physical qualities and intellectual content of his theological rhetoric can each be cause and effect to the other. The physical and spiritual could not be one, but, in language, they could be *at* one.

Wimsatt frequently speaks of the "tensile" nature of iconic language, in its twofold and simultaneous existence as physical object and as intellectual referent to something other than this physical being.[180] He also stresses the binding effect of poetic language and notes that, as in rhyme, "where there is need for binding there must be some difference or separation between the things to be bound."[181] Indeed, "iconicity enforces disparity."[182] In alliteration, much more in the formal structures of his sentences and groups of sentences, and very much in his use of the parallelisms of isocolon, Calvin's writing is a binding of opposites, the emphatic quality of its binding nature serving to underline the distance (and it is a distance of polarities) between the things that it binds. The strings of "if . . . then" clauses to which I have referred do not merely reflect Calvin's *a priori* logic; they present an experience of inevitable, relentlessly repeated discordance; the hypnotic sense of measure they produce is not merely a response of control, but suggests an edge of numb resignation.

These clauses are also a majestic procession of sound and ideas. The rhetoric that was such a natural medium for Calvin from a psychological viewpoint, and which he could thereby elaborate so adeptly, exemplifies eminently the "interrelational density of words" that Wimsatt calls "iconic solidity."[183] Verbal iconicity serves an integrating function: it is an intelligible fusion, an "amalgam of the sensory and the logical," the "arrest and precipitation of the logical in sensory form . . . the icon in which the idea is caught."[184]

CALVINISM AND A POST-SIXTEENTH-CENTURY INTELLECTUAL ENVIRONMENT

Most conspicuously, the later course of Calvinism manifests a narrowing of emotional range, an increasing hardening of the lines of thought into a habit of rationalism and schematization, and, best known, an emphasis, first, upon surviving in adversity and, subsequently, upon worldly success as the evidence of election and calling. The elitism inherent in a doctrine of election and the qualities of narrowing and hardening (standards for admission) are very compatible. However, one may wonder whether this is the inevitable unfolding of Calvinist theology. If Calvin's intellectualism is ultimately responsible for the rigid schematizing of theology, it is equally responsible for the capacity of Calvinists, often impressive to observers of congregations, to respond to pastoral injunctions to analyze and plan their religious lives. Moreover, new conditions wrought by material and intellectual events could have played a decisive part in the development of Calvinism. The questions that need to be asked concern the relationship between Calvinist theology and its environment. Something went wrong such that the first evidences of change in Calvinism seem related as pale shadows before some distressing forms that presently exist in this world. But by many who speak in Calvin's name, he has surely been more used than applied.

Soon after Calvin's death, something once very central and marked in his theology began to recede, and continued to do so incrementally. I want to raise the question of why Calvin's rhetoric ceased to have the sound and intensity that seem to have resonated, earlier, with a changed sense of complexity, and with uncertainty about the implications of that complexity, in the wake of high Renaissance thought and sensibilities. Among changes in the post-Renaissance world, that which corresponds most closely, as a reversal, to Calvin's insistence on a comprehensive view of human nature is a deliberate separation of reason and emotion. Calvin's insistence upon human complexity was accompanied by his reiterated concern to hold together the polarities in which he perceived this complexity to reside and by what I see as an intuitive effort to bridge them through his rhetoric. Just this concern seemed very soon to lose its import to an audience that had once responded to it. Thus it seems to be the case that, as Calvin perforce did some editing of Luther when he stressed the communal experiences least threatening to his introversion, later Calvinists edited Calvin. It can correspondingly be assumed that there were compelling reasons for this, and they seem to constitute the major problem in later history for Calvin historians and, conversely, a problem that the perspective of Calvin historians could address.

In theology, a subtle shift by Beza may have had wide-ranging effects upon Calvinism and may mirror a change not limited to theology. Following medieval scholasticism, he placed the idea of predestination under the doctrines of God and providence, in contrast to its location by Calvin — for whom it was a deliberate deviation from the Schoolmen — under the doctrine of salvation. There, its implications had been for the faith and life of the believer, and Calvin also surrounded it with prohibitions against presumptuous curiosity: it was specifically separated from the realm of speculative theology.[185] Beza also emphasized the importance of works, along with perseverance, as evidence of election.[186] An accompanying restoration of Aristotelianism superseded Calvin's mode of biblical exegesis[187]—there is at least an increasing preponderance of intellectualization, classifying, and measuring here.

This tendency continued more sharply after 1600. The comprehensive academies of the French Renaissance, grounded in an integrated conception of knowledge, were superseded by separate institutions.[188] Literary theory moved, in the late sixteenth century, to a psychology that separated imagination from reason or intellect.[189] Parallel to the rigidity and general hardening of thought that is part of all these shifts, the rules as well as schematized regularity in orthodoxy became pervasive and constituted a restraint upon intellectual adventurousness.[190]

Ramism, especially popular in areas that favored Calvinism,[191] manifests the same characteristics and may point to the most significant change in the world of thought and culture at the end of the sixteenth century. Ramus relegated rhetoric to the aesthetic functions of oratory—to the problems and tasks of style and delivery—while he annexed for logic (that is Walter Ong's phrase) not just the analysis but also the intellectual design of argument.[192] What was important to Ramus were the results of the rigid, bipartite divisions of his famous method.[193] This could seem a rejection of Calvinism in Calvin's spirit. But one could also see it as a more basic rejection, a radical transformation that only rather ironically preserves some vestiges of Calvin's sense of dualistic complexity, for Ramus specifically separated language and reason. Theological faculties in universities and the Genevan Academy itself reflected this shift: the major single development in curriculum is a decline in the philological study that Calvin always had wanted side by side with the teaching of theology.[194]

The separation of language and reason coincided, at the advent of the seventeenth century, with a separation, within the realm of language, of human and divine speech. God's speech was redefined in a realm outside that of discourse. The way in which God imparts knowledge to us is, essentially, not through Scripture but in and through the Book of Nature.[195] The book of the world, written in the language of mathematics, was proclaimed unambiguous, clearer, and in fact at a higher intellectual level than Scripture, in which God had had variously to accommodate himself to the rudeness of the life of his people.[196] Moreover, (and Margreta De Grazia suggests this to be a reason for the change), human language was not just overshadowed by a superior means of communication, but was found to be inherently inferior. It was flawed; it led to confusion; it obfuscated truths; it was deceptive.[197]

De Grazia abstracts from the proliferation of negative views about human speech in the seventeenth century the idea of a secularization of language. The traditional links between human and divine speech had, of course, been severed in nominalism. However, that revision was part of an apprehension of radical distance between man and God; it neither proceeded from nor led to a negative view of language. And for Calvin, accommodation was indeed lowering, but it was effective translation rather than compromise. In its human parameters, language had the greatest importance. In contrast, in the seventeenth century, it was the flawed quality of language that indicated its human origins.[198] Numerous reworkings of the Tower of Babel story made explicit the total, irreplaceable loss by man of a language with any resemblance to divine speech.[199]

The decoding of the Book of Nature promised control of nature; knowledge was power. The new view of human language was certainly an essential part of the shift to the language of mathematics; it was a concomitant of the development of a newly honed instrument of knowledge. However, there is considerable continuity between seventeenth-century science and that of the Renaissance. Agrippa, too, had sought to control nature, and, to this end, he called upon the power manifested in Adam's language.[200] Yet language came to be rejected by scientists for use toward the same goal. There is ample evidence that language was felt to be not too weak, but too strong, for such use. To Bacon, the human understanding was like a false mirror which, receiving rays irregularly, distorts the nature of things by "mingling its own nature with it."[201] To rely upon human perception is to capitulate to an inner nature:

But the *Idols of the Market Place* are the most troublesome of all—idols which have crept into the understanding through the alliance of words and names. For men believe that their reason governs words; but it is also true that words react on the understanding; and this it is that has rendered philosophy and the sciences sophistical and inactive. Now words, being commonly framed and applied according to the capacity of the vulgar, follow those lines of division which are most obvious to the vulgar understanding. And whenever an understanding of greater acuteness or a more diligent observation would alter those lines to suit the true divisions of nature, words stand in the way and resist the change. Whence it comes to pass that the high and formal discussions of learned men end oftentimes in disputes about words and names; with which (according to the use and wisdom of the mathematicians) it would be more prudent to begin, and so by means of definitions reduce them to order. Yet even definitions cannot cure this evil in dealing with natural and material things, since the definitions themselves consist of words, and those words beget others.

There are two kinds of idols "imposed by words on the understanding." They are:

either names of things which do not exist (for as there are things left unnamed through lack of observation, so likewise are there names which result from fantastic suppositions and to which nothing in reality corresponds), or they are names of things which exist, but yet confused and ill-defined, and hastily and irregularly derived from realities. . . without any due verification."

There is some small hope for securing minimal harm from language:

There are, however, in words certain degrees of distortion and error. One of the least faulty kinds is that of names of substances, especially of lowest species and well-deduced (for the notion of *chalk* and of *mud* is good, of *earth* bad); a more faulty kind is that of actions, as *to generate, to corrupt, to alter*; the most faulty is of qualities (except such as are the immediate objects of the sense) as *heavy, light, rare, dense,* and the like. Yet in all these cases some notions are of necessity a little better than others, in proportion to the greater variety of subjects that fall within the range of the human sense.[202]

So words are put in their place. One wonders whether Ockham's explanation of the obfuscating plurality of terms was deliberately discarded: if Ockham came into his own during the scientific revolution, it was, like (indeed very much like) the post-Renaissance Calvin, in an edited version.

A conception widespread in early modern science of the hardness of nature was certainly an impetus to the development of instruments that might increasingly penetrate it.[203] It may also be a compensatory counterpart to awareness of an unknown realm that eludes penetration by any known means. Directly calling upon that realm, emphatically personal and experimental ways of communication with God—often, idiosyncratic ways—characterize much seventeenth-century literature: some of George Herbert's poetry is part of this development, and is marked also, De Grazia notes, by strong doubts that he may not have found the right code toward that end.[204] Psyche and cosmos seem to be disevered in seventeenth-century thought,[205] and it looks as if the demystifying of the physical universe is the counterpart to an actually heightened sense of the elusive and enormous mysteries of an inner universe. Renaissance and Reformation theory of rhetoric evidences awareness of this universe and its reflection in language—and its shadow-side, the source of the power to deceive that demagogues could use and that we might not ourselves be able to avoid. I think Calvin, with quick intuition, availed himself of the relation between self and language. But it seems to be the case that reflection of an inner person came to be seen, in the mainstream of seventeenth-century thought, as intrusion. Thus the specific and reiterated separations of power and language, in that century, and the newly asserted and encouraged ability to escape the hold of language suggest, in considerable part, the psychological phenomenon of negation.

A sharply attenuated Calvinist scholasticism is not the only form of Calvinism in this environment. In isolation, or fragmented, some of Calvin's most characteristic and difficult doctrines and concepts are present in seventeenth-century minds, some not formally Calvinistic. It has been suggested that Hobbes's determinism was good Reformation thinking.[206] His view of the human will, articulated in controversy with Bishop Bramhall, would have been very familiar to Calvin. "When first a man hath an *appetite* or *will* to something, to which immediately before he had not appetite nor will, the *cause* of his *will*, is not the *will* itself, but *something else not in his disposing*."[207] We are "like a wooden top that is lashed by boys" and that nevertheless imagines itself to proceed by its will: man thinks he does something "without other cause than his own will and seeth not what are the lashings that cause his will."[208] That opinion applies to everyone; Hobbes tells Bramhall, "I have no dominion over my will."[209]

Sensibilities that are characteristically Calvinistic are likewise present outside orthodox Calvinism. The inescapable sense of distance between man and God in Calvin reappears in Pascal: "Le silence éternel de ces espaces infinis m'effraie."[210] The inner world of man is as much an abyss and an impenetrable secret as that outer universe. In what seems an ironic rewriting of Pico's oration on the dignity of man, Pascal asks an imaginary person to narrow his focus increasingly, working toward the smallest, most delicate thing he might examine. As we are as nothing before the universe, the smallest things and the things we find to be still smaller are infinite in comparison with that which exists further within them. The descent to the smallest moves inward, and we encounter "a colossus, a world, or rather a whole, in respect of the nothingness which we cannot reach." To the question, "in fact what is man in nature?" Pascal answers, "a Nothing in comparison with the Infinite, an All in Comparison with Nothing, a mean between nothing and everything. Since he is infinitely removed from comprehending the extremes, the end of things and their beginning are hopelessly hidden from him in an impenetrable secret; he is equally incapable of seeing the Nothing from which he was made, and the Infinite in which he is swallowed up."[211]

In a quite dualistic way, *le vide* was a positive reality to Pascal.[212]

His voice was a reaction to the content of much of post-Renaissance philosophy and science. One legacy of Reformation history may be to have established the predictability of successive oscillations between inclination to monism and inclination to dualism, with extreme counterstatements (such as Pascal's) often simultaneous with a prevailing position. One might see as evidence of these successive relations the emphatic monism of Thomas Traherne, cast in language that in 1675 must still have evoked Calvin and consists, in some part, in a specific reversal of him:

> It is the Glory of man, that his *Avarice* is insatiable, and *Ambition* infinite, that his *Appetite* carries him to innumerable Pleasures, and that his Curiosity is so Endless, that were he Monarch of the World, it could not satisfie his Soul, but he would be curiously inquisitive into the original and End of Things, and be concerned in the Nature of those that are beyond the Heavens. For having met with an infinite Benefactor, he would not be fit for his Bounty, could any finite Object satisfie his Desire.[213]

All sense of separation between inner and outer reality, between self and other, between mind and matter is denied: "I could not tell, / Whether the Things did there / Themselves appear, / Which in my Spirit *truly* seemd to dwell; / Or whether my conforming Mind / Were not alone even all that shind."[214]

Against this background, the phenomenon in the early modern period that a Calvin historian may find most striking is the loss of the original form and sound of Calvin's theology. This, with the evidence we have that the power of language evoked fear and unease, suggests a willed movement to safer ground. There seems also to have been a genuine loss of the sixteenth-century understanding of language, through effective burial by others, to thinkers who might not have so reacted. Pascal, close in many ways to Calvin's sense of man and God, complains about the ambiguity of language: he wishes God would say all or nothing; ambiguous speech is not a significant alternative to nothing.[215] Much later developments that formally link language and the unconscious could be more congenial to the coherent literary and psychological phenomenon of Calvinist rhetoric or to the set of ideas about human values, expression, and experience that it seems to represent.

DUALISM AND DUALITY

Dualism in its religious sense in western culture (as I have been using the term), and sometimes as used philosophically, divides reality into two forms or qualities—that is, reality is dyadic—with ontological parity and with opposite moral valuation. Dualism in scientific thought and, in philosophy, in the classic *res cogitans / res extensa* distinction of Descartes, is also a division of reality into two kinds: they have ontological parity; they do not have implicit valuation. Both dualisms constitute a metaphysics; the presence of the moral aspect renders the first also a world view. The two forms of which reality consists are distinct; in moral dualism they will also be seen and felt to be sharply disconnected and incompatible, and in potential or overt conflict with each other.[216]

Sometimes the valuative properties in moral dualism are unwarrantedly conveyed by any use of the term and seem often, in the history of science, to have been alienating. But displeasure with moralism is not the only reaction that dualism has evoked. The human appropriateness of the dyadic mode, of duality itself, presupposed in both valuative and nonvaluative dualism, may have evoked the weightiest suspicion and criticism—though it is very likely that some of the suspicion is an educated concern for what may lie behind or ahead of it.

One of our keenest historians of rhetoric, Nancy Struever, has associated a "disabling polarity" with the extreme stances that classical and Italian rhetoric theory urged and facilitated toward the end of irrefutable persuasion.[217] Yet one cannot escape the evidence that thinking and seeing in dualities is a strong human tendency. The similarities asserted in classical rhetoric theory among the structures of language, the human mind, and the cosmos always tended to be dyadic.[218] It is a truism that we need to organize experience but noteworthy that the dyadic mode of division for such organizing is everywhere—a familiar example is in the divisions in Ecclesiastes. Perceptions of sex differences habitually get into the more extended lists, as they provide fuel for moral dualisms.

The models that are posited in structuralist linguistics and anthropology are pervasively dyadic.[219] Independent philosophers and literary theorists following Jung may also view language and psychic structure as dyadic.[220] Further, the dualities of which mental and cultural structures are held to be composed, by such theorists, are mutually exclusive opposites and are characterized by a dynamics of opposition. The particular congeniality of psychology and structuralist linguistics is no surprise. It has been recognized in psychoanalytic theory since its beginnings in Freud that many of the basic psychological defense mechanisms are dialectical in nature.

It seems possible to accept the propensity toward dyadic patterns in thought, feeling, and expression in these models and still balk at the transition to the pattern of religious dualism—to balk at the inevitability, totality, and constancy of the dual vision and experience they posit and at the premises that identity is contrast and that differences are oppositions. There is evidence in modern philosophy of science of nonevaluative bases for seeing reality dualistically, and it is likely that these bases have reinforced, if not in part caused, a propensity to see dyadically which can veer easily into moral dualism. The bases, upon which consensus has emerged in this century, are the field/particle duality in the structuring of matter and the concomitant modes, and cognitive premises, of continuity and discontinuity.[221] This dualism sheds light especially upon the set of problems traditionally formulated as those of mind versus body or mind versus matter. In its light, the problems seem to constitute a *question mal-posée*. What remains within and after the *question mal-posée* is the phenomenon and experience of distinction, disparity, and separateness — some dual, as in disparity between mind and matter, in gender, and in much of psychodynamics, and some not dual, as in disparities within the self, among kinds of mental processes, and between mind and other minds.

The experience of separateness presents the problem of accessibility, a problem of knowledge and a form of the subject/object problem even when the object is also the self. Confrontation by gulfs and by gaps that want bridging seems both part of and prior to confrontation by opposites. Indeed the antagonistic premise seems qualified by the work of many who assert it, suggesting further the absorption of evidences for dyadic division into minds tempered by the good versus evil dichotomy in which, in western history, statements challenging monism have been conceptualized and formulated. Thus Jacques Lacan seems clearly to be dealing with a differentiation neither dualistic nor dyadic in his reading of Freud as the discoverer of the radical heteronomy in man, of the confrontation by man of "the self's radical ex-centricity to itself."[222] In a similarly less constraining way, Lévi-Strauss extrapolated from the primitive experience of the hostility of nature evidence not only for his dyadic view of mental structures but for an inherent human sense of separation from nature: the purpose of myth is to dissolve the distinction between nature and culture.[223]

Structuralist thought is also a meditation on the distinction between signs and objects; metaphor and metonymy identify the contextual, subjective realities that modify or transform signs. The subjective realities happen to be defined as polarized and recognized by that character. Calvin's thought was also informed by a polarized, indeed antagonistic view of reality, and the conventions of rhetoric that he used and the style in which he wrote expressed that view. But the sound and cadences of his writing can be regarded from a different perspective. Calvin's asceticism stopped before language. With control and abstraction, he used pure sound to evoke the love of God; in the physical arrangement of his words, he seems to be evoking something within human consciousness, and highlighting it, to persuade men further to love God. There is in all his writings a nonimmediate, nonovert presence that forms a modifying context for his direct and overt statements: the possibility of this kind of interaction of different levels of reality remains if one is not convinced that reality is always polarized.

In experiencing inner and outer boundaries so strongly and asserting them in a conceptual language of moral dualism, Calvin—though I think an edited Calvin—played a major role in giving us our puritanism. I have suggested also that the post-Renaissance world needed the challenge within Calvinism to the validity and viability—certainly to the claims of exclusive validity—of a monist view of human life. Luther's reformulation of the medieval dichotomy between the human and the divine was a historically decisive correction of a schematization that had proven impossible either to maintain or to assert consistently. However, Luther may have obliterated a perception in medieval thought of a division that corresponds more closely than his to nonmoral levels of existence. In relation to it, Calvin's insistence upon the experiences of disparity and disjunction appears to be an important internecine adjustment.

The apparent melodrama of rhetoric was reality for Calvin, yet it is in some way formalized reality, not merely formalization, for anyone. The impact of his rhetoric may be attributable to the close realism of its incorporation of dualism; a decisive intellectual context of that dualism is a belief in the human origins of words and in their power even in the world as he saw it.

The later history of the *Institutes*, which can be correlated with post-sixteenth-century attitudes toward language, seems to indicate a reaction against Calvin's insistence upon the radical complexity of experience. Twentieth-century thought in diverse fields has returned to it. It is surely significant that Lacan has characterized the intention of Freudian analysis of the assertions of the unconscious and the ego to be "one of integration and of harmony, I could even say of reconciliation (*Versöhnung*)."[224] One might also see the Augustinian idea of Christian rhetoric and Renaissance rhetoric theory—both present in Calvin—in only new formulations in Roland Barthes's opposition of the unsettling "writerly" text of erotic *jouissance* to the mere "readerly" text of comfortable *plaisir*,[225] or—with attention to the Gospel echoes—in the description by William Gass of both writer and reader in the autonomous world of literature:

> Though at first it might seem as if the richness of life had been replaced by something less so—senseless noises, abstract meanings, mere shadows of worldly employment—yet the new self with which fine fiction and good poetry should provide you is as wide as the mind is, and musicked deep with feeling. While listening to such symbols sounding, the blind perceive; thought seems to grow a body; and the will is at rest amid that moving like a gull asleep on the sea.[226]

CALVIN IN INTELLECTUAL HISTORY

The linguistic analysts of the early twentieth century were concerned with the question whether meaningful communication was possible. The roots of the question lay in Kant's analysis of the limits of pure reason in light of the active involvement of the knower in perception. The subjectivity this seemed to point to was glorified by the Romantics. Their position is merely the counterpole to that of the linguistic analysts, who were equally impressed by the fact of subjectivity and retreated into the few small areas apparently susceptible to rule. They were curiously oblivious to, or uninterested in, the positive answer to the problem of subjectivity in Freud. Subjectivity was far more radical in Freud than in Kant: it was the individual's unconscious that mediated experience, as distinct from the precisely definable categories. Yet, for Freud, this absolute individualism was also lawful, and could be analyzed and reached through its language—the symbolization the unconscious presented to the conscious. The symbolizations can be "translated," and the relation between signified and signifier in the displacements can be analyzed.

Taken together and not seeing one as simply the product of the history of psychology and the other of the history of philosophy, Freud and Kant have important predecessors who seem to fall into logical groupings. First, Ockham, and then Luther and Calvin, present the concept of the limits of knowledge, the idea of self-knowledge as the paradigmatic problem in knowledge, and the discovery, with the significance it has in modern times, of the unconscious. Secondly, the view of language as human in origin and the conception of it as a basic mediator of our experience also go back to Ockham. More specifically, this line of development is characterized by concern with language as part of the problem of self-knowledge and delusion. Descriptively, the movement is from the logical treatment of language in Ockham, to its historical treatment in Renaissance philology, to its psychological treatment, the possibility opened by Freud. All the rhetoricians, including Calvin, valued language for its creative and expressive power. The power of symbolism was clearest in consciously chosen imagery. Freud extended the significance of symbolizing to the unintentional realm: to the way in which the unconscious asserts itself. Lacan and others have carried further and made still more central the study of the language of the unconscious.

Thirdly, language was not just a preface to further knowledge, but was significant in itself. Here, the most important moment preliminary to Freud was the Romantic theory of expressionism. A glorification of, rather than a solution to, the problem of subjectivity (in holding that what all men shared was the ideal of self-realization), it is important here for its conception of language as self-expression and, as such, self-realization.[227] But this rebellion against the Enlightenment had earlier roots. The Renaissance rhetoricians exalted the power of language, and they related this power partly to a correspondence between language and the human mind. However they came to have doubts about language, and rhetoric was allowed to recede from the cultural forefront. Renaissance poets, and also Calvin, did not succumb to the doubts that they, too, had; their works were widely read in the late Renaissance; they seem more directly ancestors of the expressionists. The poets feared seduction by beauty from truth to illusion. Calvin feared the physical in general. They thought at the same time that language could, as realistically, serve the good and the true—in light of their fears, this service was all the more necessary. Language could be transformative; its effects were tantamount to psychic integration. There is a line leading from them to the expressionist idea of self-realization through language and to modern poetics, parallel and related to the line from them to Romantic expressionism and then to Freud, who read widely and claimed to have learned much from Romantic literature.

Luther was enormously important for the modern understanding of the unconscious. However, the line of development leading to modern philosophy and psychology, insofar as they are grounded in the analysis of, first, subjectivity in perception and, then, the symbolic mediation of the unconscious, might more exactly be seen as running through three key points, Ockham, Kant, and Freud, with Calvin as a very important, necessary moment, embodying all the significance for this line of Renaissance and Reformation alike.

Calvin's significance can be seen still more broadly and exactly. Secularism is the determining background of modern philosophy and psychology in regard both to the limits of the sphere of knowledge and to its content. It asserts the facticity for human life of the impersonal body and environment, directly and as hidden determinants; the possibility of their positive use is the foundation for the idea of change. But there are different understandings and versions of secularism. Calvin's secularism is quintessentially exemplified in his theological rhetoric—in the deliberate beauty of his writing about the absolute gulf between man and God. He saw the physical as real, unavoidable, and potentially healthy despite, and in relation to, the impulses that made him resist seeing it positively. His positive attitude toward the world was hard won and peculiarly more comprehensive than other secularisms insofar as it included internal resistance. Just in this regard, it is more akin to twentieth-century thought and its dominant mood than were the high Renaissance, Lutheranism, or later, the Enlightenment.

I think it is not so much Calvin's famous certainty that has been persuasive, and the decisive factor in his historical success, as his unwavering commitment to and practice of a world view involving uncertainty. He is certain that the secular life can be positive, but not that it *will* be. His persuasiveness is in the recognition not just of the possibility, but also of the apparent implausibility, that it can be so: there are real dangers inherent in the world and human nature. What he sees as the problem of evil is a reality to him. But the problem is as much in the possibility of a life of piety perverted as in the loss of a soul: human potential, learning, charity, and creativity are also real to him, and one tends, with Calvin, to trust that this is not an illusion.

Notes

INTRODUCTION

1. See, for example, A.G. Dickens, *Reformation and Society in Sixteenth-Century Europe*, chap. 8, esp. pp. 155ff., and Erwin Mülhaupt, "Luther und Calvin," in *Luther. Mitteilungen der Luthergesellschaft* 30 (1959): 97–113. The representatives of the principal variant see (and present it as the effect of Calvin's legalistic mind) a shift in emphasis to the doctrine of election, an emphasis that is reflected historically in the discipline and activism of the elect. See, for example, H. G. Koenigsberger and G. L. Mosse, *Europe in the Sixteenth Century*, chap. 7, esp. pp. 145ff. There is also a cluster of statements which present the Calvin-Luther relationship in the form of juxtaposed portraits or character sketches. The qualities most often stressed are Luther's New Testament versus Calvin's Old Testament orientation, Luther's warmth versus Calvin's coldness, and Luther's less strict biblicism versus Calvin's very strict biblicism. In these statements, Calvin's legal training is generally stressed in regard to his practicality. See, for example, J. A. K. Zimmerman, "Christian Life in Luther and Calvin," *Lutheran Quarterly* 16 (1964): 222–30; John Dillenberger and Claude Welch, *Protestant Christianity Interpreted through its Development*, chap. 2, "A New Theology Develops: Luther and Calvin."

2. An enthusiastic version of this view is presented in T. H. L. Parker, *John Calvin*. The synthesis is characterized as the purification and reshaping of a deteriorated religion, a return to genuine Christianity. Lefèvre and Briçonnet are considered important for all the Reformers (pp. xiv ff.); it was Calvin who reached back to the early centuries of the church and also gave real form to the cardinal doctrines of the Reformation (p. 50). Variants of this view shift the proportions and identity of the many influences Calvin brought together. To some (see Roland H. Bainton, *The Reformation of the Sixteenth Century*, ch. 6, pp. 110ff.), Calvin synthesized the ideas of the Protestant reformers who preceded him—Luther, Zwingli, and the Anabaptists. François Wendel, *Calvin: The Origins and Development of His Religious Thought*, sees Luther as of great importance for Calvin's ideas, but sees several other sources of comparable importance. Wendel

emphasizes Scotus and, on the visible church (with many other historians), Bucer (but see, for its stress on the importance of Luther for Bucer, Ernst-Wilhelm Kohls, "Martin Bucer als Anhänger Luthers," *Theologische Zeitschrift* 33 [1977]: 210–18). For Calvin and Saint Augustine, see Luchesius Smits, *Saint Augustin dans l'oeuvre de Jean Calvin*, and Joseph Fitzer, "The Augustinian Roots of Calvin's Eucharistic Thought," *Augustinian Studies* 7 (1976): 69–98. (I shall, of course, be concerned with Calvin and Saint Augustine — and with what seem to me the limiting conditions of the influence — at several points in the chapters that follow.) The view of Calvin the synthesizer is, I think, best stated by W. Nijenhuis, "Der ökumenische Calvin," *Nederlands theologisch Tijdschrift* (1980), pp. 191–212, who applies to him Schweitzer's characterization of Bach: "Es geht nichts von ihm aus: alles führt nur auf ihn hin" (p. 197). Calvin's theology is often seen as in large part a return to Catholicism; see, for an approving statement of that view, Charles Boyer, *Calvin et Luther*. See also Steven E. Ozment, *The Age of Reform, 1250–1550*, chap. 11, esp. pp. 372–80 ("Were Calvinists Really Protestants?"), who finds regression in Calvin's stress upon works.

3. See, for example, Joachim Rogge, "Kritik Calvins an Luthers Zwei-Reiche-Lehre?" in *Theologie in Geschichte und Kunst. Walter Elliger zum 65. Geburtstag*, pp. 152–68, for the practical differences between launching reform and preserving and developing it.

4. Owen Chadwick presents a predominantly negative personal charac-terization and incorporates material from early modern portrayals (such as the influential life of Calvin by one of his banished enemies, Bolsec), in *The Reformation*, chap. 3, esp. pp. 85ff. In *The Travail of Religious Liberty*, Roland Bainton qualifies his presentation of Calvin as "the peak of Protestant intolerance" with recognition of the dangerous political situation that threatened the church of Geneva, engendering "all the tension of a wartime psychology" (p. 71). Georgia Harkness maintains a positive view in the frequently encountered framework of a worthwhile trade-off — the good in Calvin weighed against the bad — throughout her *John Calvin*.

5. There is a good survey article by Simone Pétrement, "Dualism in Philosophy and Religion," in the *Dictionary of the History of Ideas*, vol. 2, pp. 38–44. See also Henri-Charles Puech, "The Concept of Redemption in Manichaeism," *The Mystic Vision*, vol. 6, pp. 247–314, esp. pp. 262f.

6. On the earlier history of the idea of evil as privation, see Arthur O. Lovejoy, *The Great Chain of Being*, pp. 59–64. See also John Hick, *Evil and the God of Love*, a general discussion, with historical survey, of Christianity and the problem of dualism.

7. See Charles Partee, *Calvin and Classical Philosophy*, pp. 59ff, and Heinrich Quistorp, *Calvin's Doctrine of the Last Things*. Quistorp finds the tendency strong, but also finds it constantly corrected by biblical realism (pp. 192–93).

8. Nicole Malet, *Dieu selon Calvin*.

9. Gerd Babelotsky, *Platonischer Bilder und Gedankengänge in Calvins Lehre vom Menschen*. Margaret R. Miles, too, argues this point in "Theology, Anthropology, and the Human Body in Calvin's *Institutes of the Christian Religion*," *Harvard Theological Review* 74 (1981): 303–323. She stresses Calvin's distinction between "the body" and "the flesh" — for him the flesh, like the spirit, is located in the soul; the body is merely the habitation of the soul. The apparent ambiguities in Calvin on body and soul are to be understood in this framework. I think Miles disregards the relative weight and emotional content of the sides of the ambiguities and thus overlooks the psychological context of the formal anthropology with which she is dealing. See also Hick, *Evil and the God of Love*,

which places Calvin together with Augustine and the Augustinian Luther; for the purpose of emphasizing God's transcendence, the three may veer somewhat too far in the direction of dualism, but, to Hick, never dangerously so.

10. Thomas N. Tentler, *Sin and Confession on the Eve of the Reformation.*

11. Ozment, *Age of Reform*, pp. 20–21, 134. See also his discussion of the institutional background of the medieval value system, esp. chaps. 1 and 4.

12. Jill Raitt, "Three Inter-related Principles in Calvin's Unique Doctrine of Infant Baptism," *Sixteenth Century Journal* (1980): 53, n. 8.

13. Charles Partee, "Calvin, Calvinism, and Philosophy: A Prolusion," *Reformed Review* 33 (1980): 134.

14. See Richard Stauffer, "Un Calvin méconnu: Le prédicateur de Genève," *Bulletin historique et littéraire de la Société de l'histoire du protestantisme français* 123 (1977): 184–203; "Dieu, la création et la providence dans l'oeuvre homilétique de Calvin, *La Revue reformée* 28 (1977): 196–203; "Plaidoyer pour une lecture non-calviniste de Calvin," *Supplément à la Revue reformée* 120 (1979): 2–11. See also the response by Pierre Marcel, "Une lecture non-calviniste de Calvin?" ibid., pp. 1–2, 11–16.

15. See F. M. Higman, *The Style of John Calvin in his French Polemical Treatises.* For the distinctiveness of Calvin's style and its use as an identification tool for hitherto anonymous sources, see Higman's "Un pamphlet de Calvin restitué à son auteur," *Revue d'histoire et de philosophie religieuses* 60 (1980): 167–80, 327–37. See also Rodolphe Peter, "Rhétorique et prédication selon Calvin," *Revue d'histoire et de philosophie religieuses* 55 (1975): 249–72. For a literary historian's analysis, see the chapter on Calvin and French literature in I. D. McFarlane, *Renaissance France, 1470–1589*, pp. 336ff. See also Nicole Malet's analysis of Calvin's vocabulary, *Dieu selon Calvin.* For a linguistic analysis, see Gilbert Vincent, "La théologie calvinienne du sacrement à la lumière de la linguistique," in *Calvinus Ecclesiae Doctor*, pp. 145–58. On logic, see Robert H. Ayers, "Language, Logic and Reason in Calvin's *Institutes*," *Religious Studies* 16 (1980): 283–97 (in which Calvin's rigorous and subtle logic is presented as compensation for the "irrationalities" in his theology) and Ford Lewis Battles, "Calculus Fidei," *Calvinus Ecclesiae Doctor*, pp. 85–110. Battles, Malet, and Vincent specifically use their analyses for new access to Calvin's theology. In contrast, Benoît Girardin argues, in his *Rhétorique et théologique: Calvin, le commentaire de l'Épître aux Romains*, that the forensic rhetoric of the commentary confers contraints as well as coherence upon the author's thinking. Girardin finds the constraints in the arrangement and strategies prescribed by "*l'ordre rhétorique*," and he is asking for a reconsideration of Calvin in the light of his findings—that is, a Calvin lifted out of a rather contaminating vehicle of expression. It will be clear that I would not concur with this suggestion. However, it should be noted that Girardin's conception of rhetoric is focused upon *dispositio*, to the practical exclusion of *elocutio*. Thus our subjects (even narrowly conceived) are as different as the direction of our interpretations.

16. See Partee, *Calvin and Classical Philosophy.* Basil Hall surveys this area historiographically in "From Biblical Humanism to Calvinist Orthodoxy," *Journal of Ecclesiastical History* 31 (1980): 335–36, 339–40.

17. See commentary on the Weber thesis in Benjamin Nelson, "Weber's Protestant Ethic," in *Beyond the Classics?* ed. Charles Young Glock and P. E. Hammond, pp. 71–130; *Protestantisme et capitalisme*, ed. Philippe Besnard; *Seminar: Religion und Gesellschaftliche Entwicklung*, ed. Constans Seyfarth and Walter M. Sprondel. The generalized view is very frequently found. An older and typical statement of the importance of the calling and the "heroic certainty" of

the elect, manifested in their activism, is in Harold J. Grimm, *The Reformation Era 1500–1650*, pp. 349f. See Koenigsberger and Mosse, *Europe in the Sixteenth Century*, pp. 145–47, for a succinct statement on the joining, for God, of inward battle against Satan with outward struggle against him in the world. It has been interestingly suggested that the social activism of Calvinism was helpful in placing the irrational within clear bounds, in contrast to the more demanding individual introspection in Lutheranism (Donald J. Wilcox, *In Search of God and Self*, p. 374). See also the conception of Calvinist secularism as an *Entzauberung* of the world in Walter M. Sprondel, "Sozialer Wandel, Ideen und Interessen, in *Seminar: Religion und Gesellschaftliche Entwicklung*, pp. 206–24, and the characterization of the concrete changes Calvinism wrought in Geneva as the equivalent of a radical revolution in Robert M. Kingdon, "Was the Protestant Reformation a Revolution? The Case of Geneva," in *Studies in Church History*, vol. 12, pp. 203–22.

18. William J. Bouwsma, "Changing Assumptions in Later Renaissance Culture," *Viator* 7 (1976): 421–40, esp. pp. 438–39. Denys Hay stresses the compatibility of late Italian Renaissance culture with northern society, "which in the main was princely and aristocratic," in *The Italian Renaissance in its Historical Background*, chap. 8, "The Reception of the Renaissance in the North," p. 188.

19. William J. Bouwsma, "The Two Faces of Humanism," in *Itinerarium Italicum*, ed. Heiko A. Oberman and Thomas A. Brady, Jr., pp. 3–60.

20. Bouwsma, "Changing Assumptions," p. 437.

21. Paul Oskar Kristeller's work was early and basic for the study of Renaissance rhetoric. See his *Renaissance Thought*. See also Hanna H. Gray, "Renaissance Humanism," *Journal of the History of Ideas* 24 (1963): 497–514; Jerrold E. Seigel, *Rhetoric and Philosophy in Renaissance Humanism*; Nancy S. Struever, *The Language of History in the Renaissance*; William J. Bouwsma, "The Renaissance and the Drama of Western History," *American Historical Review* 84 (1979): 1–15 and the essays cited in notes 18, 19, and 27.

22. I am following the lines drawn in Bouwsma's "Renaissance and the Drama of Western History."

23. A basic theme in Marcia Colish, *The Mirror of Language* and Marjorie O'Rourke Boyle, *Erasmus on Language and Method in Theology*.

24. Jung may have been the first to observe explicity that "it frequently happens that, when a problem that is at bottom personal, and therefore apparently subjective, impinges upon outer events which contain the same psychic elements as the personal conflict, it is suddenly transformed into a general question that embraces the whole of society" (C. G. Jung, *Psychological Types or the Psychology of Individuation*, p. 103). See also E. Harris Harbison, *The Christian Scholar in the Age of Reformation*, and, of course, Erik H. Erikson, *Young Man Luther*.

25. "The causation or production of a specific symptom, item of behavior, or any element of psychic life, by a variable number of intersecting causal paths." (The term is derived from geometry: "two intersecting lines determine a point; three lines intersecting at a point overdetermine the point. However, in psychoanalytic usage the term implies several lines but does not necessarily imply more than necessary"; some writers, therefore, prefer the term "multidetermination.") *Glossary of Psychoanalytic Terms and Concepts*, s.v. "overdetermination."

26. The work of William J. Courtenay has been especially important here: see "Covenant and Causality in Pierre D'Ailly," *Speculum* 46 (1971): 94–119; "Nominalism and Late Medieval Religion," in *The Pursuit of Holiness in Late Medieval and Renaissance Religion*, ed. Charles Trinkaus with Heiko A. Oberman. For nominalism and the Renaissance and Reformation, see Charles Trinkaus, "The

Religious Thought of the Italian Humanists and the Reformers," *The Pursuit of Holiness*, pp. 347, 350. Bouwsma characterizes the relation between nominalism and Renaissance humanism as a collaboration, however unwitting, to focus attention upon the significance of language as a human phenomenon (see "Anxiety and the Formation of Early Modern Culture," in *After the Reformation*, ed. Barbara C. Malament, pp. 233–34). Alternatively, nominalism and early humanism have been viewed as parts of a larger whole consisting of the many late medieval religious and spiritual reactions, all antimetaphysical, against scholastic thought and the culture of which it was part. See Heiko A. Oberman, "The Shape of Late Medieval Thought," *The Pursuit of Holiness*, pp. 3–25.

27. See Trinkaus ("Religious Thought," pp. 339–66), who concludes that the religious thought of the Italian humanists anticipated Reformation ideas but did not seek reform in drastic ways. Rather, it looked to "a milder spiritual transformation and quickening" (p. 366). Bouwsma, in "Renaissance and Reformation," in *Luther and the Dawn of the Modern Era*, ed. Heiko A. Oberman, pp. 127–49, sees the Pelagian tendencies in Renaissance thought as the limiting condition in the community between Renaissance religiosity and Reformation theology. Ozment, in *Age of Reform*, sees "the persistence of scholasticism" in Protestantism, precluding moral critique, as a further limiting condition (p. 315).

28. See, for example, Steven E. Ozment, *The Reformation in the Cities*, p. 48 and passim.

29. Ozment, *Age of Reform*, p. 204.

30. Olivier Fatio, "Présence de Calvin à l'époque de l'orthodoxie réformée," in *Calvinus Ecclesiae Doctor*, p. 199 and passim.

31. Robert M. Kingdon, "Protestant Parishes in the Old World and the New," *Church History* 48 (1979): 297ff.

32. Richard A. Muller, "*Duplex cognitio dei* in the Theology of Early Reformed Orthodoxy," *Sixteenth Century Journal* 10 (1979): 59–61.

CHAPTER 1

1. Jean Calvin, *Theological Treatises*, p. 185.

2. Quoted in B. A. Gerrish, "John Calvin on Luther," *Interpreters of Luther*, ed. Jaroslav Pelikan, p. 69.

3. Ibid.

4. Quoted in ibid., p. 79.

5. Quoted in E. W. Zeeden, "Das Bild Martin Luthers in den Briefen Calvins," *Archiv für Reformationsgeschichte* 49 (1958): 180.

6. Quoted in Gerrish, "Calvin on Luther," p. 79.

7. Quoted in ibid., p. 80.

8. Quoted in ibid., p. 79.

9. Quoted in ibid., pp. 71, 76.

10. Quoted in ibid., p. 85.

11. Quoted in ibid., p. 82.

12. Quoted in ibid., pp. 84, 72. Joseph N. Tylenda ("The Ecumenical Intention of Calvin's Early Eucharistic Teaching," *Reformatio Perennis*, ed. B. A. Gerrish, pp. 27ff.) thinks it may be either the "Reply to Sadolet" or the 1536 or 1539 edition of the *Institutes*.

13. Jean Calvin, *Letters of John Calvin*, letter to Melanchthon, 28 June 1545.

14. Father reference in the sole letter of Calvin to Luther (not delivered, at

Melanchthon's decision) in *Letters*, 21 Jan. 1545; apostle reference quoted in Gerrish, "Calvin on Luther," p. 79.

15. Karl Reuter, *Das Grundverständnis des Theologie Calvins*, pp. 59–70.

16. Ibid., p. 74; Heribert Schützeichel, *Die Glaubenstheologie Calvins*, p. 44.

17. Kilian McDonnell, *John Calvin, the Church, and the Eucharist*, p. 78. Tjarko Stadtland rejects the Bucer influence in his *Rechtfertigung und Heiligung bei Calvin*, pp. 1f.

18. S. E. Ozment has emphasized this for Luther: see his *Homo Spiritualis*, passim.

19. Jean Calvin, *Institutes of the Christian Religion*, III, xi, 1. Henceforth, this edition [See below, Works Cited] will be referred to as *Institutes*. When included, Latin texts are from Jean Calvin, *Institutio christianae religionis . . . 1559*, in *Ioannis Calvini opera quae supersunt omnia*, vol. 2, ed. Guilelmus Baum, Eduardus Cunitz, and Eduardus Reuss.

20. Ibid., III, xi, 19: "Si manifestatur in evangelio iustitia, certe non lacera nec dimidia, sed plena et absoluta illic continetur."

21. Gerrish, "Calvin on Luther," p. 86.

22. Peter Meinhold, "Calvin und Luther," *Lutherische Monatshefte*, 1964, pp. 264ff.

23. Stated in seminar at Yale Graduate School, 1962.

24. Meinhold's short article comes closest, but only points to common themes, and, for example, the basis of the common theme of predestination in their conception of God (which is helpful), but not the place of predestination (or the other common themes) in their theology as a whole. He also rejects psychology to explain differences—indeed the differences are seen mainly in the concept of the visible church.

25. Quoted in B. A. Gerrish, "To the Unknown God: Luther and Calvin on the Hiddenness of God," *Journal of Religion* 53 (1973): 269.

26. *Institutes*, p. 5.

27. T. F. Torrance, "Infinitive and Abstractive Knowledge from Duns Scotus to John Calvin," *De doctrina Iohannis Scoti*, vol. 4, pp. 295, 301. See discussion in T. H. L. Parker, *John Calvin*, p. 11.

28. Stadtland, *Rechtfertigung und Heiligung*, pp. 1f.

29. That the Reformers could often be entirely unchronological and undistinguishing in their identification of earlier church thinkers, including nominalist theologians, as Schoolmen, does not belie a more discriminate reading, and, in nonpolemical contexts, the evaluations are different: one must distinguish between strategy and conviction.

30. Reuter, *Grundverständnis*, p. 180.

31. Jean Calvin, *Commentary on the Book of Psalms*, vol. 4, p. 366.

32. Martin Luther, "Commentary on Galatians," in *Martin Luther*, ed. John Dillenberger, p. 153.

33. Ibid., p. 101.

34. Ibid., p. 69–70.

35. Ibid., p. 50.

36. Luther, *Commentary on Galatians*, p. 112.

37. Jean Calvin, *Commentary on Galatians*, in *Commentaries on the Epistles of Paul to the Galatians and Ephesians*, p. 77.

38. *Institutes*, III, i, 1: "ac de arcana spiritus efficacia inquirere, qua fit ut Christo bonisque eius omnibus fruamur."

39. Ibid., II, iii, 5.

40. Ibid., III, xxiii, 7.

41. Ibid., I, ii, 1–2: "En quid sit pura germanaque religio, nempe fides cum serio Dei timore coniuncta."

42. Ibid., III, xxiii, 7: "unde factum est ut tot gentes una cum liberis eorum infantibus aeternae morti involveret lapsus Adae absque remedio, nisi quia Deo ita visum est? Hic obmutescere oportet tam dicaces alioqui linguas. Decretum quidem horribile, fateor."

43. Ibid., II, iv, 1.

44. From "Scholia on Psalm 84," quoted in Ozment, *Homo Spiritualis*, p. 171.

45. Martin Luther, "The Bondage of the Will," in *Erasmus-Luther*, p. 112.

46. Ibid., p. 130.

47. Martin Luther, "Preface to Romans," in *Martin Luther*, p. 32.

48. *Institutes*, III, xxi, 1.

49. Ibid., III, xxi, 1; III, xxii, 4; III, xxiii, 2.

50. Luther, "Preface to Romans," p. 32.

51. Quoted in Ozment, *Homo Spiritualis*, p. 200.

52. *Institutes*, III, ii, 14.

53. Ibid., III, xxiii, 4.

54. Ibid., III, xxiii, 2.

55. Ibid.

56. Martin Luther, "The Freedom of a Christian," in *Martin Luther*, p. 59.

57. *Institutes*, III, xxi, 1: "sapientiae sublimitatem (quam adorari et non apprehendi voluit, ut per ipsam quoque admirabilis nobis foret)."

58. Ibid., III, xxiv, 3.

59. Ibid., III, xxiv, 17.

60. See Heiko Oberman, "Die 'Extra'-Dimension in der Theologie Calvins," *Geist und Geschichte der Reformation*, ed. Heinz Liebing and Klaus Scholder, pp. 323ff.

61. Torrance, "Infinitive and Abstractive Knowledge," p. 300.

62. Reuter, *Grundverständnis*, p. 142.

63. Ibid.

64. Ibid.

65. *Institutes*, I, xvii, 2.

66. Ibid., I, xviii, 3.

67. Ibid., III, xx, 43.

68. Quoted in Paul Tillich, "Die Wiederentdeckung der prophetischen Tradition in der Reformation," *Gesammelte Werke*, vol. 7, section 1, p. 176.

69. Gerrish, "To the Unknown God," p. 270.

70. Ibid., p. 276.

71. Ibid., p. 290.

72. Quoted in Tillich, *Wiederentdeckung*, vol. 7, section 1, pp. 176–77.

73. Quoted in Ozment, *Homo Spiritualis*, p. 200.

74. Gerrish, "To the Unknown God," p. 292.

75. T. F. Torrance, "Knowledge of God and Speech about Him according to John Calvin," *Regards contemporaines sur Jean Calvin*, p. 143.

76. Torrance, "Infinitive and Abstractive Knowledge," pp. 300–01.

77. Ibid., p. 291.

78. Ibid., p. 298.

79. Ibid., p. 297.

80. Ozment, *Homo Spiritualis*, pp. 44ff.

81. Calvin, *Commentary on Psalms*, vol. 4, p. 450.

82. McDonnell, *John Calvin*, p. 26; Ozment, *Homo Spiritualis*, passim.

83. Torrance, "Infinitive and Abstractive Knowledge," pp. 303–04.

84. Ozment, *Homo Spiritualis*, p. 1.

85. Luther, "Bondage of the Will," p. 100.

86. Ibid., p. 103.

87. Motif in *Institutes* noted in Torrance, "Knowledge of God," p. 148; Reuter, *Grundverständnis*, p. 22.

88. Quoted in E. D. Willis, *Calvin's Catholic Christology*, p. 61 (from *Commentary on John*).

89. *Institutes*, III, i, 4.

90. Luther, "Freedom of a Christian," pp. 60–61.

91. Stadtland, *Rechtfertigung und Heiligung*, p. 119; *Institutes*, IV, xvii, 2: "quod filius hominis nobiscum factus nos secum Dei filios fecerit; quod suo in terras descensu ascensum nobis in coelum straverit; quod accepta nostra mortalitate suam nobis immortalitatem contulerit; quod suscepta nostra imbecillitate sua nos virtute confirmaverit; quod nostra in se recepta paupertate, suam ad nos opulentiam transtulerit; quod recepta ad se qua premebamur iniustitiae nostrae mole sua nos iustitia induerit."

92. See Steven E. Ozment, *The Age of Reform*, p. 117.

93. Quoted in ibid., p. 130.

94. Quoted in ibid., p. 242.

95. Jean Calvin, *Commentaries on the Epistle of Paul the Apostle to the Romans*, p. 210.

96. Jean Calvin, *Commentaries: The Gospel according to Saint John*, vol. 2, p. 136.

97. Thomas N. Tentler, *Sin and Confession on the Eve of the Reformation*, p. 167.

98. Ibid., pp. 167, 165.

99. Ozment, *Age of Reform*, pp. 242 f.; this is a major thesis throughout.

100. Ozment, *Homo Spiritualis*, p. 202.

101. Jean Calvin, *Commentaries: The First Epistle of Paul the Apostle to the Corinthians*, p. 355.

102. Quoted in T. F. Torrance, *Calvin's Doctrine of Man*, p. 112.

103. Luther, *Commentary on Galatians*, p. 131.

104. Ibid., p. 140.

105. Ibid., p. 141.

106. *Institutes*, I, i, 1.

107. Ibid., "Prefatory Address to King Francis," p. 13: "Quid enim melius atque aptius fidei convenit quam agnoscere nos omni virtute nudos, ut a Deo vestiamur? omni bono vacuos, ut ab ipso impleamur? nos peccati servos, ut ab ipso liberemur? nos caecos, ut ab ipso illuminemur? nos claudos, ut ab ipso dirigamur? nos debiles, ut ab ipso sustentemur? nobis omnem gloriandi materiam detrahere, ut solus ipse gloriosus emineat et nos in ipso gloriemur?"

108. Ibid., I, i, 2.

109. Ibid.

110. Ibid., I, i, 1.

111. Ibid., "John Calvin to the Reader," p. 3.

112. McNeill's editorial apparatus to the *Institutes* records the changes.

113. *Institutes*, II, vii, 7.

114. Ibid.

115. Luther, "Preface to Romans," p. 26.

116. Luther, "Freedom of a Christian," p. 55.

117. Ibid., p. 85.

118. Ibid., p. 21.

119. Ibid., p. 22.

120. Luther, "Commentary on Galatians," p. 107.

121. Ibid., pp. 141–42.

122. Ozment, *Homo Spiritualis*, pp. 154–56.

123. Luther, "Freedom of a Christian," pp. 55–56.

124. Heiko A. Oberman, *The Harvest of Medieval Theology*, pp. 107, 67–68.

125. Frederick Copleston, *A History of Philosophy*, vol. 3, part 1, p. 60.

126. Quoted in ibid., p. 68.

127. Ibid., p. 80.

128. William of Ockham, *Predestination, God's Foreknowledge, and Future Contingents*, trans. Marilyn McCord Adams and Norman Kretzmann, p. 89.

129. Oberman, *Harvest of Medieval Theology*, p. 360.

130. Examples in Ockham, *Quodlibeta*, I, in *Philosophical Writings*, trans. Philotheus Boehner, pp. 158–60; p. 90.

131. "There cannot be different acts of knowledge of one conclusion, since plurality must not be asserted without necessity." From *Quodlibeta*, V, in *Philosophical Writings*, p. 109.

132. Ibid., pp. 109–10.

133. Quoted in Copleston, *History of Philosophy*, vol. 3, part 1, p. 98.

134. William J. Courtenay, "Nominalism and Late Medieval Religion," in *The Pursuit of Holiness in Late Medieval and Renaissance Religion*, ed. Charles Trinkaus, p. 42.

135. Julius R. Weinberg, *Ockham, Descartes, and Hume*, pp. 27–28.

136. Copleston, *History of Philosophy*, vol. 3, part 1, p. 78.

137. Courtenay, "Nominalism," p. 44.

138. Ibid., p. 56. Gordon Leff extensively correlates the nominalist sense of contingency with the late medieval environment in *The Dissolution of the Medieval Outlook*, and indeed Heiko Oberman notes that contingency would be the best one-word summary of the nominalist program, in "The Shape of Late Medieval Thought, in *Pursuit of Holiness*, p. 13.

139. Jean Calvin, *Commentaries on the First Book of Moses called Genesis*, p. 76; John H. Leith ("The Doctrine of the Will in the *Institutes of the Christian Religion*," in *Reformatio Perennis*, pp. 49–50) also notes the relation between dependency and direct causality.

140. Quoted in Copleston, *History of Philosophy*, vol. 3, part 1, p. 99.

141. F. Edward Cranz, "Cusanus, Luther, and the Mystical Tradition," in *Pursuit of Holiness*, p. 94. "Rapport between being and thinking" is Gordon Leff's phrase; *William of Ockham*, pp. 124–25.

142. F. Edward Cranz, "The Renaissance Reading of the *De Anima*," in *Platon et Aristote à la Renaissance*, p. 369.

143. See, for example, Ozment, *Age of Reform*, pp. 61–62.

144. Quoted in Raymond Klibansky, Erwin Panofsky, and Fritz Saxl, *Saturn and Melancholy*, p. 363.

145. Quoted in Donald J. Wilcox, *In Search of God and Self*, p. 384.

146. Quoted in Joseph Fitzer, "The Augustinian Roots of Calvin's Eucharistic Thought," *Augustinian Studies* 7 (1976): 71.

147. Luchesius Smits, *Saint Augustin dans l'oeuvre de Jean Calvin*; Fitzer, "Augustinian Roots," pp. 69–98.

148. On Augustine's concept of divine illumination, see Copleston, *History of Philosophy*, vol. 2, part 1, pp. 78ff.

149. Gerd Babelotsky, *Platonische Bilder und Gedankengänge in Calvins Lehre vom Menschen*, p. 53.

150. Ozment, *Age of Reform*, p. 7.

151. Luther, "Commentary on Galatians," p. 148.

152. Martin Luther, "Preface to the Complete Edition of Luther's Latin Writings, Wittenberg, 1545," in *Martin Luther*, p. 11.

153. Jean Calvin, "Reply to Sadolet," in *Theological Treatises*, p. 251.

154. Luther, "Freedom of a Christian," p. 69.

155. *Institutes*, III, iv, 18.

156. Luther, "Preface to Romans," p. 25.

157. *Institutes*, II, i, 4.

158. Ibid., II, i, 9: "totum hominem quasi diluvio a capite ad pedes sic fuisse obrutum, ut nulla pars a peccato sit immunis; ac proinde quidquid ab eo procedit in peccatum imputari. Sicut dicit Paulus (Rom. 8, 7), omnes affectus carnis, vel cogitationes, esse inimicitias adversus Deum, et ideo mortem."

159. Luther, "Commentary on Galatians," p. 130.

160. Ozment, *The Reformation in the Cities*, passim.

161. Calvin, "Reply to Sadolet," p. 251.

162. Calvin, *Commentary on Psalms*, vol. 1, p. 330.

163. Ozment notes this general trend, and Miriam Chrisman (*Strasbourg and the Reform*) has studied it in particular in Strasbourg.

164. Leff, *Dissolution of the Medieval Outlook*, chap. 2, "Knowledge and Belief".

165. *Institutes*, II, iii, 2. Psychoanalytic theory presupposes the lack of distinction by the superego between wish and deed. See Charles Brenner, *An Elementary Textbook of Psychoanalysis*, rev. ed., pp. 121–22.

166. *Institutes*, IV, x, 3.

167. Examples in ibid.

168. Luther, "Commentary on Galatians," p. 146: "the ungodly do not complain of the rebellion of their flesh, of any battle or conflict, or of the captivity and bondage of sin: for sin mightily reigneth in them."

169. In *Institutes*, III, xix, 5. Calvin points out that God's children know their Father will measure only their intention, not their accomplishment, in contrast to the servants who can never satisfy their masters.

170. Luther, "Preface to Romans," p. 25.

171. Quoted in Ozment, *Homo Spiritualis*, p. 208.

172. Luther, "Commentary on Galatians," p. 111.

173. Luther, "Preface to Romans," p. 31.

174. Luther, "Freedom of a Christian," p. 67.

175. Luther, "Commentary on Galatians," p. 151.

176. Ibid., p. 106.

177. Ozment, *Homo Spiritualis*, pp. 132–33

178. *Institutes*, III, iii, 14.

179. Ibid., III, iii, 14: "Quo fit ut longo intervallo a perfectione dissiti proficere semper aliquid et vitiis irretiti cum illis quotidie luctari necesse habeamus. Unde etiam consequitur, excussa desidia et securitate, intentis animis vigilandum esse, ne carnis nostrae insidiis incauti circumveniamur. Nisi forte confidimus nos maiores progressus fecisse quam apostolum, qui tamen fatigabatur ab angelo satanae, quo virtus in infirmitate perficeretur (2 Cor. 12, 7); et qui illam carnis et spiritus divisionem in sua carne non ficte repraesentabat (Rom. 7, 7seqq.)."

180. Ibid., III, ii, 17: "Nos certe, dum fidem docemus esse debere certam ac securam, non certitudinem aliquam imaginamur, quae nulla tangatur

dubitatione, nec securitatem quae nulla sollicitudine impetatur; quin potius dicimus perpetuum esse fidelibus certamen cum sua ipsorum diffidentia. Tantum abest ut eorum conscientias in placida aliqua quiete collocemus, quae nullis omnino turbis interpelletur. Rursum tamen, qualemcunque in modum afflictentur, decidere ac desciscere negamus, a certa illa, quam de misericordia Dei conceperunt, fiducia."

181. Ibid., III, ii, 18: "Sentit ergo in se divisionem pium pectus, quod partim ob divinae bonitatis agnitionem suavitate perfunditur, partim ob suae calamitatis sensum amaritudine angitur; partim in evangelii promissionem recumbit, partim suae iniquitatis testimonio trepidat; partim vitae apprehensione exsultat, partim mortem exhorrescit. Quae variatio ex fidei imperfectione contingit, quando nunquam tam bene in praesentis vitae cursu nobiscum agitur, ut omni diffidentiae morbo curati fide toti repleamur et occupemur. Hinc conflictus illi: ubi quae in reliquiis carnis haeret diffidentia, ad oppugnandam quae intus concepta est fidem insurgit."

182. Ibid., III, ii, 19: "Quantum deinde proficimus, ut nos assidue proficere decet, quasi progressu facto, in propiorem eius conspectum eoque certiorem venimus, et ipsa etiam continuatione familiarior nobis redditur."

183. Ibid.: "sic terrei corporis compedibus vincti, utcunque multa obscuritate undique obumbremur, luce tamen Dei vel pusillum ad exserendam eius misericordiam irradiante, quantum satis est ad solidam securitatem illuminamur."

184. Ibid., III, xx, 51: "Quin potius spem nostram bene temperata animi aequitate differendo, in eam perseverantiam insistamus, quae tantopere nobis commendatur in scripturis. Nam in Psalmis frequenter videre licet, ut David et reliqui fideles, dum precando fere lassi videntur aërem verberasse, quia Deo surdo verba sparserint, non tamen a precando desistunt."

185. Calvin, *Commentary on John*, vol. 2, p. 37. Charles Partee, "Calvin and Experience," *Scottish Journal of Theology* 26 (1973): 172.

186. *Institutes*, III, viii, 8: "in eo elucet alacritas, si tristitia et moerore vulneratus in spirituali Dei consolatione acquiescit."

187. Ibid., III, xi, 5.

188. Luther, "Commentary on Galatians," p. 108.

189. Ibid., p. 119.

190. Calvin, *Commentary on Galatians*, pp. 109–10.

191. Ibid., p. 119.

192. Luther, "Commentary on Galatians," p. 147.

193. Ibid., p. 107.

194. Ibid., p. 119

195. Ibid., p. 158

196. Luther, "Preface to Romans," p. 32.

197. Luther, "Commentary on Galatians," p. 148.

198. Luther, "Freedom of a Christian," p. 66.

199. Luther, "Commentary on Galatians," p. 128: "we, excluding all works, do go to the very head of this beast which is called Reason, which is the fountain and headspring of all mischiefs."

200. Ibid., p. 135.

201. Luther, "Preface to Romans," p. 33.

CHAPTER 2

1. Calvin, *Commentary on Psalms*, vol. 4, p. 494.

2. Jean Calvin, *Commentaries*, ed. J. Haroutunian, p. 242.

3. Quoted in F. -M. Higman, *The Style of John Calvin in his French Polemical Treatises*, p. 122: "qu'on mette en oubli toute humanité, quand il est question de combattre pour sa gloire."

4. A basic theme in Klaus Bannach, *Die Lehre von der doppelten Macht Gottes bei Wilhelm von Ockham*.

5. *Institutes*, III, xiii, 1.

6. Ibid., III, xv, 6.

7. Calvin, *Commentary on Psalms*, vol. 1, p. xxxvii.

8. Ibid., vol. 2, p. 289.

9. Ibid., vol. 1, p. 287.

10. Ibid., vol. 2, p. 306.

11. *Institutes*, IV, v, 18.

12. Ibid., IV, xii, 16.

13. "The Catechism of the Church of Geneva," in Jean Calvin, *Theological Treatises*, ed. J. K. S. Reid, pp. 128, 132–33.

14. Cf. "For the desires of the flesh are against the Spirit, and the desires of the Spirit are against the flesh; for these are opposed to each other, to prevent you from doing what you would." Gal. 5:17.

15. Calvin, *Commentary on Psalms*, vol. 3, p. 374.

16. Calvin, *Commentary on Genesis*, p. 92; *Institutes*, I, xv, 3.

17. W. Niesel, *The Theology of Calvin*, p. 68.

18. *Institutes*, I, xv, 4.

19. Torrance, *Calvin's Doctrine of Man*, p. 35.

20. Willis, *Calvin's Catholic Christology*, pp. 110–11.

21. *Institutes*, II, viii, 57.

22. Luther, "Preface to the Complete Edition of Luther's Latin Writings," p. 11; Calvin's account of his conversion in "Preface to Psalms" (also included in *Commentaries*, pp. 51–57, and L. W. Spitz, ed., *The Protestant Reformation*, pp. 110–14).

23. Calvin, *Commentary on Psalms*, vol. 1, p. 267.

24. Ibid., vol. 4, p. 145.

25. C. G. Jung, *Psychological Types or the Psychology of Individuation*, trans. H. G. Baynes, p. 23.

26. *Institutes*, II, xiv, 1.

27. Ibid., I, xiv, 16.

28. Ibid.

29. Ibid., II, xiii, 4.

30. Quoted in Paul Van Buren, *Christ in Our Place*, p. 13.

31. Discussed in Willis, *Calvin's Catholic Christology*, pp. 69ff.

32. Ibid., pp. 135–36.

33. Oberman, "Die 'Extra'-Dimension," pp. 323ff.

34. Calvin, *Commentary on John*, p. 167.

35. Ibid., p. 167.

36. *Institutes*, II, xvii, 1.

37. Quoted in McDonnell, *John Calvin*, p. 10.

38. *Institutes*, III, ii, 33.

39. Quoted in Van Buren, *Christ in Our Place*, p. 15.

40. Calvin, *Commentary on Psalms*, vol. 1, p. 361.

41. Calvin, *Commentary on John*, vol. 2, p. 12.

42. Quoted in Van Buren, *Christ in Our Place*, p. 16.

43. *Institutes*, II, xiii, 4.

44. Quoted in Alexandre Ganoczy, *Calvin, théologien de l'église et du*

ministère, p. 81.
45. Quoted in ibid., p. 88.
46. Quoted in Van Buren, *Christ in Our Place*, p. 38.
47. Quoted in ibid., p. 48.
48. Quoted in ibid., p. 49.
49. *Institutes*, II, xvi, 14.
50. Calvin, *Commentary on John*, vol. 2, p. 80.
51. *Institutes*, III, xx, 18.
52. Ibid., IV, xvii, 36.
53. Quoted in Willis, *Calvin's Catholic Christology*, p. 98.
54. *Institutes*, I, v, 9.
55. Quoted in Higman, *Style of John Calvin*, p. 123: "Le Seigneur sachent bien que, s'il parloit à nous selon qu'il convient à sa majesté, nostre intelligence n'est point capable d'atteindre si haut, s'accommode à nostre petitesse: et. . .il use envers nous d'une façon grossiere de parler, à fin d'estre entendu."
56. *Institutes*, III, xx, 40: "Verum quia aliter inenarrabilem eius gloriam mens nostra pro sua crassitie concipere non poterat, nobis per coelum designata est, quo nihil augustius aut maiestate plenius sub aspectum nostrum venire potest."
57. Ibid., III, xi, 8: "ac proinde non secundum divinam naturam hoc nobis praestare, sed pro dispensationis sibi iniunctae ratione. Etsi enim solus Deus fons est iustitiae, nec aliter quam eius participatione sumus iusti; quia tamen infelici dissidio ab eius iustitia alienati sumus, necesse est descendere ad hoc inferius remedium, ut nos Christus mortis et resurrectionis suae virtute iustificet."
58. Quoted in Ganoczy, *Calvin*, p. 166: "ceste condition abjecte et contemptible, laquelle il avoit vestue avec nostre chair."
59. *Institutes*, IV, xiv, 3: "Atque ita quidem hic se captui nostro pro immensa sua indulgentia attemperat misericors Dominus, ut quando animales sumus, qui humi semper adrepentes et in carne haerentes, nihil spirituale cogitamus, ac ne concipimus quidem, elementis etiam istis terrenis nos ad se deducere non gravetur, atque in ipsa carne proponere bonorum spiritualium speculum."
60. Calvin, *Commentary on Psalms*, vol. 4, p. 138
61. See Jürgen Moltmann, *Prädestination und Perseveranz*, passim.
62. *Institutes*, I, xv, 3.
63. Ibid.
64. Calvin, *Commentary on Genesis*, p. 111.
65. *Institutes*, I, xv, 5.
66. Calvin, *Commentary on Psalms*, vol. 4, p. 242.
67. Noted by Stadtland, *Rechtfertigung und Heiligung*, p. 182.
68. *Institutes*, II, iii, 13.
69. Calvin, *Commentary on Genesis*, p. 112.
70. Torrance, *Calvin's Doctrine of Man*, p. 40.
71. Quoted in Willis, *Calvin's Catholic Christology*, p. 70.
72. Quoted in ibid.
73. Quoted in ibid., p. 68.
74. Luther, "Commentary on Galatians," p. 158.
75. Calvin, *Commentary on Psalms*, vol. 1, p. xxxvii.
76. Ibid., vol. 3, p. 338.
77. Quoted in H. G. Haile, *Luther: An Experiment in Biography*, pp. 129–30.
78. Erik H. Erikson, *Young Man Luther*, pp. 213, 192.
79. Calvin, *Commentary on Corinthians*, p. 335.
80. W. Fred Graham, *The Constructive Revolutionary*; the quotation, which Graham italicizes, is on p. 179.

81. From his student years onward, Calvin drove himself and would deal with the apparent effects of this abuse with stringent dietary measures. To Farel in 1540 he reports that, when he is angry or more anxious than usual, he eats to excess and then has indigestion the next day, which he cures by fasting (*Letters*, vol. I, Oct. 1540). His attitude toward the insomnia, headaches, and indigestion that retarded his work (or forced him to slow down) was one of irritation or regret: he who needed so much more stamina than others had less. This is a recurrent theme in his letters.

82. Far less puzzling is the extremism in his treatment of heresy: here, he was proceeding consistently as a theologian and administrator with sixteenth-century mental équipage for decision making.

83. *Glossary of Psychoanalytic Terms and Concepts*, ed. Burness E. Moore and Bernard D. Fine, 2nd ed., s.v. "Character." (Hereafter cited as *Glossary*.)

84. David Shapiro, *Neurotic Styles*, chap. 2, "Obsessive-Compulsive Style," pp. 23–53.

85. Ibid., chap. 3, "Paranoid Style," pp. 54–107.

86. As throughout Jung, *Psychological Types*.

87. Charles Brenner, *An Elementary Textbook of Psychoanalysis*, rev. ed., p. 98.

88. *Glossary*, s.v. "Character formation."

89. See Shapiro, *Neurotic Styles*, chap. 7, "General and Theoretical Considerations," pp. 176–99, and survey of theory in chap. 1, Introduction, pp. 1–22.

90. Ibid., p. 177; *Glossary*, s.v. "Character formation."

91. Shapiro, *Neurotic Styles*, chap. 7, pp. 176–81.

92. Ibid., p. 180.

93. Tendency noted in Higman, *Style of John Calvin*, p. 158. Aristotelian formulation in *Institutes*, III, xiv, 17.

94. Calvin, "Preface to Psalms," in Spitz, *Protestant Reformation*, p. 111. In the absence of specific evidence of anything else, I conjecture that the human mechanism through which Calvin was able to move from one set of ideas to another was skeptical curiosity. The Lutherans, heretical and probably annoying, if not as upsetting as they were to his teachers at Montaigu, were nevertheless increasingly making decisive impressions on people he trusted greatly (Olivétan and Wolmar). That was a puzzle, and the way to solve puzzles was through texts. I suspect he got hold of some of the heretical texts, moved from skepticism to absorption, then realized, with surprise, that he agreed and felt at one with what he was reading, and just continued to read.

95. Calvin, "Preface to Psalms," in Spitz, *Protestant Reformation*, p. 111.

96. Calvin, *Letters*, pp. 71–72.

97. Erich Neumann, "Mystical Man," in *The Mystic Vision*, pp. 381, 397.

98. Henri-Charles Puech, "The Concept of Redemption in Manichaeism," in *The Mystic Vision*, p. 262.

99. C. G. Jung, "Aion," in *Psyche and Symbol*, ed. Violet S. de Laszlo, pp. 7–8.

100. Kenneth Joel Shapiro and Irving E. Alexander, *The Experience of Introversion*, pp. 153–60.

101. Ibid., p. 152.

102. Ibid., p. 144.

103. Jung, *Psychological Types*, p. 12.

104. Ibid., p. 412.

105. Ibid., p. 120.

106. Ibid., p. 481.
107. Ibid., p. 482.
108. Ibid., p. 120.
109. Ibid., p. 193.
110. 7 April 1549: letter to Viret, *Ioannis Calvini opera*, vol. 13, no. 1173, "Nosti animi mei teneritudinem, vel mollitiem potius. Quare nisi valida moderatio adhibita fuisset, non ita hactenus stetissem."
111. Jung, *Psychological Types*, p. 195.
112. Ibid., p. 479.
113. Quoted in Torrance, "Knowledge of God," p. 233.
114. Jung, *Psychological Types*, pp. 348, 356.
115. Calvin, *Commentary on Psalms*, vol. 3, p. 488.
116. Quoted in Heinrich Quistorp, *Calvin's Doctrine of the Last Things*, p. 57.
117. *Institutes*, I, xiv, 13.
118. Calvin, *Commentary on Genesis*, p. 529.
119. Quoted in Torrance, *Calvin's Doctrine of Man*, pp. 117, 124.
120. Quoted in ibid., p. 123.
121. See, for example, Calvin, *Letters*, vol. 1, pp. 71–72 (10 July 1538, to du Tillet).
122. Calvin, *Commentary on Psalms*, vol. 3, p. 255.
123. Ibid., vol. 4, p. 411.
124. Ibid., vol. 2, p. 133.
125. Ibid., vol. 1, p. 432.
126. Roland Bainton, *Here I Stand: A Life of Martin Luther*, pp. 31, 283.
127. *Institutes*, IV, xiv, 21.
128. Quoted in John Hick, *Evil and the God of Love*, p. 121n.
129. Bennett Simon, *Mind and Madness in Ancient Greece*, p. 174.
130. *Institutes*, IV, i, 1.
131. Ibid., II, viii, 6.
132. Ibid., II, xvi, 2: "Verum audiat rursum quod scriptura docet, se alienatum fuisse a Deo per peccatum, haeredem irae, mortis aeternae maledictioni obnoxium, exclusum ab omni spe salutis, extraneum ab omni benedictione Dei, satanae mancipium, sub peccati iugo captivum, horribili denique exitio destinatum et iam implicitum: hic Christum deprecatorem intercessisse, poenam in se recepisse ac luisse, quae ex iusto Dei iudicio peccatoribus omnibus imminebat; mala, quae Deo exosos illos reddebant, sanguine suo expiasse; hoc piaculo satisfactum ac rite litatum Deo patri esse; hoc intercessore iram eius fuisse placatam; hoc fundamento pacem Dei cum hominibus esse subnixam; hoc vinculo benevolentiam illius erga ipsos contineri: his nonne eo magis permovebitur, quo melius ad vivum repraesentatur quanta e calamitate ereptus fuerit? In summa, quoniam non potest animus noster vitam in Dei misericordia vel satis cupide apprehendere vel qua decet gratitudine excipere, nisi formidine irae Dei et aeternae mortis horrore ante perculsus et consternatus, sic instituimur sacra doctrina, ut sine Christo Deum nobis quodammodo infestum cernamus, et eius manum in exitium nostrum armatam, benevolentiam eius paternamque caritatem non nisi in Christo amplexemur."

I encountered Ford Lewis Battles's article, "God was Accommodating Himself to Human Capacity," *Interpretation*, 31 (1977): 19–38, after I wrote this. We are in agreement about accommodation as lowering, as we are in agreement about the extent of accommodation. I think our treatments are complementary; in fact, we seem to get to several of the same things by different routes (cf. my textual analysis, above, p. 32, with his analysis of the intellectual structure in the *Institutes* on page 33 of this article and with Brian A. Gerrish's development of this in "Theology within the Limits of Piety Alone," *Reformatio Perennis*, pp. 67–87).

133. Brenner, *Elementary Textbook*, pp. 103ff.

134. Ibid., p. 106.

135. I am informed by Robert Ostroff that this is an ordinary aspect of childhood grief.

136. Georgia Harkness, *John Calvin: The Man and his Ethics*, p. 4.

137. T. H. L. Parker, *John Calvin*, pp. 3–4.

138. Psychologists now use the term "splitting" for this phenomenon. Freud described a version of it in existence in his own life, stemming from his highly ambivalent relationship with a childhood friend who was also (as the result of a previous marriage by his father much earlier in life) his nephew: "An intimate friend and a hated enemy have always been indispensable to my emotional life; I have always been able to create them anew, and not infrequently my childish ideal has been so closely approached that friend and enemy have coincided in the same person; but not simultaneously, of course, as was the case in my early childhood." Quoted in Ernst Jones, *The Life and Work of Sigmund Freud*, p. 8.

139. Calvin, *Letters*, letter to Farel, 11 April 1549.

140. Ibid., letter to Viret, 7 April 1549.

141. Jung, *Psychological Types*, p. 300.

142. Ibid., p. 116.

143. Ibid., p. 120.

144. Alexandre Ganoczy, *Le jeune Calvin*, p. 346: "l'action que le Seigneur m'a mise entre les mains."

145. *Institutes*, IV, xii, 5.

146. Ibid., IV, xx, 10: "aut superstitiosa clementiae affectatione in crudelissimam incidat humanitatem, si molli dissolutaque indulgentia cum multorum pernicie diffluat."

147. Ibid., IV, xii, 5: "ne cum Dei contumelia inter Christianos nominentur, qui turpem ac flagitiosam vitam agunt, ac si sancta eius ecclesia foret improborum et sceleratorum hominum coniuratio."

148. Ganoczy, *Le Jeune Calvin*, p. 354: "Je parle: mais il faut que je m'escoute, estant enseigné par l'esprit de Dieu."

149. *Institutes*, III, viii, 11.

150. Ibid., III, xx, 44.

151. Ibid., III, xxv, 12.

152. Text included in note 107, chapter 1.

153. Ibid., III, viii, 7: "si penatibus nostris extrudimur, eo interius recipimur in Dei familiam; si vexamur et contemnimur, eo firmiores agimus in Christo radices; si probris ac ignominia notamur, eo ampliore loco sumus in regno Dei; si trucidamur, ita nobis ingressus patefit ad beatam vitam."

154. Quoted in Van Buren, *Christ in Our Place*, p. 4.

155. Calvin, *Commentary on John*, vol. 1, p. 223.

156. Leslie Armour, *Logic and Reality*, pp. 33ff. Armour rejects (without giving it much voice) the argument that things might be described by plurality of attributes, without limit and to satisfaction of the requirements of communication (pp. 156ff.).

157. Quoted at the end of Calvin's preface to the 1559 *Institutes*.

158. Ford Lewis Battles, "Calculus Fidei," in *Calvinus Ecclesiae Doctor*, pp. 85–110, esp. p. 100.

159. *Institutes*, II, iii, 1.

160. Ibid., IV, v, 15: "Quemadmodum enim latrones iugulatis hominibus praedam inter se dividunt, ita isti post exstinctum verbi Dei lumen, quasi iugulata ecclesia, putarunt expositum esse praedae ac direptioni, quidquid in sanctos usus dicatum erat."

161. Ibid., III, xvii, 1: "Sed quia aliis praeterea machinis, ut dictum est, nos impetunt, age, in illis quoque propulsandis pergamus."

162. See, for example, his final answer to objections to the doctrine of predestination as contradictory to God's love for all mankind: "as Augustine truly contends, they who measure divine justice by the standard of human justice are acting perversely" (III, xxiv, 17).

163. Not surprisingly, of one to whom personal display of emotion was uncongenial, his lecture style was described as old fashioned in comparison with that of many of his contemporaries (T. H. L. Parker, *John Calvin*, 132).

164. *Institutes*, III, v, 3: "Unum, unum illum praedicari decebat, unum proponi, unum nominari, unum respici quum de obtinenda peccatorum remissione, expiatione, sanctificatione agitur."

165. Ibid., IV, x, 10: "Sed quomodo excusarent, quum immenso apud eos sceleratius sit auricularem confessionem vertente anno praetermisisse, quam nequissimam vitam in solidum annum produxisse? linguam die veneris infecisse modico carnis gusto, quam totum corpus diebus omnibus scortando foedasse? manum, die sanctulis nescio quibus consecrato, admovisse honesto operi, quam pessimis facinoribus assidue membra omnia exercuisse?"

166. Ibid., III, ii, 18; the Latin text is included above in note 181, chapter 1.

167. Ibid., II, viii, 41; II, viii, 43.

168. Ibid., II, xiii, 4.

169. Calvin, *Commentary on Corinthians*, pp. 140–41.

170. Ibid., p. 166.

171. Ibid., pp. 137, 142, 145, 163.

172. Sexual passion is sinful in its inordinateness; "more than that, this feeling, I grant you, is more violent than others, and almost bestial (ibid., p. 140). While knowing that it is a trick of Satan to make us feel so, it is still the case that "there are few who are not sometimes waylaid by [the] feeling of distaste for their wives" (ibid., p. 137).

173. Ibid., p. 135.

174. Ibid., p. 144.

175. This is a recurrent concept in the *Institutes*. See especially II, ii, 12–13, 20; III, vi, 2–4; II, vii, 1.

176. See fuller discussion below, pp. 101–05.

177. Calvin, *Commentary on Psalms,* vol. 2, p. 70.

178. See, for example, note 110 in this chapter.

179. Calvin, *Commentary on Psalms,* vol. 5, p. 204; vol. 1, p. 528. See also quotations above, pp. 58–59.

180. For example: "But 'assurance' I do not understand to mean that which soothes our minds with sweet and perfect repose, releasing it from every anxiety. For to repose so peacefully is the part of those who, when all affairs are flowing to their liking, are touched by no care, burn with no desire, toss with no fear. But for the saints, the occasion that best stimulates them to call upon God is when, distressed by their own need, they are troubled by the greatest unrest, and are almost driven out of their senses until faith opportunely comes to their relief" (*Institutes*, III, xx, 11).

181. Calvin, *Commentary on Genesis*, p. 471.

182. Rosalie L. Colie, *Paradoxia Epidemica*, esp. chap. 3, pp. 96ff.

183. Calvin, *Commentary on Romans*, p. 429: "Vult enim miseram naturae nostrae conditionem a nobis perpetuo reputari: illa nihil quam horrorem, taedium, anxietatem, desperationem parere potest: atque ita sane expedit prosterni nos penitus ac conteri, quo tandem ad ipsum ingemiscamus. Caeterum nihil obest horror ille a nostri recognitione conceptus, quin animi nostri eius bonitate freti placide resideant: nihil obstat taedium illud quominus plena in ipso consolatione fruamur: nihil illa anxietas, nihil desperatio, quin solida et laetitia et spe apud ipsum potiamur" (*Ioannis Calvini opera*, vol. 49:222).

184. Ibid., p. 175.

185. Calvin, *Commentary on John*, vol. 2, p. 9.

186. Calvin, *Commentary on Genesis*, p. 127.

187. For examples, see *Commentary on Psalms*, vol. 1, pp. 8, 29f; *Commentary on Romans*, pp. 468–70.

188. *Commentary on Psalms*, vol. 1, pp. 9–10; vol. 3, p. 109.

189. Ibid., vol. 1, p. 20.

190. Ibid.

191. "Reply to Sadolet," in *Theological Treatises*, p. 233.

192. Quoted in T. H. L. Parker, *John Calvin*, p. 108.

193. *Institutes*, III, ii, 41: "Proinde mirum non est si perversum cor et obliquum nunquam subit hic affectus: quo in coelum ipsum traducti, ad reconditissimos Dei thesauros admittimur, et ad sacratissima regni eius adyta, quae profanari impuri cordis ingressu non decet."

194. T. H. L. Parker, *John Calvin*, p. 92.

195. *Institutes*, III, ii, 36.

196. Ibid., IV, xix, 10: "constituunt, sacram hanc unctionem maiori in veneratione habendam esse quam baptismum, quod illa summorum pontificum manibus peculiariter administratur, baptismus ab omnibus vulgariter sacerdotibus distribuitur. Quid hic dicas nisi plane furiosos esse, qui suis inventionibus ita blandiuntur ut prae ipsis sacrosanctas Dei institutiones secure contemnant? Os sacrilegum, tune pinguedinem foetore duntaxat anhelitus tui inquinatam, et verborum murmure incantatam, audes Christi sacramento opponere, et conferre cum aqua verbo Dei sanctificata?"

197. Ibid., p. 27 (Prefatory Address to King Francis): "Ipsam, ipsam doctrinam, cui id deberi aiunt quod sunt ecclesia, exitialem animarum carnificinam, facem, ruinam, et excidium ecclesiae esse non obscure cognosces, si legendis nostris aliquantum otii tui decidas."

198. Jung, *Psychological Types*, p. 151.

199. Luther, "Secular Authority," in *Martin Luther*, p. 373.

200. *Institutes*, IV, xx, 2.

201. Calvin, *Commentary on Corinthians*, p. 274.

202. *Institutes*, III, vii, 6.

203. Ibid., III, xix, 11.

204. Calvin, *Commentary on Genesis*, p. 529.

205. *Institutes*, III, xix, 13.

206. T. H. L. Parker, *John Calvin*, pp. 99–100.

207. Calvin, *Commentary on Psalms*, vol. 3, p. 54.

208. *Institutes*, III, xviii, 8.

209. Calvin, *Commentary on Genesis*, p. 482.

210. Calvin, *Commentary on Psalms*, vol. 3, p. 484.

211. T. H. L. Parker, *John Calvin*, p. 153.

212. Ibid., p. 145.

213. Ibid., p. 110.

214. Ibid., p. 102.

215. Quoted in ibid., p. 110.

216. Ibid., p. 153.

217. Ibid., p. 78.

218. Harkness (*John Calvin*, p. 17, n. 43) thinks so. See also note 12 in chapter 1, above.

219. "Reply to Sadolet," in *Theological Treatises*, pp. 222–223.

220. T. H. L. Parker, *John Calvin*, p. 80.

221. Ibid., p. 80.

222. E. Doumergue, *Jean Calvin*, vol. 2, pp. 701f.

223. Ibid., p. 705.

224. Ibid., p. 704.

225. Ibid., pp. 705–06.

226. T. H. L. Parker, *John Calvin*, p. 155.

227. *Institutes*, IV, xvii, 30.

228. Ibid., II, xiv, 1: "Si quid in rebus humanis tanto mysterio simile potest reperiri, hominis similitudo appositissima videtur, quem ex duabus substantiis conspicimus constare; quarum neutra tamen sic alteri permixta est, ut non retineat naturae suae proprietatem. Neque enim aut anima corpus aut corpus anima est. Quare et de anima seorsum dicitur quod in corpus nullo modo cadere potest; et de corpore rursus, quod nulla ratione animae conveniat; de toto homine, quod nec de anima seorsum, nec de corpore, nisi inepte, accipi possit. Postremo animi propria transferuntur ad corpus, et propria corporis ad animam. Qui tamen iis constat, unus homo est, non plures. Huiusmodi vero loquendi formulae et unam esse in homine personam ex duobus connexis compositam significant, et duas subesse diversas naturas, quae hanc constituant. Ita et de Christo scripturae loquuntur. Attribuunt illi interdum quae ad humanitatem singulariter referri oporteat, interdum quae divinitati peculiariter competant: nonnunquam quae utramque naturam complectantur, neutri seorsum satis conveniant. Atque istam quidem duplicis naturae coniunctionem, quae in Christo subest, tanta religione exprimunt, ut eas quandoque inter se communicent; qui tropus veteribus [idiōmatōn koinōnia] dictus est."

229. Ibid., II, xvi, 11–12: "Vincere ergo metum oportuit, qui naturaliter cunctos mortales assidue angit ac urget; quod fieri non potuit nisi pugnando. Porro fuisse non vulgarem aut levi de causa conceptum moerorem, mox clarius patebit. Ita cum diaboli potestate, cum mortis horrore, cum inferorum doloribus manum conserendo, factum est ut et referret de illis victoriam et triumphum ageret, ne iam in morte ea formidemus, quae princeps noster deglutivit. . . . Et sane nisi poenae fuisset particeps anima, corporibus tantum fuisset redemptor. Luctari autem oportuit ut erigeret, qui prostrati iacebant; adeoque nihil inde coelesti eius gloriae decedit, ut in hac parte refulgeat bonitas nunquam satis laudata, quod infirmitates nostras in se suscipere gravatus non est. . . . Unde . . . nobis proponit apostolus (Hebr. 4, 15) mediatorem hunc expertum esse nostras infirmitates, ut ad succurrendum miseris propensior sit."

230. Calvin, *Commentary on John*, vol. 1, p. 171. In "Negation" (*General Psychological Theory*, ed. Philip Rieff, pp. 213–17), Freud maintained that conscious and gratuitously asserted denials may be the only way in which a desire or belief that is, for various possible reasons, intolerable to the speaker, can be manifested.

231. Nicole Malet, *Dieu selon Calvin*.

232. T. H. L. Parker, *John Calvin*, p. 88; and W. Stanford Reid, "The Battle

Hymns of the Lord," in *Sixteenth Century Essays and Studies*, vol. 2, ed. Carl S. Meyer, p. 40.

233. Calvin, *Commentary on Romans*, p. 459.

234. See, for example, quotations above, p. 91, and below, p. 119.

235. See especially Jacques Lacan, "The Insistence of the Letter in the Unconscious," in *The Structuralists from Marx to Lévi-Strauss*, edited by Richard and Fernande De George, pp. 287–323.

236. Colie, *Paradoxia Epidemica*, esp. chap. 3, on Donne.

237. Quoted in Gerrish, "John Calvin on Luther," p. 81.

238. *Institutes*, IV, xiv, 9: "cuius unius virtute et corda penetrantur, et affectus permoventur, et sacramentis in animas nostras aditus patet. Si desit ille, nihil sacramenta plus praestare mentibus nostris possunt, quam si vel solis splendor caecis oculis affulgeat, vel surdis auribus vox insonet. Itaque sic inter spiritum sacramentaque partior, ut penes illum agendi virtus resideat, his ministerium duntaxat relinquatur: idque sine spiritus actione inane ac frivolum; illo vero intus agente vimque suam exserente, multae energiae refertum."

239. Ibid., IV, xvii, 5.

240. Ibid., IV, xvii, 39.

241. Ibid., IV, xvii, 26.

242. Ibid., IV, xvii, 10.

243. Ibid., IV, xvii, 32.

244. Ibid., IV, xvii, 2: "quod testimonium habent in unum corpus nos cum Christo coaluisse, ut quidquid ipsius est, nostrum vocare liceat. Hinc sequitur ut nobis secure spondere audeamus, vitam aeternam nostram esse, cuius ipse est haeres; nec regnum coelorum, quo iam ingressus est, posse magis nobis excidere quam ipsi; rursum, peccatis nostris non posse nos damnari a quorum reatu nos absolvit, quum ea sibi imputari voluerit ac si sua essent. Haec est mirifica commutatio, qua pro immensa sua benignitate nobiscum usus est."

245. Calvin, *Commentary on Corinthians*, p. 246.

246. *Institutes*, IV, xvii, 19.

247. Jung, *Psychological Types*, pp. 84–85.

248. *Institutes*, IV, xvii, 10: "Etsi autem incredibile videtur in tanta locorum distantia penetrare ad nos Christi carnem ut nobis sit in cibum, meminerimus quantum supra sensus omnes nostros emineat arcana spiritus sancti virtus, et quam stultum sit eius immensitatem modo nostro velle metiri. Quod ergo mens nostra non comprehendit, concipiat fides, spiritum vere unire quae locis disiuncta sunt."

249. Ibid., IV, xvii, 32.

250. Ibid., IV, xvii, 38: "Praeclare vero in sacramento profecerimus, si impressa insculptaque animis nostris fuerit haec cogitatio, non posse a nobis quemquam ex fratribus laedi, contemni, reiici, violari, aut ullo modo offendi, quin simul in eo Christum laedamus, spernamus, violemus nostris iniuriis; non posse nos a fratribus dissidere, quin simul a Christo dissideamus; Christum a nobis diligi non posse, quin diligatur in fratribus; qualem corporis nostri curam gerimus, talem fratrum quoque gerendam, qui membra sunt corporis nostri; quomodo nulla corporis nostri pars aliquo doloris sensu tangitur, qui non in alias omnes diffundatur, ita non ferendum esse fratrem malo aliquo affici, cuius non et ipsi compassione tangamur. Quamobrem non abs re Augustinus toties sacramentum hoc appellat caritatis vinculum."

251. Ibid., IV, xvii, 19.

252. Ibid., IV, xvii, 29.

253. Ibid.

254. Noted in McDonnell, *John Calvin*, pp. 210–11.

255. *Institutes*, IV, xvii, 40.

256. Ibid, IV, xvii, 30.

257. See discussion above, pp. 109–10.

258. *Institutes*, IV, xvii, 33.

259. Ibid., IV, xvii, 42: "Quare ea est dignitas, quam unam et optimam afferre Deo possumus, si nostram ei vilitatem et, ut ita loquar, indignitatem offeramus, ut sua misericordia nos se dignos faciat; si animos in nobis despondeamus, ut nos in ipso consolemur; si nos humiliemus, ut ab ipso erigamur; si nos accusemus, ut ab ipso iustificemur; praeterea, si ad eam quam in sua coena nobis commendat unitatem aspiremus; et, quemadmodum nos omnes unum in se ipso esse facit, ita unam omnino animam, cor unum, linguam unam nobis omnibus optemus. Haec si perpensa et meditata habuerimus, nunquam nos illae cogitationes, etiamsi concutiant, prosternent. Nos bonorum omnium egeni et nudi, nos peccatorum sordibus inquinati, nos semimortui, quomodo corpus Domini digne manducaremus? Magis cogitabimus nos pauperes venire ad benignum largitorem, aegros ad medicum, peccatores ad iustitiae autorem, mortuos denique ad eum qui vivificat."

260. *Glossary*, s.v. "Character."

261. *Institutes*, IV, vii, 23.

262. Ibid., III, xx, 8.

263. Ibid., II, xii, 3: "Quum denique mortem nec solus Deus sentire, nec solus homo superare posset, humanam naturam cum divina sociavit, ut alterius imbecillitatem morti subiiceret, ad expianda, peccata alterius virtute luctam cum morte suscipiens nobis victoriam acquireret."

264. Ibid., III, iv, 2: "Si quid autem in tota religione scire nostra refert, id certe refert maxime, nempe intelligere ac probe tenere, qua ratione, qua lege, qua conditione, qua facilitate aut difficultate obtineatur peccatorum remissio. Haec notitia nisi perspicua certaque constat, nullam omnino requiem, nullam cum Deo pacem, nullam fiduciam aut securitatem habere potest conscientia; sed assidue trepidat, fluctuatur, aestuat, cruciatur, divexatur, horret, odit ac fugit conspectum Dei."

265. "Ergo non est, quod pacificum adeo vobis regnum tribuas: ubi non alia ratione quies fuit, nisi quia Christus conticebat" *Ioannis Calvini opera*, vol. 5, "Responsio ad Sadoleti epistolam," p. 415.

266. *Institutes*, II, xvi, 19: "Si salus quaeritur, ipso nomine Iesu docemur penes eum esse; si spiritus alia quaelibet dona, in eius unctione reperientur; si fortitudo, in eius dominio; si puritas, in eius conceptione; si indulgentia, in eius nativitate se profert, qua factus est nobis per omnia similis, ut condolescere disceret; si redemptio, in eius passione; si absolutio, in eius damnatione; si maledictionis remissio, in eius cruce; si satisfactio, in eius sacrificio; si purgatio, in eius sanguine; si reconciliatio, in descensu ad inferos; si mortificatio carnis, in eius sepulcro; si vitae novitas, in eius resurrectione; si immortalitas, in eadem; si haereditas regni coelestis, in coeli ingressu; si praesidium, si securitas, si bonorum omnium copia et facultas, in eius regno; si secura iudicii exspectatio, in potestate iudicandi illi tradita. Denique in ipso thesauri omne genus bonorum quum sint, inde ad satietatem hauriantur, non aliunde."

267. Ozment has also stressed, with other historians, the growing literacy among townspeople. Literacy and printing helped disseminate a highly responsive theology; pride in literacy, as well as access to Scripture, probably bolstered confidence in the questioning of church authority (*Age of Reform*, pp. 201–04).

268. From *Avertissement contre l'astrologie judiciaire*, quoted in Higman, *Style of John Calvin*, p. 138: "De fait, puisque ceux qui ont de l'argent sont tant

soigneux à le bien garder, c'estoit bien raison que ce thresor inestimable de l'Evangile, quand Dieu nous en a enrichis, fust comme enfermé en bonne conscience, qui est, par manière de dire, le vray cofre, pour le tenir en bonne garde et seure, à ce qui'il ne nous soit ravy par Sathan."

269. *Institutes*, II, viii, 45.

270. E. H. Harbison, *The Christian Scholar in the Age of Reformation*, p. 158.

271. Quoted in ibid., p. 159, though I have changed the translation slightly.

272. Quoted in ibid., p. 161.

273. Ibid., pp. 162–63.

274. *Institutes*, IV, xi, 16.

275. Ibid., IV, xx, 3: "non minor inter homines quam panis, aquae, solis et aeris; dignitas quidem multo etiam praestantior. Non enim (quae illorum omnium commoditas est) huc spectat duntaxat ut spirent homines, edant, bibant, foveantur (quanquam haec certe omnia complectitur, dum efficit ut simul vivant), non tamen, inquam, huc spectat solum: sed ne idolatria, ne in Dei nomen sacrilegia, ne adversus eius veritatem blasphemiae aliaeque religionis offensiones publice emergant ac in populum spargantur; ne publica quies perturbetur; ut suum cuique salvum sit et incolume; ut innoxia inter se commercia homines agitent; ut honestas et modestia inter ipsos colatur. Denique, ut inter Christianos publica religionis facies exsistat, inter homines constet humanitas."

276. Ibid., IV, xx, 8.

277. Ibid., IV, xx, 21.

278. Ibid., III, ix, 3.

279. Ibid., III, ix, 4: "Nam si coelum patria est, quid aliud terra quam exsilium? Si migratio e mundo est in vitam ingressus, quid aliud mundus quam sepulcrum? in ipso manere, quid aliud quam in morte demersum esse? Si liberari a corpore, est asseri in solidam libertatem, quid aliud est corpus quam carcer? Si Dei praesentia frui suprema felicitatis summa est, nonne ea carere miserum? Atqui, donec e mundo evaserimus, peregrinamur a Domino (2 Cor. 5, 6). Ergo, si cum coelesti vita terrena comparetur, non dubium quin facile et contemnenda et proculcanda sit."

280. Ibid., III, ix, 2.

281. Ibid., IV, xx, 31.

282. Ibid., IV, xx, 25.

283. Ibid., IV, xx, 23.

284. Jung, *Psychological Types*, chap. 1, "The Problem of Types in the History of Classical and Medieval Thought."

285. Ernst Cassirer, *The Individual and the Cosmos in Renaissance Philosophy*, trans. Mario Domandi, esp. chap. 2, "Cusanus in Italy."

286. F. Edward Cranz, "Cusanus, Luther, and the Mystical Tradition," *The Pursuit of Holiness in Late Medieval and Renaissance Religion*, ed. Charles Trinkaus with Heiko A. Oberman, p. 99.

287. Colie, *Paradoxia Epidemica*, p. 29; Edgar Wind, *Pagan Mysteries in the Renaissance*, p. 158.

288. See Charles Trinkaus, *The Poet as Philosopher*.

289. Ibid. See especially the discussion of Petrarch's antiurbanism in chap. 3, "Petrarch's Critique of Self and Society," pp. 71ff.

290. Ibid., pp. 89, 119.

291. There is a good list of techniques of argument in Richard Lanham, *A Handlist of Rhetorical Terms*, pp. 125–28.

292. For Neumann's analysis, see "Leonardo da Vinci and the Mother

Archetype," in his *Art and the Creative Unconscious*. For the historiographical disputes over Freud's treatment of what he, too, considers to be a vulture, see the introduction by Alan Tyson to Freud's *Leonardo da Vinci and a Memory of his Childhood*, pp. 8–10.

293. I. D. McFarlane, *Renaissance France, 1470–1589*, p. 509.

294. The literary historian Wylie Sypher has also traced a dialectical development from medieval to Renaissance culture and from the culture of the Renaissance to that of the late Renaissance, and correlated Mannerist art (and late sixteenth- and seventeenth-century English literature) with aspects of the Calvinist God of predestination—with his inscrutability and irrationality—in *Four Stages of Renaissance Style*. Sypher regards Mannerism as a symptomatic link in a chain leading to the culture of Cartesian thought and late Baroque art and literature, when the dual dimensions of human life were finally comprised and subjected to clear and thorough analysis. It should be evident that I see sixteenth-century culture positively rather than symptomatically, and it will become evident below that the rejection of the claims of the unconscious—and the wiles of rhetoric—in seventeenth-century culture seem wishful and fearful to me. There is more than a difference in taste and temperament here—historians, some two decades after Sypher wrote his book in 1955, are working with different historiographical equipment.

295. McFarlane, *Renaissance France*, pp. 501–10, discusses the extremely unsettling nature of the loss of traditional moorings and senses of identity in this period of cultural and political flux in France—and also sees it as the stimulus to the great reassessments of human nature in later sixteenth-century French literature.

CHAPTER 3

1. Max Dvorak, "El Greco and Mannerism," *Magazine of Art* (Jan., 1953): 18.

2. Walter Friedlaender, *Mannerism and Anti-Mannerism in Italian Painting*, p. 3.

3. See introduction by Donald Posner (pp. xi–xix) to ibid.

4. Erwin Panofsky, *Idea*, chap. 5, esp. pp. 83f.

5. Quoted in ibid., pp. 90–91.

6. Quoted in ibid., p. 153.

7. Quoted in ibid., p. 143.

8. Quoted in ibid., pp. 87–88.

9. Ibid., chap 5, passim.

10. Sypher, *Four Stages of Renaissance Style*, esp. pp. 117, 130, 162ff.

11. Ibid., pp. 81, 99.

12. Noted by Arnold Hauser, in *Mannerism*, p. 71. He mentions Luther here.

13. Nikolaus Pevsner, "Gegenreformation und Manierismus," *Repertorium für Kunstwissenschaft* 46: 243–61.

14. Quoted in Ozment, *Age of Reform*, p. 416.

15. T. M. Parker, chap. 3, "The Papacy, Catholic Reform, and Christian Missions," in *The New Cambridge Modern History*, vol. 3, pp. 59–69.

16. Hauser, *Mannerism*, p. 20.

17. Ibid., pp. 123f.; Sypher, *Four Stages of Renaissance Style*, p. 176.

18. Hauser, *Mannerism*, p. 278.

19. Ibid., pp. 115ff.

20. Ibid., p. 118.

21. Ibid., pp. 118f., 279.
22. Ibid., p. 111.
23. Otto Benesch, *The Art of the Renaissance in Northern Europe*, pp. 88–95.
24. Nikolaus Pevsner, *Academies of Art, Past and Present*, p. 7.
25. Ibid., p. 12.
26. Ibid., p. 66.
27. Ibid., pp. 54–55.
28. Ibid., p. 42.
29. Selection from Vasari in E. G. Holt, *A Documentary History of Art*, vol. 2, pp. 25ff.
30. Hauser, *Mannerism*, p. 280.
31. Frederick Hartt, "Power and the Individual in Mannerist Art," in *Acts of the Twentieth International Congress of the History of Art*, pp. 222ff.
32. Selection from Guicciardini in J. B. Ross and M. M. McLaughlin, eds., *The Portable Renaissance Reader*, p. 279.
33. Ibid., p. 283.
34. Ibid., p. 284.
35. Hans Baron, *The Crisis of the Early Italian Renaissance*.
36. My last phrase is adapted from Ozment, *Age of Reform*, p. 198. Ozment stresses this theme in his treatment of the period.
37. M. D. Feld, "Revolution and Reaction in Early Modern Europe," *Journal of the History of Ideas* 38 (1977): 175–84.
38. Ibid., p. 175.
39. Ibid., p. 181.
40. Ibid., p. 178.
41. Ibid., p. 183.
42. H. G. Koenigsberger and G. L. Mosse, *Europe in the Sixteenth Century*, pp. 227f.
43. G. E. Swanson, in *Religion and Regime*, has argued that participants in municipal government in sixteenth-century Europe had profound doubts about the legitimacy as well as the viability of urban democracy.
44. Koenigsberger and Mosse, *Europe in the Sixteenth Century*, p. 218.
45. Feld, "Revolution and Reaction," p. 179.
46. Hauser, *Mannerism*, pp. 96f.
47. By Bernd Moeller, quoted in Ozment, *Age of Reform*, p. 192.
48. Henry Kamen, "Golden Age, Iron Age," *Journal of Medieval and Renaissance Studies* 4 (1974): 141.
49. Ibid., p. 154.
50. Ibid., pp. 144–49.
51. Ibid., pp. 149–50.
52. Ibid., p. 150.
53. Ibid., p. 151.
54. Hartt, "Power and the Individual," pp. 222f.
55. Ibid., p. 233.
56. Selection from Loys Le Roy in Ross and McLaughlin, *Portable Renaissance Reader*, p. 107.
57. Michael Walzer, *The Revolution of the Saints*, pp. 22–27.
58. Ibid., p. 27.
59. Ibid., p. 247.
60. Ibid., p. 30.
61. Ibid., pp. 31–45. See also W. J. Bouwsma, "Anxiety and the Formation of Early Modern Culture," in *After the Reformation*, ed. Barbara C. Malament,

pp. 215–46, which traces the origins of the character of modern society to the anxiety precipitated by discrepancies between a changing historical world and the medieval organization and guidelines for the life of soul and society — guidelines never fully redrawn.

62. Walzer, *Revolution of the Saints*, p. 308.

63. Ibid.

64. Ibid., p. 61.

65. Ozment, *Age of Reform*, pp. 220–22.

66. "Doctrine and life are to be distinguished. Life is as bad among us as among the papists. Hence we do not fight and damn them because of their bad lives. Wyclif and Hus, who fought over the moral quality of life, failed to understand this. I do not consider myself to be pious. But when it comes to whether one teaches correctly about the Word of God, there I take my stand and fight. To contest doctrine has never happened until now. Others have fought over life, but to take on doctrine — that is to grab the goose by the neck! Truly the kingdom and office of the papists is evil. Once we have demonstrated that, it is easy to go on and prove that their lives are also bad. But when the word of God remains pure, even if the quality of life fails us, life is placed in a position to become what it ought. That is why everything hinges on the purity of the Word. I have succeeded only if I have taught correctly." Quoted from the *Tischreden* in Ozment, *Age of Reform*, p. 316.

67. Oberman, *Harvest of Medieval Theology*, pp. 106ff.

68. Ibid., p. 346.

69. Ford Lewis Battles has pointed out that his scriptural exegesis is an analysis of ideas in relation to the mode of discourse that is God's particular form of accommodation in a given instance ("God Was Accommodating Himself to Human Capacity," pp. 20ff.). Gilbert Vincent has observed that his understanding of the Eucharist is in part an analysis of what is implied by a particular mode of discourse in its historical context — and Vincent suggests that Calvin's juridical training was influential in forming his awareness of the effect of the institutional contexts of words upon their meanings ("La théologie calvinienne," p. 152 and passim).

70. This is Marcia Colish's point of departure in her study of medieval sign theory, *The Mirror of Language*.

71. Lucien Richard, *The Spirituality of John Calvin*, pp. 146–48.

72. Ibid., pp. 151–52.

73. E. David Willis has linked Calvin's and Augustine's use of rhetoric through these concepts. See his "Rhetoric and Responsibility in Calvin's Theology," in *The Context of Contemporary Theology*, ed. Alexander J. McKelway and E. David Willis, pp. 49–50.

74. Colish, *Mirror of Language*, chap. 1, "Saint Augustine: The Expression of the Word," pp. 18ff.

75. Ibid., pp. 33–35.

76. From *Enarratio in Psalmum XCIX*, 6, quoted in ibid., p. 35.

77. Ibid. See list with references on p. 35, n. 70; the works cited include the *Confessiones, De vera religione, Tractatus in Ioannem, De fide et symbolo*, and *De civitate dei*.

78. Quoted in ibid., pp. 37–38.

79. From *De Trinitate*, quoted in Robert L. Montgomery, *The Reader's Eye*, p. 33.

80. Quoted in Rodolphe Peter, "Rhétorique et prédication selon Calvin," *Revue d'histoire et de philosophie religieuses* 55 (1975): 252–53.

81. Ibid., p. 250.

82. Ibid., p. 249: "l'éloquence qui convient à l'Esprit de Dieu, c'est celle qui n'est point enflée d'ostentation et ne se perd point en l'air par vaines bouffés, mais est solide et pleine d'efficace, et a plus de sincérité que d'élégance."

83. Colish's paraphrase of the passage in the *Confessions* (*Mirror of Language*, p. 25).

84. Ibid., p. 61.

85. Gal. 6:11. Madolene Stone called my attention to this verse.

86. Gal. 6:15.

87. Leff, *Dissolution of the Medieval Outlook*, pp. 67–69.

88. Julius R. Weinberg, *Ockham, Descartes, and Hume*, p. 128.

89. Leff, *Dissolution of the Medieval Outlook*, pp. 69–70.

90. Struever, *Language of History*, p. 45.

91. William J. Courtenay, "Covenant and Causality in Pierre D'Ailly," *Speculum* 46 (1971): 116–19 and passim.

92. William of Ockham, *Philosophical Writings*, p. 52 (from *Summa totius logicae*).

93. See discussion in Gordon Leff, *William of Ockham*, pp. 70, 236ff. A list of the syncategorematic terms (such as "some," "whole," "beside") is in William of Ockham, *Philosophical Writings*, p. 55 (*Summa totius logicae*).

94. Nancy Streuver, *Language of History*, passim; Kelley, *Foundations of Modern Historical Scholarship*, passim.

95. James Anderson Winn, *Unsuspected Eloquence*, p. 157.

96. Quoted in ibid., p. 162.

97. Barbara Kiefer Lewalski, *Protestant Poetics and the Seventeenth-Century Religious Lyric*, p. 120.

98. See R. Waswo, "The 'Ordinary Language Philosophy' of Lorenzo Valla," *Bibliothèque d'Humanisme et Renaissance* 41 (1979): pp. 255–71. The wider setting of Valla's ideas on language would have been congenial to Calvin. Language is the way we know and orient ourselves in the world; at the same time, Valla is explicit about the limits of self-knowledge and supports this awareness with the evidence of human language. Truth and falsehood, we are told in the *Dialecticae*, "are in ourselves, that is, of our mind. Sometimes these are not manifested in the mind but in the mouth. Therefore an utterance can be false while the mind is not mistaken—when someone speaks otherwise than he feels—and can likewise be true while the mind is mistaken—when someone deceives not another, as before, but rather himself" (quoted on p. 258).

99. The discussion from the *Institutes* is at IV, xvii, 21. Cf. presentation of the idea in *Commentary on Genesis*: "Externis symbolis Deus verbum suum illustrat et ornat ut maior illi tum claritas tum autoritas accedit" (quoted in Wallace, *Calvin's Doctrine of the Word and Sacrament*, p. 73), and a motif in Calvin. See also Joseph N. Tylenda, "Ecumenical Intention," pp. 27–47.

100. The *Dialecticae* was widely available. An edition of Valla which includes it was published in Basel in 1543; an edition of the *Dialecticae* alone was published in Paris in 1509. (See Cosenza's *Biographical and Bibliographical Dictionary of the Italian Humanists*, and the Bibliothèque Nationale catalog.)

101. *Institutes*, III, xxiii, 6.

102. See Quirinus Breen, *John Calvin*, pp. 102–13.

103. "It is peculiar to the poet in metric and figurative speech to move the imaginative faculty in such a way that our intellect sees the words themselves by a certain similitude and perceives what is said and understands something other than what is narrated." From Salutati, *De laboribus herculis*, quoted in Montgomery, *Reader's Eye*, p. 47.

104. "Vox humana naturalis illa quidem est, sed eius significatio ab institutione descendit: homines enim rebus cognitis, voces quas adaptarent invenerunt. Quorum primus fuit Adam deo autore: easque cum suis significationibus posteros docuerunt. Ut soni quidem sint a natura, voces autem et significationes ab artifice: quorum sonus auris, significationes animus, voces ambo percipiunt. Postremo inventae sunt literae quasi mutae voces, sive vocum imagines: ut ipse voces sunt quasi imagines significationum quae iam proprie dicuntur vocabula." Quoted in Waswo, "'Ordinary Language Philosophy,'" p. 265. It is also interesting to a historian analyzing the rhetoric of the *Institutes* that, while most theory in the sixteenth century did not distinguish between spoken and written rhetoric, focusing upon the former and considering that approach applicable to the latter, Valla considered written words, just insofar as they lacked vocalized sounds, to have a distanced but permanent physical presence (ibid., pp. 266–67).

105. *Institutes*, IV, xvii, 21.

106. "Restat igitur ut propter affinitatem quam habent cum suis symbolis res signatae, nomen ipsum rei fateamur attributum fuisse symbolo: figurate id quidem, sed non sine aptissima analogia. . . . Dico metonymicum esse hunc sermonem, qui usitatus est passim in Scriptura, ubi de mysteriis agitur." Ibid.

107. "Neque enim aliter accipere possis quod dicitur, circumcisionem esse foedus, agnum esse transitum, sacrificia legis esse expiationes: denique petram, ex qua in deserto aqua profluebat, fuisse Christum, nisi translatitie dictum accipias. Nec modo a superiore ad inferius nomen transfertur: sed contra, etiam rei signatae tribuitur nomen signi visibilis." Ibid.

108. ". . . non figurat tantum ceu nuda et inanis tessera, sed vere etiam exhibet." Ibid.

109. Ibid., 20.

110. "Quod si humanitus excogitata symbola, quae imagines sunt rerum absentium potius quam notae praesentium, quas etiam ipsas fallaciter saepissime adumbrant, earum tamen titulis interdum ornantur: quae a Deo sunt instituta, multa maiori ratione rerum nomina mutuantur, quarum et certam minimeque fallacem significationem semper gerunt, et adiunctam habent secum veritatem. Tanta est similitudo et vicinitas alterius ad alterum, ut proclivis ultro citroque sit deductio." Ibid., 21.

111. "Nam quum in multis sacramenta simul conveniunt, tum in hac metonymia quaedam est ipsis omnibus inter se communitas." Ibid.

112. Wallace, *Calvin's Doctrine*, p. 167.

113. Ibid., p. 167. See my discussion of this analogy above, pp. 109–10.

114. John Calvin, "The Form of Prayers and Songs in the Church," trans. Ford Lewis Battles, *Calvin Theological Journal* 15 (1980): 164.

115. Struever, *Language of History*, p. 32.

116. Ibid., p. 161.

117. Ibid., p. 157.

118. Ibid., see, for example, pp. 17, 45, 87.

119. Ibid., pp. 29, 50.

120. Ibid., pp. 129–31, 140, 74, 89.

121. Bouwsma, "Changing Assumptions," p. 422.

122. Struever, *Language of History*, p. 60.

123. Ibid., p. 54.

124. Ibid., p. 60.

125. Ibid., p. 61.

126. Bouwsma, "Changing Assumptions," p. 425.

127. Struever, *Language of History*, p. 155.

128. Ibid., p. 107.

129. Bouwsma, "Changing Assumptions," p. 427.

130. Struever, *Language of History*, p. 120.

131. Ibid., p. 57.

132. Klibansky, Panofsky, and Saxl, *Saturn and Melancholy*, pp. 360–61.

133. Bouwsma, "Renaissance and Reformation," p. 140.

134. Struever, *Language of History*, p. 59.

135. See Bouwsma, "Changing Assumptions," p. 431.

136. Ibid., p. 437.

137. Ibid., p. 438.

138. Ibid.

139. Denys Hay, *The Italian Renaissance in Its Historical Background*, chap. 7, "The Reception of the Renaissance in the North," p. 188; Bouwsma, "Changing Assumptions," esp. pp. 438–39.

140. Struever sees it this way, as a general cultural phenomenon (*Language of History*, pp. 8, 23, 24, 27).

141. Bouwsma, "Changing Assumptions," p. 427.

142. Ibid., p. 431.

143. Ibid.

144. Ibid., pp. 431–33.

145. Ibid., pp. 434–36.

146. Frances A. Yates, *The French Academies of the Sixteenth Century*, pp. 73ff.

147. Ibid., p. 76.

148. Ibid., pp. 76ff.

149. Winn, *Unsuspected Eloquence*, pp. 166ff.

150. Yates, *French Academies*, p. 141.

151. Cf. ibid., p. 235: "The academic initiate reached levels of hidden truth, only to be expressed in images, known under the influence of poetry and music, and impossible to explain, or even to remember, when one came out into a world in which the Massacre of St. Bartholemew's had just taken place. In that lower world, the academicians too oft reverted to their party cries. Yet to an academic philosopher, harmony must always have been the groundwork of thought, and so he can never have been able to avoid the problem presented by the religious differences, which broke the universal harmony of Christendom."

152. Oberman, *Harvest of Medieval Theology*, pp. 67–68.

153. Ozment, *Age of Reform*, pp. 121–25.

154. Oberman, *Harvest of Medieval Theology*, pp. 346, 265. Biel's Mariology further reflects reserve on the humanity of Christ: Mary, in her bodily assumption into heaven, is more the Hope of the World than Christ, "who was not a pure man but a man-God" (p. 315).

155. William of Ockham, *Predestination*, pp. 46, 54, 101.

156. See, for example, the discussion of Spenser and mutability in A. Bartlett Giamatti, *Play of Double Senses*, chap. 4.

157. Montgomery, *Reader's Eye*, passim.

158. Ibid., pp. 66f., 84f., 88.

159. See, for example, the chapters on Ariosto and Tasso in A. Bartlett Giamatti, *The Earthly Paradise and the Renaissance Epic*.

160. Montgomery, *Reader's Eye*, pp. 171, 203.

161. Edmund Spenser, "A Letter of the Authors to Sir Walter Raleigh," p. 407.

162. Montgomery, *Reader's Eye*, p. 136.

163. Lewalski, *Protestant Poetics*, passim.

164. Lewalski begins her analysis of it with George Herbert's question, "Must all be vail'd, while he that reades, divines / Catching the sense at two removes?" Quoted in ibid., pp. 3–4.

165. Ibid., pp. 120–21.

166. Lewalski (ibid., pp. 77–78) considers the passage on metonymy in regard to the Eucharist to be limited to sacramental signification, though very important for its concept of "exhibiting," later to be extended by others.

167. Colie, *Paradoxia Epidemica*, pp. 199–201, 207ff.

168. Richard A. Lanham, *The Motives of Eloquence*, p. 175.

169. Quoted in Lanham, *Motives of Eloquence*, p. 160.

170. Winn, *Unsuspected Eloquence*, p. 168.

171. See Harbison, *Christian Scholar*, for the Athens-Jerusalem theme.

172. John Hollander, *Vision and Resonance*, pp. 93, 96.

173. Ibid., pp. 117ff., especially 120f. Hollander is following Wimsatt's observation of an "almost magic" relation (Wimsatt is speaking here of Pope) "of phonetic likeness which encourages us to perceive and believe in a meaning otherwise asserted by the words" (W. K. Wimsatt, *The Verbal Icon*, p. 181, and also the chapters entitled "One Relation of Rhyme to Reason" and "Rhetoric and Poems").

174. *Institutes*, III, xx, 40.

175. Ibid., II, xvi, 2.

176. Ibid., III, xxiv, 17.

177. Ibid., III, xxv, i: "Etsi Christus, sol iustitiae, morte devicta per evangelium illucens, vitam nobis illuminavit, teste Paulo, unde et credendo dicimur transiisse a morte in vitam, non iam peregrini et advenae, sed cives sanctorum et domestici Dei, qui nos cum ipso unigenito sedere fecit in coelestibus, ut ad plenam felicitatem nihil desit."

178. Ibid.: "Denique sursum et deorsum, a fronte et a tergo violentae nos tentationes obsident, quibus sustinendis longe essent animi nostri impares, nisi expliciti rebus terrenis, coelesti vitae, quae in speciem procul remota est, devincti essent." (I have changed the Battles translation somewhat.)

179. Ibid., III, xxv, 3.

180. Wimsatt, *Verbal Icon*; see, for example, p. 175.

181. Ibid., p. 164.

182. Ibid., p. 217.

183. Ibid., p. 231

184. Ibid., p. 165.

185. Basil Hall, "Calvin against the Calvinists," in *Courtenay Studies in Reformation Theology*, vol. 1, *John Calvin*, ed. G. E. Duffield, chap. 2, pp. 25ff.

186. Basil Hall, "From Biblical Humanism to Calvinist Orthodoxy," *Journal of Ecclesiastical History* 31 (1980): pp. 341–42.

187. Hall, "Calvin against the Calvinists," p. 25.

188. Yates, *French Academies*, p. 311 and passim.

189. Montgomery, *Reader's Eye*, pp. 176ff.

190. Ibid., p. 167

191. Walter Jackson Ong, "Ramism," *Dictionary of the History of Ideas*, vol. 4.

192. Walter Jackson Ong, *Ramus, Method, and the Decay of Dialogue*, esp. book 1.

193. Ong, "Ramism," p. 43; and *Ramus, Method, and the Decay of Dialogue*:

diagrams from early printed texts of Ramus are included in the latter.

194. Richard Stauffer, "Le calvinisme et les universités," *Bulletin historique et littéraire de la Société de l'Histoire du Protestantisme Français* 126 (1980): esp. pp. 48–50.

195. Margreta De Grazia, "The Secularization of Language in the Seventeenth Century," *Journal of the History of Ideas* 41 (1980): 319–20.

196. Ibid., p. 322.

197. Ibid., pp. 319, 327.

198. Ibid., p. 325.

199. Ibid.

200. Ibid., p. 324.

201. Francis Bacon, *The New Organon and Related Writings*, ed. Fulton H. Anderson, p. 48 (Book One, Aphorism XLI).

202. Ibid., pp. 56–58 (Book One, Aphorisms LIX, LX).

203. On the concept of hardness, see Agnes Heller, *Renaissance Man*, trans. Richard E. Allen, p. 425.

204. De Grazia, "Secularization of Language," p. 328.

205. Frances Yates, *Occult Philosophy in the Elizabethan Age*, p. 174.

206. Leopold Damrosch, "Hobbes as Reformation Theologian," *Journal of the History of Ideas* 40 (1979): 339–52.

207. Ibid., p. 348.

208. Ibid., p. 349.

209. Ibid., p. 348.

210. Quoted in Colie, *Paradoxia Epidemica*, p. 268 (Pensée no. 206).

211. Quoted in ibid., p. 263.

212. Ibid., p. 253.

213. Quoted in ibid., pp. 164–65.

214. Quoted in ibid., p. 161.

215. De Grazia, "Secularization of Language," pp. 328–29.

216. See the article by Simone Pétrement, "Dualism in Philosophy and Religion," in the *Dictionary of the History of Ideas*, vol. 2. The article includes a bibliography.

217. Struever, *Language of History*, p. 197.

218. Ibid., pp, 12, 29.

219. Terence Hawkes, *Structuralism and Semiotics*, chap. 2.

220. For example, Paul Ricoeur (*Freud and Philosophy*, trans. Denis Savage), and Paolo Valesio (*Novantiqua*).

221. Especially in physics, a nineteenth-century view of continuity has been, not superseded, but balanced with an equally viable and fruitful view of discreteness; "the whole structure of physics has been brought to rest on a duality between the continuous and the discrete." (Salomon Bochner, "Continuity and Discontinuity in Nature and Knowledge," in *Dictionary of the History of Ideas*, vol. 1, pp. 493–94). It could be noted that scientists have tended to find dualism uncongenial; however, confirmation from within, rather than external challenge, has been persuasive, sometimes against admitted resistance. The psychiatrist Silvano Arieti has written (of the question for which his field has often been an arena for debate) that, for reasons that probably have to do with his biological training, he would be inclined to prefer the monist to the dualist view. But he considers the major attempts to overcome dualism to be failures and that "dualism is inescapable. We have confused our state of understanding with our wishes" (Silvano Arieti, *Abraham and the Contemporary Mind*, pp. 22–23).

222. Lacan, "Insistence of the Letter," p. 318. Lacan's own theory of the

stade du miroir is an analysis of the origin of the sense of disjunction and desire for cohesion within the self, a sense he finds mediated by and through the symbolic dimensions of language (ibid., p. 319, and *The Language of the Self*, trans. and ed. Anthony Wilden, passim). See also the commentary by the editor, *Language of the Self*, pp. 262–70, on the concept of the Other.

223. Hawkes, *Structuralism and Semiotics*, pp. 41ff.
224. Lacan, "Insistence of the Letter," p. 318.
225. Hawkes, *Structuralism and Semiotics*, p. 115.
226. William H. Gass, *Fiction and the Figures of Life*, p. 33.
227. Charles Taylor, "Aims of a New Epoch," *Hegel*, pp. 19–28.

Works Cited

Arieti, Silvano. *Abraham and the Contemporary Mind*. New York: Basic Books, 1981.

Armour, Leslie. *Logic and Reality: An Investigation into the Idea of a Dialectical System*. Assen: Van Gorcum, 1972.

Auerbach, Erich. *Mimesis*. Translated by Willard Trask. Garden City, N.Y.: Anchor Books, 1957.

Ayers, Robert H. "Language, Logic and Reason in Calvin's *Institutes*." *Religious Studies* 16 (1980): 283–97.

Babelotsky, Gerd. *Platonischer Bilder und Gedankengänge in Calvins Lehre vom Menschen*. Wiesbaden: Franz Steiner Verlag, 1977.

Bacon, Francis. *The New Organon and Related Writings*. Edited by Fulton H. Anderson. Indianapolis: Bobbs-Merrill Co., 1960.

Bainton, Roland H. *Here I Stand: A Life of Martin Luther*. New York: Mentor Books, 1955.

_____. *The Reformation of the Sixteenth Century*. Boston: Beacon Press, 1952.

_____. *The Travail of Religious Liberty*. New York: Harper Torchbooks, 1958.

Bannach, Klaus. *Die Lehre von der doppelten Macht Gottes bei Wilhelm von Ockham*. Wiesbaden: Steiner, 1975.

Baron, Hans. *The Crisis of the Early Italian Renaissance: Civic Humanism and Republican Liberty in an Age of Classicism and Tyranny*. Princeton: Princeton University Press, 1966.

Battles, Ford Lewis. "Calculus Fidei." In *Calvinus Ecclesiae Doctor*, pp. 85–110.

_____. "God Was Accommodating Himself to Human Capacity." *Interpretation* 31 (1977): 19–38.

Bauke, Hermann. *Die Probleme der Theologie Calvins*. Leipzig: J. C. Hinrichs'schen, 1922.

Benesch, Otto. *The Art of the Renaissance in Northern Europe: Its Relation to the Contemporary Spiritual and Intellectual Movement*. Hamden, Conn.: Archon Books, 1964.

Bochner, Salomon. "Continuity and Discontinuity in Nature and Knowledge." In *Dictionary of the History of Ideas*, vol. 1, pp. 492–504.

Bouwsma, William J. "Anxiety and the Formation of Early Modern Culture." In *After the Reformation: Essays in Honor of J. H. Hexter*, edited by Barbara C. Malament, pp. 215–46. Philadelphia: University of Pennsylvania Press, 1980.

————. "Changing Assumptions in Later Renaissance Culture." *Viator* 7 (1976): 421–40.

————. "Renaissance and Reformation: An Essay in their Affinities and Connections." In *Luther and the Dawn of the Modern Era*, edited by Heiko A. Oberman, pp. 127–49. Leiden: E. J. Brill, 1974.

————. "The Renaissance and the Drama of Western History." *American Historical Review* 84 (1979): 1–15.

————. "The Two Faces of Humanism: Stoicism and Augustinianism in Renaissance Thought." In *Itinerarium Italicum: The Profile of the Italian Renaissance in the Mirror of Its European Transformations*, edited by Heiko A. Oberman and Thomas A. Brady, Jr., pp. 3–60. Leiden: E. J. Brill, 1975.

Boyer, Charles. *Calvin et Luther: Accords et différences*. Rome: Universitá Gregoriana Editrice, 1973.

Boyle, Marjorie O'Rourke. *Erasmus on Language and Method in Theology*. Toronto: University of Toronto Press, 1977.

Breen, Quirinus. *John Calvin: A Study in French Humanism*. Hamden, Conn.: Archon Books, 1968.

Brenner, Charles. *An Elementary Textbook of Psychoanalysis*. Rev. ed. Garden City, N.Y.: Anchor Books, 1974.

Calvin, Jean.

Collected Works; Collections

————. *Ioannis Calvini opera quae supersunt omnia*. Edited by G. Baum, E. Cunitz, and E. Reuss. 59 vols. Brunswick and Berlin: Schwetschke, 1863–1900. (*Corpus Reformatorum*).

————. *Ioannis Calvini opera selecta*. Edited by P. Barth, W. Niesel, and D. Scheuner. 5 vols. Munich: 1926–62.

————. *Commentaries*. Edited by J. Haroutunian. Philadelphia: The Westminster Press, n.d.

————. *Theological Treatises*. Edited by J. K. S. Reid. Philadelphia: The Westminster Press, 1954.

————. *Letters of John Calvin*. 4 vols. Philadelphia: Presbyterian Board of Publication, 1858.

Institutes

————. *Institutes of the Christian Religion*. Edited by J. T. McNeill and translated by Ford Lewis Battles. 2 vols. Philadelphia: The Westminster Press, 1967.

————. *Institutio christianae religionis . . . 1559*. In *Ioannis Calvini opera quae supersunt omnia*, vol. 2.

Other Works

————. *Commentaries on the First Book of Moses Called Genesis*. Edinburgh: The Calvin Translation Society, 1847.

————. *Commentary on The Book of Psalms*. 5 vols. Edinburgh: The Calvin Translation Society, 1845–48.

————. *Commentaries: The Gospel according to Saint John*. 2 vols. London: Oliver and Boyd, 1959–61.

————. *Commentaries on the Epistle of Paul the Apostle to the Romans*. Edinburgh: The Calvin Translation Society, 1849.

————. *Commentaries: The First Epistle of Paul the Apostle to the Corinthians*. London: Oliver and Boyd, 1960.

_____. *Commentaries on the Epistles of Paul to the Galatians and Ephesians.* Edinburgh: The Calvin Translation Society, 1854.

_____. "The Form of Prayers and Songs of the Church. Letter to the Reader, 1542." Translated by Ford Lewis Battles. *Calvin Theological Journal* 15 (1980): 160–65.

Calvinus Ecclesiae Doctor. Die Referate des Internationalen Kongresses für Calvinforschung, Amsterdam, 1978. Edited by Wilhelm H. Neuser, Kampen: J. H. Kok, 1980.

Cassirer, Ernst. *The Individual and the Cosmos in Renaissance Philosophy.* Translated by Mario Domandi. New York: Harper Torchbooks, 1964. (German ed., 1927.)

Chadwick, Owen. *The Reformation.* Middlesex: Penguin Books, 1964.

Chrisman, Miriam Usher. *Strasbourg and the Reform: A Study in the Process of Change.* New Haven: Yale University Press, 1967.

Colie, Rosalie L. *Paradoxia Epidemica: The Renaissance Tradition of Paradox,* 1966. Reprint. Hamden, Conn.: Archon Books, 1976.

Colish, Marcia L. *The Mirror of Language: A Study in the Medieval Theory of Knowledge.* New Haven: Yale University Press, 1968.

Copleston, Frederick. *A History of Philosophy.* Vol. 2, *Medieval Philosophy,* Part 1: *Augustine to Bonaventura.* Garden City: Doubleday and Co., 1962. Vol. 3, *Late Medieval and Renaissance Philosophy,* Part 1: *Ockham to the Speculative Mystics.* Garden City: Doubleday and Co., 1963.

Courtenay, William J. "Covenant and Causality in Pierre D'Ailly." *Speculum* 46 (1971): 94–119.

_____. "Nominalism and Late Medieval Religion." In *The Pursuit of Holiness in Late Medieval and Renaissance Religion,* edited by Charles Trinkaus and Heiko A. Oberman, pp. 26–59.

Cranz, F. Edward. "Cusanus, Luther, and the Mystical Tradition." In *The Pursuit of Holiness,* edited by Charles Trinkaus and Heiko A. Oberman, pp. 93–102.

_____. "The Renaissance Reading of the *De Anima.*" In *Platon et Aristote à la Renaissance,* pp. 359–76. Paris: Librairie Philosophique, J. Vrin, 1976.

Damrosch, Leopold. "Hobbes as Reformation Theologian: Implications of the Free-Will Controversy." *Journal of the History of Ideas* 40 (1979): 339–52.

De Grazia, Margreta. "The Secularization of Language in the Seventeenth Century." *Journal of the History of Ideas* 41 (1980): 319–29.

Dickens, A. G. *Reformation and Society in Sixteenth-Century Europe.* London: Thames and Hudson, 1966.

Dictionary of the History of Ideas: Studies of Selected Pivotal Ideas. Edited by Philip S. Weiner. 5 vols. New York: Charles Scribner's Sons, 1968–73.

Dillenberger, John, and Claude Welch. *Protestant Christianity Interpreted through Its Development.* New York: Charles Scribners' Sons, 1954.

Donnelly, John. "Italian Influences on the Development of Calvinist Scholasticism." *Sixteenth Century Journal* 7 (1976): 81–101.

Doumergue, E. *Jean Calvin: Les hommes et les choses de son temps.* 7 vols. Lausanne: G. Bridel, 1899–1927.

Dvorak, Max. "El Greco and Mannerism." *Magazine of Art* (Jan. 1953): 18–23.

Erikson, Erik H. *Young Man Luther: A Study in Psychoanalysis and History.* New York: W. W. Norton, 1962.

Fatio, Olivier. "Présence de Calvin à l'époque de l'orthodoxie réformée: Les abrégés de Calvin à la fin du 16ᵉ au 17ᵉ siècle." In *Calvinus Ecclesiae Doctor,* pp. 171–207.

Feld, M. D. "Revolution and Reaction in Early Modern Europe." *Journal of the*

History of Ideas 38 (1977): 175–84.

Fitzer, Joseph. "The Augustinian Roots of Calvin's Eucharistic Thought." *Augustinian Studies* 7 (1976): 69–98.

Freud, Sigmund. "The Economic Problem in Masochism." *General Psychological Theory: Papers on Metapsychology*, edited by Philip Rieff, pp. 190–201. New York: Collier Books, 1963.

———. *Leonardo da Vinci and a Memory of His Childhood*. Trans. Alan Tyson. From *The Standard Edition*. New York: W. W. Norton, 1964.

———. "Negation." In *General Psychological Theory*, pp. 213–17.

Friedlaender, Walter. *Mannerism and Anti-Mannerism in Italian Painting*. New York: Schocken Books, 1965.

Ganoczy, Alexandre. *Calvin, théologien de l'église et du ministère*. Paris: Les Éditions du Cerf, 1964.

———. *Le jeune Calvin: genèse et évolution de sa vocation reformatrice*. Wiesbaden: Franz Steiner Verlag, 1966.

Gass, William H. *Fiction and the Figures of Life*. Boston: Nonpareil Books, 1958.

Gerrish, B. A. "John Calvin on Luther." In *Interpreters of Luther*, edited by Jaroslav Pelikan, pp. 67–96. Philadelphia: Fortress Press, 1968.

———. "Theology within the Limits of Piety Alone: Schleiermacher and Calvin's Doctrine of God." In *Reformatio Perennis*, pp. 67–87.

———. "To the Unknown God: Luther and Calvin on the Hiddenness of God." *Journal of Religion* 53 (1973): 263–92.

Giamatti, A. Bartlett. *The Earthly Paradise and the Renaissance Epic*. Princeton: Princeton University Press, 1966.

———. *Play of Double Senses: Spenser's "Faerie Queene."* Englewood Cliffs, N. J.: Prentice-Hall, 1975.

Girardin, Benoît. *Rhétorique et théologique: Calvin, le commentaire de l'Épître aux Romains*. Paris: Éditions Beauchesne, 1979.

Glossary of Psychoanalytic Terms and Concepts. 2nd ed. Edited by Burness E. Moore and Bernard D. Fine. New York: American Psychoanalytic Association, 1968.

Graham, W. Fred. *The Constructive Revolutionary: John Calvin and his Socio-economic Impact*. Richmond: John Knox Press, 1971.

Gray, Hanna H. "Renaissance Humanism." *Journal of the History of Ideas* 24 (1963): 497–514.

Grimm, Harold J. *The Reformation Era, 1500–1650*. New York: Macmillan, 1954.

Haile, H. G. *Luther: An Experiment in Biography*. New York: Doubleday, 1980.

Hall, Basil. "Calvin against the Calvinists." In *Courtenay Studies in Reformation Theology: I. John Calvin*, edited by G. E. Duffield, chap. 2. Grand Rapids, Mich.: Eerdmans, 1966.

———. "From Biblical Humanism to Calvinist Orthodoxy." *Journal of Ecclesiastical History* 31 (1980): 331–43.

Harbison, E. H. *The Christian Scholar in the Age of the Reformation*. New York: Charles Scribner's Sons, 1956.

Harkness, Georgia. *John Calvin: The Man and his Ethics*. New York: Abingdon Press, 1958.

Hartt, Frederick. "Power and the Individual in Mannerist Art." In *Acts of the Twentieth International Congress of the History of Art*, pp. 222–38. Princeton: Princeton University Press, 1963.

Hauser, Arnold. *Mannerism: The Crisis of the Renaissance and the Origin of Modern Art*. London: Routledge and Kegan Paul, 1965.

Hawkes, Terence. *Structuralism and Semiotics*. Berkeley and Los Angeles: University of California Press, 1977.

Hay, Denys. *The Italian Renaissance in Its Historical Background*. Cambridge: Cambridge University Press, 1961.

Heller, Agnes. *Renaissance Man*. Translated by Richard E. Allen. London: Routledge and Kegan Paul, 1978. (Hungarian ed., 1967.)

Hick, John. *Evil and the God of Love*. London: Macmillan, 1966.

Higman, F. -M. "Un pamphlet de Calvin restitué à son auteur." *Revue d'histoire et de philosophie religieuses* 60 (1980): 167–80, 327–37.

———. *The Style of John Calvin in his French Polemical Treatises*. New York: Oxford University Press, 1967.

Hollander, John. *Vision and Resonance: Two Senses of Poetic Form*. New York: Oxford University Press, 1975.

Holt, E. G. *A Documentary History of Art*. Vol. 2, *Michelangelo and the Mannerists; the Baroque and the Eighteenth Century*. Garden City, N.Y.: Anchor Books, 1958. (Selections from Vasari, *Lives of the Most Eminent Painters, Sculptors, and Architects*, pp. 24–34.)

Jones, Ernst. *The Life and Work of Sigmund Freud*. Edited and abridged by Lionel Trilling and Steven Marcus. Garden City, N.Y.: Anchor Books, 1963.

Jung, C. G. "Aion." In *Psyche and Symbol: A Selection from the Writings of C. G. Jung*, edited by Violet S. de Laszlo, pp. 1–60. Garden City, N.Y.: Anchor Books, 1958.

———. *Psychological Types or the Psychology of Individuation*. Translated by H. G. Baynes. New York: Harcourt, Brace and Co., 1923.

Kamen, Henry. "Golden Age, Iron Age: A Conflict of Concepts in the Renaissance." *Journal of Medieval and Renaissance Studies* 4 (1974): 135–55.

Kelley, Donald R. *Foundations of Modern Historical Scholarship: Language, Law, and History in the French Renaissance*. New York: Columbia University Press, 1970.

———. "*Vera Philosophia*: The Philosophical Significance of Renaissance Jurisprudence." *Journal of the History of Philosophy* 14 (1976): 267–79.

Kelly, L. G. "*Modus Significandi*. An Interdisciplinary Concept." *Historiographia Linguistica* 6 (1979): 159–80.

Kingdon, Robert M. "Protestant Parishes in the Old World and the New: The Cases of Geneva and Boston." *Church History* 48 (1979): 290–304.

———. "Was the Protestant Reformation a Revolution? The Case of Geneva." In *Studies in Church History*, vol. 12, pp. 203–22. Oxford: Published for the Ecclesiastical History Society by Basil Blackwell, 1975.

Klibansky, Raymond, Erwin Panofsky, and Fritz Saxl. *Saturn and Melancholy: Studies in the History of Natural Philosophy, Religion, and Art*. New York: Basic Books, 1964.

Koenigsberger, H. G., and G. L. Mosse. *Europe in the Sixteenth Century*. New York: Holt, Rinehart and Winston, 1968.

Kohls, Ernst-Wilhelm. "Martin Bucer als Anhänger Luthers." *Theologische Zeitschrift* 33 (1977): 210–18.

Kristeller, Paul Oskar. *Renaissance Thought: The Classic, Scholastic, and Humanistic Strains*. New York: Harper and Brothers, 1961.

Lacan, Jacques. "The Insistence of the Letter in the Unconscious." In *The Structuralists from Marx to Lévi-Strauss*, edited by Richard and Fernande De George, pp. 287–323. Garden City: Doubleday, Anchor Books, 1972.

_____. *The Language of the Self: The Function of Language in Psychoanalysis.* Translated and edited by Anthony Wilden. New York: Dell Publishing Co., 1968.

Lanham, Richard A. *A Handlist of Rhetorical Terms: A Guide for Students of English Literature.* Berkeley and Los Angeles: University of California Press, 1969.

_____. *The Motives of Eloquence: Literary Rhetoric in the Renaissance.* New Haven: Yale University Press, 1976.

La Vallée, Armand Aimé. "Calvin's Criticism of Scholastic Theology." Ph.D. dissertation, Harvard University, 1967.

Leff, Gordon. *The Dissolution of the Medieval Outlook: An Essay on the Intellectual and Spiritual Change in the Fourteenth Century.* New York: Harper Torchbooks, 1976.

_____. *William of Ockham: The Metamorphosis of Scholastic Discourse.* Manchester: Manchester University Press, 1975.

Leith, John H. "The Doctrine of the Will in the *Institutes of the Christian Religion.*" In *Reformatio Perennis,* pp. 49–66.

Lewalski, Barbara Kiefer. *Protestant Poetics and the Seventeenth-Century Religious Lyric.* Princeton: Princeton University Press, 1979.

Lovejoy, Arthor O. *The Great Chain of Being: A Study of the History of an Idea.* New York: Harper Torchbooks, 1960.

Luther, Martin. "The Bondage of the Will." In *Erasmus-Luther: Discourse on Free Will.* New York: Frederick Ungar Publishing Co., 1961.

_____. *Martin Luther: Selections From His Writings.* Edited by John Dillenberger. Garden City, N.Y.: Anchor Books, 1961.

McDonnell, Kilian. *John Calvin, the Church, and the Eucharist.* Princeton: Princeton University Press, 1967.

McFarlane, I. D. *Renaissance France, 1470–1589.* London: Ernest Benn, 1974.

Malet, Nicole. *Dieu selon Calvin. Des mots à la doctrine.* Lausanne: L'Age d'Homme, 1977.

Meinhold, Peter. "Calvin und Luther." *Lutherische Monatshefte,* 1964: 264–69.

Miles, Margaret R. "Theology, Anthropology, and the Human Body in Calvin's *Institutes of the Christian Religion.*" *Harvard Theological Review* 74 (1981): 303–23.

Moltmann, Jürgen. *Prädestination und Perseveranz: Geschichte und Bedeutung der reformierten Lehre 'de perseverantia sanctorum'.* Neukirchen: Kreis Moers, 1961.

Montgomery, Robert L. *The Reader's Eye: Studies in Didactic Literary Theory from Dante to Tasso.* Berkeley and Los Angeles: University of California Press, 1979.

Mülhaupt, Erwin. "Luther und Calvin." In *Luther: Mitteilungen der Luthergesellschaft* 30 (1959): 97–113.

Muller, Richard A. "*Duplex Cognitio Dei* in the Theology of Early Reformed Orthodoxy." *Sixteenth Century Journal* 10 (1979): 51–61.

Nelson, Benjamin. "Weber's Protestant Ethic: Its Origins, Wanderings, and Foreseeable Futures." In *Beyond the Classics? Essays in the Scientific Study of Religion,* edited by Charles Young Glock and P. E. Hammond, pp. 71–130. New York: Harper and Row, 1973.

Neumann, Erich. "Leonardo da Vinci and the Mother Archetype." In *Art and the Creative Unconscious: Four Essays.* New York: Pantheon, 1959.

_____. "Mystical Man." In *The Mystic Vision: Papers from the Eranos Yearbooks,* vol. 6, pp. 375–418. Princeton: Princeton University Press, 1968.

Niesel, W. *The Theology of Calvin.* London: Lutterworth Press, 1956.

Nijenhuis, W. "Der ökumenische Calvin: Calvin, Luther und das Luthertum." *Nederlands theologisch Tijdschrift*, 1980: 191–212.

Oberman, Heiko A. "Die 'Extra'-Dimension in der Theologie Calvins." In *Geist und Geschichte der Reformation*, edited by Heinz Liebing and Klaus Scholder, pp. 323–56. Berlin: Walter De Gruyter, 1966.

_____. *The Harvest of Medieval Theology: Gabriel Biel and Late Medieval Nominalism.* Cambridge: Harvard University Press, 1963.

_____. "The Shape of Late Medieval Thought: the Birthpangs of the Modern Era." In *The Pursuit of Holiness*, edited by Charles Trinkaus and Heiko A. Obermann, pp. 3–25.

Ockham, William of. *Philosophical Writings: A Selection.* Translated by Philotheus Boehner. Indianapolis: Bobbs-Merrill Co., 1979.

_____. *Predestination, God's Foreknowledge, and Future Contingents.* Translated by Marilyn McCord Adams and Norman Kretzmann. New York: Appleton-Century-Crofts, 1969.

Ong, Walter Jackson. *Ramus, Method, and the Decay of Dialogue: From the Art of Discourse to the Art of Reason.* 1958. Reprint. New York: Octagon Books, 1979.

_____. "Ramism." *Dictionary of the History of Ideas*, vol. 4.

Ozment, Steven E. *The Age of Reform, 1250–1550: An Intellectual and Religious History of Late Medieval and Reformation Europe.* New Haven: Yale University Press, 1980.

_____. *Homo Spiritualis. A Comparative Study of the Anthropology of Johannes Tauler, Jean Gerson, and Martin Luther (1509–16) in the Context of their Theological Thought.* Leiden: E. J. Brill, 1969.

_____. *The Reformation in the Cities.* New Haven: Yale University Press, 1975.

Panofsky, Erwin. *Idea: A Concept in Art Theory.* Columbia: University of South Carolina Press, 1968.

Parker, T. H. L. *John Calvin: A Biography.* Philadelphia: Westminster Press, 1975.

Parker, T. M. "The Papacy, Catholic Reform, and Christian Missions." In *The New Cambridge Modern History*, vol. 3, chap. 3. Cambridge: Cambridge University Press, 1968.

Partee, Charles. *Calvin and Classical Philosophy.* Leiden: E. J. Brill, 1977.

_____. "Calvin and Experience." *Scottish Journal of Theology* 26 (1973): 169–81.

_____. "Calvin, Calvinism, and Philosophy: A Prolusion." *Reformed Review* 33 (1980): 129–35.

Peter, Rodolphe. "Rhétorique et prédication selon Calvin." *Revue d'histoire et de philosophie religieuses* 55 (1975): 249–72.

Pétrement, Simone. "Dualism in Philosophy and Religion." In *Dictionary of the History of Ideas*, vol. 2.

Pevsner, Nikolaus. *Academies of Art, Past and Present.* Cambridge: Cambridge University Press, 1940.

_____. "Gegenreformation und Manierismus." *Repertorium für Kunstwissenschaft* 46: 243–61.

Protestantisme et capitalisme. La controverse post-Weberienne. Edited by Philippe Besnard. Paris: Librairie Armand Colin, 1970.

Puech, Henri-Charles. "The Concept of Redemption in Manichaeism." In *The Mystic Vision: Papers from the Eranos Yearbooks*, vol. 6, pp. 247–314. Princeton: Princeton University Press, 1968.

The Pursuit of Holiness in Late Medieval and Renaissance Religion. Edited by Charles Trinkaus and Heiko A. Oberman. Leiden: E. J. Brill, 1974.

Quistorp, Heinrich. *Calvin's Doctrine of the Last Things*. London: Lutterworth Press, 1935.

Raitt, Jill. "Three Inter-related Principles in Calvin's Unique Doctrine of Infant Baptism." *Sixteenth Century Journal* 11 (1980): 51–61.

Reformatio Perennis: Essays on Calvin and the Reformation in Honor of Ford Lewis Battles. Edited by B. A. Gerrish. Pittsburgh: The Pickwick Press, 1981.

Reid, W. Stanford. "The Battle Hymns of the Lord: Calvinist Psalmody of the Sixteenth Century." In *Sixteenth Century Essays and Studies*, vol. 2, edited by Carl S. Meyer, pp. 36–54. St. Louis: The Foundation for Reformation Research, 1971.

Reuter, Karl. *Das Grundverständnis des Theologie Calvins: Unter Einbeziehung ihrer geschichtlichen Abhängigkeiten*. Neukirchen-Vluyn: Neukirchener Verlag, 1963.

Richard, Lucien. *The Spirituality of John Calvin*. Atlanta: John Knox Press, 1974.

Ricoeur, Paul. *Freud and Philosophy: An Essay on Interpretation*. Translated by Denis Savage. New Haven: Yale University Press, 1970.

Rogge, Joachim. "Kritik Calvins an Luthers Zwei-Reich-Lehre?" In *Theologie in Geschichte und Kunst. Walter Elliger zum 65. Geburtstag*, pp. 152–68. Witten: Luther-Verlag, 1968.

Ross, J. B., and M. M. McLaughlin, eds. *The Portable Renaissance Reader*. New York: Viking Press, 1953. (Selections from Guicciardini, *Storia d'Italia*, pp. 279–84; Loys Le Roy, *De la vicissitude ou variété des choses en l'univers*, pp. 91–108.)

Schützeichel, Heribert. *Die Glaubenstheologie Calvins*. Munich: Max Hueber Verlag, 1972.

Seigel, Jerrold E. *Rhetoric and Philosophy in Renaissance Humanism: The Union of Eloquence and Wisdom, Petrarch to Valla*. Princeton: Princeton University Press, 1968.

Seminar: Religion und Gesellschaftliche Entwicklung. Studien zur Protestantismus-Kapitalismus-These Max Webers. Edited by Constans Seyfarth and Walter M. Sprondel. Frankfurt am Main: Suhrkamp Verlag, 1973.

Shapiro, David. *Neurotic Styles*. New York: Basic Books, 1965.

Shapiro, Kenneth Joel, and Irving E. Alexander. *The Experience of Introversion: An Integration of Phenomenological, Empirical, and Jungian Approaches*. Durham, N.C.: Duke University Press, 1975.

Simon, Bennett. *Mind and Madness in Ancient Greece: The Classical Roots of Modern Psychiatry.*. Ithaca: Cornell University Press, 1978.

Smits, Luchesius, *Saint Augustin dans l'oeuvre de Jean Calvin*. Vol. 1, *Étude de critique littéraire. Vol. 2, Table des références augustiniennes*. Assen: Van Gorcum, 1956.

Spenser, Edmund. "A Letter of the Authors to Sir Walter Raleigh." (Appended to Book VII of the *Faerie Queene*.) In *The Poetical Works of Edmund Spenser*, Edited by J. C. Smith and E. De Selincourt, pp. 407–08. London: Oxford University Press, 1957.

Spitz, L. W., ed. *The Protestant Reformation*. Englewood Cliffs, N.J.: Prentice-Hall 1966.

Sprondel, Walter M. "Sozialer Wandel, Ideen und Interessen: Systematisierung zu Max Webers Protestantischer Ethik." In *Seminar: Religion und Gesellschaftliche Entwicklung*, pp. 206–24.

Stadtland, Tjarko. *Rechtfertigung und Heiligung bei Calvin*. Neukirchen-Vluyn: Neukirchener Verlag, 1972.

Stauffer, Richard. "Un Calvin méconnu: Le prédicateur de Génève." *Bulletin historique et littéraire de la Société de l'Histoire du Protestantisme Français* 123 (1977): 184–203.

_____."Le calvinisme et les universités." *Bulletin historique et littéraire de la Société de l'Histoire du Protestantisme Français* 126 (1980): 27–51.

_____."Dieu, la création et la providence dans l'oeuvre homilétique de Calvin." *La Revue reformée 28 (1977): 196–203.*

_____."Plaidoyer pour une lecture non-calviniste de Calvin." *Supplément à la Revue réformée* 120 (1979): pp. 1–16. (Also includes response by Pierre Marcel, "Une lecture non-calviniste de Calvin?".)

Struever, Nancy S. *The Language of History in the Renaissance: Rhetoric and Historical Consciousness in Florentine Humanism.* Princeton: Princeton University Press, 1970.

Swanson, G. E. *Religion and Regime: A Sociological Account of the Reformation.* Ann Arbor: University of Michigan Press, 1967.

Sypher, Wylie. *Four Stages of Renaissance Style: Transformations in Art and Literature, 1400–1700.* 1955. Reprint. Gloucester, Mass.: Peter Smith, 1978.

Taylor, Charles. *Hegel.* Cambridge: Cambridge University Press, 1975.

Tentler, Thomas N. *Sin and Confession on the Eve of the Reformation.* Princeton: Princeton University Press, 1977

Tillich, Paul. "Die Wiederentdeckung der prophetischen Tradition in der Reformation." In *Gesammelte Werke*, vol. 7, pp. 71–215. Stuttgart: Evangelisches Verlagswerk, 1962.

Torrance, T. F. *Calvin's Doctrine of Man.* London: Lutterworth Press, 1949.

_____. "Infinitive and Abstractive Knowledge from Duns Scotus to John Calvin." *De doctrina Iohannis Scoti.* Acta Congressus Scotistici Internationalis, Oxford and Edinburgh, 1966. Vol. 4, pp. 291–305. Rome, 1968.

_____. "Knowledge of God and Speech about Him according to John Calvin." In *Regards contemporaines sur Jean Calvin*, pp. 140–60. Paris: Presses Universitaires de France, 1965.

Trinkaus, Charles. *The Poet as Philosopher: Petrarch and the Formation of Renaissance Consciousness.* New Haven: Yale University Press, 1979.

_____. "The Religious Thought of the Italian Humanists and the Reformers: Anticipation or Autonomy?" In *The Pursuit of Holiness*, ed. Charles Trinkaus, and Heiko A. Oberman, pp. 339–66.

Tylenda, Joseph N. "The Ecumenical Intention of Calvin's Early Eucharistic Teaching." In *Reformatio Perennis*, pp. 27–47.

Valesio, Paolo. *Novantiqua: Rhetorics as a Contemporary Theory.* Bloomington: Indiana University Press, 1980.

Van Buren, Paul. *Christ in Our Place: The Substitutionary Character of Calvin's Doctrine of Reconciliation.* Grand Rapids, Mich.: Wm. B. Eerdmans, 1957.

Vincent, Gilbert. "La théologie calvinienne du sacrament à la lumière de la linguistique." In *Calvinus Ecclesiae Doctor*, pp. 145–158.

Wallace, Ronald S. *Calvin's Doctrine of the Word and Sacrament.* Edinburgh: Oliver and Boyd, 1953.

Walzer, Michael. *The Revolution of the Saints: A Study in the Origins of Radical Politics.* Cambridge: Harvard University Press, 1965.

Waswo, R. "The 'Ordinary Language Philosophy' of Lorenzo Valla." *Bibliothèque d'humanisme et Renaissance* 41 (1979): 255–71.

Weinberg, Julius R. *Ockham, Descartes, and Hume: Self-Knowledge, Substance, and Causality.* Madison: University of Wisconsin Press, 1977.

Wendel, François. *Calvin et l'humanisme*. Paris: Presses Universitaires de France, 1976.

———.*Calvin: The Origins and Development of His Religious Thought*. Translated by P. Mairet. New York: Harper and Row, 1963.

Wilcox, Donald J. *In Search of God and Self: Renaissance and Reformation Thought*. New York: Houghton Mifflin, 1975.

Willis, E. David. *Calvin's Catholic Christology: The Function of the So-Called Extra Calvinisticum in Calvin's Theology*. Leiden: E. J. Brill, 1966.

———. "Rhetoric and Responsibility in Calvin's Theology." In *The Context of Contemporary Theology: Essays in Honor of Paul Lehmann*, edited by Alexander J. McKelway and E. David Willis, pp. 43–63. Atlanta: John Knox Press, 1974.

Wimsatt, W. K. *The Verbal Icon*. Lexington: University of Kentucky Press, 1954.

Wind, Edgar. *Pagan Mysteries in the Renaissance*. New Haven: Yale University Press, 1958.

Winn, James Anderson. *Unsuspected Eloquence. A History of the Relations between Poetry and Music*. New Haven: Yale University Press, 1981.

Yates, Frances A. *The French Academies of the Sixteenth Century*. London: The Warburg Institute, 1947.

———. *Occult Philosophy in the Elizabethan Age*. London: Routledge and Kegan Paul, 1979.

Zeeden, E. W. "Das Bild Martin Luther in den Briefen Calvins." *Archiv für Reformationsgeschichte* 49 (1958): 177–95.

Zimmerman, J. A. K. "Christian Life in Luther and Calvin." *Lutheran Quarterly* 16 (1964): 222–30.

Index

("Calvin" within entries is abbreviated "C.")